# GAMBLING

Other Books in the Current Controversies Series:

# GAMBLING

**David Bender**, *Publisher*
**Bruno Leone**, *Executive Editor*

**Katie de Koster**, *Managing Editor*
**Scott Barbour**, *Senior Editor*

**Charles P. Cozic**, *Book Editor*
**Paul A. Winters**, *Book Editor*

Cover Photo: Uniphoto

Library of Congress Cataloging-in-Publication Data

Gambling / Charles P. Cozic & Paul A. Winters, book editors.
    p.  cm. — (Current controversies)
    Includes bibliographical references and index.
    ISBN 1-56510-235-5 (alk. paper) : ISBN 1-56510-234-7 (pbk. : alk.
paper)
    1. Gambling. [1. Gambling. ] I. Cozic, Charles P., 1957–      . II
Winters, Paul A., 1965–      . III. Series.
    HV6710.G314    1995
    363.4'2—dc20                                              94-43378
                                                                    CIP
                                                                     AC

© 1995 by Greenhaven Press, Inc., PO Box 289009, San Diego, CA 92198-9009
Printed in the U.S.A.

# Contents

## Chapter 2: Is Compulsive Gambling an Uncontrollable Disease?

### Yes: Compulsive Gambling Is an Uncontrollable Disease

are obligated to provide counseling services for those who suffer from this addiction.

## No: Compulsive Gambling Is Not an Uncontrollable Disease

# Chapter 3: Does Gambling Benefit State and Local Economies?

## Yes: Gambling Benefits State and Local Economies

## No: Gambling Does Not Benefit State and Local Economies

# Chapter 4: Does Indian Gaming Help Native Americans?

## Yes: Indian Gaming Helps Native Americans

## No: Indian Gaming May Not Help Native Americans

# Foreword

By definition, controversies are "discussions of questions in which opposing opinions clash" (Webster's Twentieth Century Dictionary Unabridged). Few would deny that controversies are a pervasive part of the human condition and exist on virtually every level of human enterprise. Controversies transpire between individuals and among groups, within nations and between nations. Controversies supply the grist necessary for progress by providing challenges and challengers to the status quo. They also create atmospheres where strife and warfare can flourish. A world without controversies would be a peaceful world; but it also would be, by and large, static and prosaic.

## The Series' Purpose

The purpose of the Current Controversies series is to explore many of the social, political, and economic controversies dominating the national and international scenes today. Titles selected for inclusion in the series are highly focused and specific. For example, from the larger category of criminal justice, Current Controversies deals with specific topics such as police brutality, gun control, white collar crime, and others. The debates in Current Controversies also are presented in a useful, timeless fashion. Articles and book excerpts included in each title are selected if they contribute valuable, long-range ideas to the overall debate. And wherever possible, current information is enhanced with historical documents and other relevant materials. Thus, while individual titles are current in focus, every effort is made to ensure that they will not become quickly outdated. Books in the Current Controversies series will remain important resources for librarians, teachers, and students for many years.

In addition to keeping the titles focused and specific, great care is taken in the editorial format of each book in the series. Book introductions and chapter prefaces are offered to provide background material for readers. Chapters are organized around several key questions that are answered with diverse opinions representing all points on the political spectrum. Materials in each chapter include opinions in which authors clearly disagree as well as alternative opinions in which authors may agree on a broader issue but disagree on the possible solutions. In this way, the content of each volume in Current Controversies mirrors the mosaic of opinions encountered in society. Readers will quickly realize that there are many viable answers to these complex issues. By questioning each author's conclusions, students and casual readers can begin to develop the critical thinking skills so important to evaluating opinionated material.

Current Controversies is also ideal for controlled research. Each anthology in the series is composed of primary sources taken from a wide gamut of informational categories including periodicals, newspapers, books, United States and foreign government documents, and the publications of private and public organizations. Readers will find factual support for reports, debates, and research papers covering all areas of important issues. In addition, an annotated table of contents, an index, a book and periodical bibliography, and a list of organizations to contact are included in each book to expedite further research.

Perhaps more than ever before in history, people are confronted with diverse and contradictory information. During the Persian Gulf War, for example, the public was not only treated to minute-to-minute coverage of the war, it was also inundated with critiques of the coverage and countless analyses of the factors motivating U.S. involvement. Being able to sort through the plethora of opinions accompanying today's major issues, and to draw one's own conclusions, can be a complicated and frustrating struggle. It is the editors' hope that Current Controversies will help readers with this struggle.

*"[The growth of gambling on Native American reservations] is related to an ongoing series of court battles between states seeking to regulate gambling and Native American tribes seeking to expand their businesses."*

# Introduction

Since the early 1980s, gambling on Native American reservations has grown from low-stakes bingo games to an estimated $7.5-billion-a-year casino industry. This growth is related to an ongoing series of court battles between states seeking to regulate gambling and Native American tribes seeking to expand their businesses. The legal wrangling reached a turning point in 1987 when the U.S. Supreme Court ruled that tribes could operate legal forms of gambling on their lands free from state regulation, taxation, and law enforcement. In response to the ruling, in 1988 the U.S. Congress passed the Indian Gaming Regulatory Act (IGRA) in an attempt to allow states and the federal government to regulate Indian gaming operations. This act merely served to intensify and expand the legal battles over Native American casinos, battles that have pitted state and local governments against Native American tribes and the federal government.

The start of Native American gaming's expansion was marked by a 1982 Florida appeals court ruling. Prior to the ruling, gaming on reservations consisted of small, low-stakes bingo operations. The case arose when the Miami Seminole tribe of Florida defied a state law that limited the size of bingo jackpots to $100. At the end of a three-year battle, the court decided in favor of the tribe, ruling that the jackpot-limit law could not be enforced on tribal lands. This decision set a precedent for the independence of Native American gaming operations from state regulation and facilitated the spread of high-stakes bingo games on reservations across America.

The next legal battle was decided in 1987. The case stemmed from the efforts of Riverside County, California, to shut down an Indian-run card room on Indian land within the county borders. Since other counties in California allow card rooms to operate, the U.S. Supreme Court ruled in the case of *California v. Cabazon Band of Mission Indians* that Riverside County could not prohibit on reservations card games that were permitted elsewhere in the state. According to Richard L. Worsnop, associate editor of the *CQ Researcher,* the ruling meant that if a state does not prohibit a form of gaming, "tribes may operate such games, and operate them free of state control." The Supreme Court ruling affirmed the sovereignty of tribes and further paved the way for the opening of high-stakes casinos.

The ruling raised for states the possibility of "the spread of casino-style gambling with little control by elected officials," according to Kathleen Sylvester, senior writer for *Governing*. Specific areas of concern for the states were their inability to tax Indian casino revenues due to tribal sovereignty, the theoretical possibility that tribes could buy land in any city or town and open a casino there, and the potential for infiltration of Native American casino operations by organized crime. To address these concerns, Congress adopted in 1988 the Indian Gaming Regulatory Act. The law defined three classes of gaming to be regulated in different ways. Class I consisted of traditional ceremonial or social games with prizes of limited value, to be regulated solely by the tribes. Class II consisted of such games as bingo and lotto (a lottery-type game)—already allowed by nearly all states—to be regulated by a federal commission appointed by the president and confirmed by the Senate. Class III consisted of slot machines, casino games, and horse and dog racing. In states where these forms of gambling were not specifically prohibited by law, the state and tribes were required to negotiate compacts for the establishment of Class III operations on Native American lands.

The law raised as many objections—from both the Native American tribes and the states—as it attempted to quell. The states felt that the law "greatly favored the tribes and allowed the proliferating of gaming activities that the states had no intention of allowing," according to New Jersey representative Robert G. Torricelli. The tribes believed that the law was an unfair attempt to curtail the sovereignty recognized in the 1987 Supreme Court decision. "Regrettably, we had to make compromises and accept restrictions on our right of self-government and sovereignty in the enactment of the Indian Gaming Regulatory Act," lamented Leonard Prescott of the National Indian Gaming Association. The states balked at negotiating compacts with the tribes; meanwhile, the tribes expanded their gaming operations, paying little heed to local or state law. A new round of court battles quickly developed.

One major ruling in the legal battles arising from the IGRA law came in January 1994. The two cases settled by the ruling arose when Native American tribes sued the states of Florida and Alabama for blocking the negotiation of gaming compacts. IGRA's provisions allowed lawsuits to be filed if a state did not negotiate in good faith, but many states claimed they were immune from these provisions under the Tenth and Eleventh Amendments to the U.S. Constitution, which, respectively, define the rights of states against the federal government and give the states immunity from certain lawsuits. The 11th U.S. Circuit Court of Appeals in Florida ruled that the states were immune from lawsuits brought under IGRA, but it also ruled that tribes could appeal to the federal government—the U.S. Department of the Interior—when states refused to negotiate compacts. Many other district and circuit courts have given rulings on the issue—some in favor of states and some in favor of Native Americans—and still others are expected to add to the debate. And according to Richard Worsnop,

"The U.S. Supreme Court may yet render a definitive judgement" on the balance of states' rights and Native American rights.

Another kind of battle between the states and tribes involves the kinds of gaming allowed by the states. This issue came to a head in 1991 when law enforcement authorities in San Diego County, California, seized slot machines from three Indian casinos. The casinos were operating the slot machines despite a California law that specifically prohibited them. But the tribes argued that the state's own lottery allowed the use of video poker machines and video lottery terminals, so slot machines should be legal as well. Senator Daniel K. Inouye of Hawaii argued in favor of the tribes, saying that "when Indian people see these games being played by everyone else in the state, we would be hard-pressed to tell them that there is or should be a different rule" applied to them. The tribes also argued that because IGRA divided gaming forms into three distinct classes, if one form of gaming were allowed, all forms of gaming in that class should be allowed. The San Diego case is scheduled to be decided by the 9th U.S. Circuit Court of Appeals in California, but each side then will have an opportunity to appeal to the U.S. Supreme Court, according to the National Indian Gaming Association. In the interim, California has not seized any other slot machines from Native American casinos, and the casinos continue to operate some slot machines but have refrained from adding to the numbers in operation.

In the absence of a definitive decision by the U.S. Supreme Court, the battle continues between states asserting their power to regulate gambling and tribes affirming their sovereignty and expanding their businesses. The beginning of the newest round was marked by the March 1995 announcement by Idaho's Coeur d'Alene tribe of plans to implement a nationwide lottery (in the thirty-six states where lotteries are legal) akin to the Powerball Lotto game now offered in nineteen states. States may win the right to regulate Native American gaming in these court battles, but it is likely that Indian gaming will continue to expand as part of the gambling boom taking place across the country. *Gambling: Current Controversies* examines this and other ethical, social, and economic impacts of gambling's spread in America.

# Chapter 1

# Is Gambling Unethical?

# Gambling and Ethics: An Overview

## by James Popkin and Katia Hetter

**About the authors:** *James Popkin is a senior editor and Katia Hetter is a reporter-researcher for* U.S. News & World Report.

No one howled in protest in February 1994 when H&R Block set up makeshift tax-preparation offices in four Nevada casinos and offered gamblers same-day "refund-anticipation loans." And few people cared when a Florida inventor won a U.S. patent that could someday enable television audiences to legally bet on game shows, football games and even beauty pageants from their homes.

### From Moral Outrage to National Pastime

What's the deal? Not that long ago, Americans held gambling in nearly the same esteem as heroin dealing and applauded when ax-wielding police paid a visit to the corner dice room. But moral outrage has become as outmoded as a penny slot machine. In 1955, for example, baseball commissioner Ford Frick considered wagering so corrupt he prohibited major leaguers from overnighting in Las Vegas. In 1993, by contrast, Americans for the first time made more trips to casinos than they did to Major League ballparks—some 92 million trips, according to one study.

It took six decades for gambling to become America's Pastime, from the legalization of Nevada casinos in 1931 to April Fool's Day 1991, when Davenport, Iowa, launched the Diamond Lady, the nation's first legal riverboat casino. The gradual creation of thirty-seven state lotteries broke down the public's mistrust, conveying a clear message that the government sanctioned gambling; indeed, is even coming to depend on it as a tax-revenue source. Corporate ownership of casinos helped in its own way, too, replacing shady operators with trusted brand names like Hilton and MGM. Casinos now operate or are authorized in twenty-three states, and 95 percent of all Americans are expected to live within a three- or four-hour drive of one by the year 2000.

Today, the Bible Belt might as well be renamed the Blackjack Belt, with floating and land-based casinos throughout Mississippi and Louisiana and plans for more in Florida, Texas, Alabama and Arkansas. Meanwhile, the Midwest is overrun with slot hogs, none of the porcine variety. Iowa, Illinois, Indiana and Missouri allow riverboat gambling, and a 50,000-square-foot land-based casino was scheduled to open in mid-May 1994 just outside Detroit, in Windsor, Ontario. Low-stakes casinos attract visitors to old mining towns in Colorado and South Dakota, and Indian tribes operate 225 casinos and high-stakes bingo halls nationwide. Add church bingo, card rooms, sports wagering, dog and horse racing and jai alai to the mix and it becomes clear why Americans legally wagered $330 billion in 1992—a 1,800 percent increase over 1976.

> *"Not that long ago, Americans held gambling in nearly the same esteem as heroin dealing."*

## Gambling and the Economy

Like the first bars that opened after Prohibition, modern gambling halls are enormously successful. "It will be impossible not to make a lot of money," one executive in New Orleans bragged before his casino had even opened. "It's like spitting and missing the floor." Such boasts—and the real possibility that the boom will create 500,000 jobs nationwide this decade—have not been lost on federal, state and local lawmakers. In the first six weeks of 1994 alone they introduced more than 200 bills regarding gambling.

But casinos and lotteries may not guarantee the jackpots many politicians expect. When urban-planning professor Robert Goodman reviewed the economic-impact studies that fourteen government agencies relied upon before deciding to embrace casino gambling, he found that most were written with a pro-industry spin and only four were balanced and factored in gambling's hidden costs. Goodman's two-year study concludes that newly opened casinos "suck money out of the local economy," away from existing movie theaters, car dealerships, clothing shops and sports arenas. In Atlantic City, for example, about 100 of 250 local restaurants have closed since the casinos debuted in 1978, says Goodman, who teaches at the University of Massachusetts at Amherst.

States that get hooked on gambling revenues soon suffer withdrawal symptoms when local competition kicks in. Although pioneering casinos and lotteries typically are profitable, gambling grosses decline when lotteries or casinos open in neighboring states. In Biloxi, Mississippi, for example, slot revenues at first topped about $207 per machine per day. A year later when competitors moved in, however, the daily win-per-machine figure dipped to $109.

States frequently overestimate the financial impact of gambling revenues, too. "Legalized gambling is never large enough to solve any social problems," says gambling-law professor and paid industry consultant I. Nelson Rose. In New Jersey, for example, horse racing alone accounted for about 10 percent of state revenue in the 1950s. Today, despite the addition of a lottery and 12 casinos, the state earns only 6 percent of its revenue through gambling. "Atlantic City used to be a slum by the sea," says Rose. "Now it's a slum by the sea with casinos."

## America's Fickle Romance with Gambling

America's love affair with dice and cards has always been a fickle romance, and some academics predict a breakup soon. Legalized gambling in America has been running on a seventy-year boom-and-bust cycle since the colonists started the first lotteries. "We're now riding the third wave of legal gambling" that began with the Depression, says Rose, who has written extensively on the subject and teaches at Whittier Law School in Los Angeles. The trend self-destructs after a few decades, when the public simply gets fed up and embraces more conservative values. Rose believes a cheating or corruption scandal will trigger the next crash in about thirty-five years, an idea that most casino officials think is ludicrous.

The sky is not falling yet. Apart from a handful of academics and the odd politician, few Americans are seriously questioning the morality of an industry that is expected to help gamblers lose a record $35 billion in 1995 alone. Religious leaders have been oddly silent, perhaps because so many churches and synagogues rely on bingo revenues. "The biggest things we have to help people are churches and temples and the government," says Arnie Wexler, executive director of the Council on Compulsive Gambling of New Jersey. "And now they're all in the gambling business."

The consequences can be damaging. Wexler says he got a phone call from a man in his seventies who ran up $150,000 in debt just by buying lottery tickets. Although most gambling experts believe that only 1 percent to 3 percent of Americans have a serious gambling problem at any given time, a July 1993 Gallup Poll funded by Wexler's group suggests that the figure may be closer to 5 percent. Regardless, now that casinos are no longer located just in Atlantic City and Nevada it's reasonable to assume that the total number of problem gamblers will soar. "If you put a guy who wouldn't cheat on his wife in a room with a gorgeous nude woman, some guys would fall by the wayside," Wexler says. "When you make gambling legal and socially acceptable, people will try it and some of them will get hooked."

But try telling that to a gambler happily feeding a slot machine and waiting for a multimillion-dollar payoff. Fifty-one percent of American adults now find casino gambling "acceptable for anyone," and 35 percent describe it as "acceptable for others but not for me." according to a recent Yankelovich Inc. survey paid for by Harrah's Casinos. The attraction is simple. "The action for them is the thrill of what's going to happen in the next pull of that slot-machine handle," explains Harrah's president, Phil Satre.

# Gambling Is Unethical

by *The Christian Science Monitor*

**About the author:** *The* Christian Science Monitor *is an international daily newspaper published by the Christian Science Publishing Society of the First Church of Christ, Scientist.*

The nation's $300 billion gambling industry is shifting its message. Gambling is not just about winning; it is also about family entertainment, civic improvements, and a region's economic well-being.

## Gambling's New Promises

The promise to individuals: It could happen! Or, if you don't win, you will at least be amused.

The promise to beleaguered state and city officials: a quick and easy way to reduce chronic state budget deficits and appease anti-tax voters.

The promise to blighted areas left behind by economic growth: new visitors, new jobs, new tax revenues, new wealth.

The traditional opponents of gambling, church and state, have largely stepped aside in the moral debate over this issue. Many churches adopted bingo or "Las Vegas nights" as a way of raising revenue, opening the door to arguments for allowing legalized gambling on Indian reservations. State governments find themselves more and more dependent on gambling revenues.

- All states but Hawaii and Utah allow some form of legalized gambling. The proceeds are usually targeted for a politically popular cause: downtown improvements, education, programs for the elderly and the disabled.
- Since New Hampshire established the first state lottery in 1964, thirty-seven states have followed suit. Lotteries provided $11.45 billion in tax revenues in 1992.
- Since Iowa started the first riverboat gambling operation in 1991, six states have launched some forty boats. Riverboat gambling is soon expected to be approved in at least eight other states.
- Connecticut, which granted a monopoly on slot machines to the Mashantucket Pequot tribe, now receives $113 million a year in revenues, making

the Foxwoods casino the state's single largest taxpayer.

Many Americans are buying the argument, directing more of their time and family resources to picking numbers, scraping tickets, and feeding slot machines. In 1938, 47 percent of those surveyed in a Gallup poll said that government lotteries "would produce an unwholesome gambling spirit" in the country. By 1993, only about one-third thought that gambling is immoral. Fifty-four percent of American adults have purchased lottery tickets, according to a 1992 survey; nearly 25 percent say they have formed a weekly lottery habit.

> *"Aggressive images reinforce the notion of gambling as crowned with victory."*

Aggressive images reinforce the notion of gambling as crowned with victory. Gambling casinos amplify the sounds of winning. Before the big-stakes tables, nickel, quarter, dollar slot machines dole out the fruits of victory one coin at a time into a metal cup. There is no sound from losing.

State lotteries send the same message: The pots get larger, faces of winners beam out from television and newspapers. Massachusetts launched its state lottery with a campaign targeted at poorer neighborhoods of the city: "If you won, think what you could say to your boss."

Is this winning?

Try another question: What is the impact on children? Does gambling treat children as precious?

What does gambling have to do with children? Note the number of children's arcades and fast food restaurants that are building the gambling habit into playtime and mealtime activities. Note the tendency in new casinos to build around themes attractive to children: castles, pirate ships, wild animals, amusements. A new generation of interactive video machines, designed to be fast and arousing, targets young audiences.

Workers at the Jellinek addiction center in the Netherlands describe the difficulties of helping young men under twenty-five overcome addiction to the "buzz" from the whirling reels, flashing lights, and noise of slot machines. In 1986, when the Dutch legalized the playing of cash-paying machines, 400 people visited the center for help with gambling addiction. By 1992, that number had risen to 6,000.

## The Drain on Income and Hope

Family income in the United States has not grown since 1971, and yet gambling expenditures are taking a deeper bite out of family budgets. Marketing outlets for gambling are often concentrated in poorer neighborhoods.

Are public officials figuring into their budget calculations the daily drain on family time, resources, and hope this habit involves?

Yes, hope. One of the most precious legacies we can give children as parents or as a civic culture is to articulate the reason for the hope that is in us. Yet the message from gambling is that hope rests with chance or luck, rather than with individual moral and spiritual growth. It is the buzz, glitz, thrill, and illusive promise of heroic reward without heroic endeavor.

As public officials and voters take a closer look at gambling proposals in their communities, they also should take a hard look at the faces that don't make it into high-gloss industry promotions: troubled faces as people scratch tickets in convenience stores or watch a pile of chips in front of a gambling spouse disappear.

Budget deficits may fall, but at what price? And on whose shoulders?

# Gambling Violates Biblical Principles

**by Lamar E. Cooper Sr.**

**About the author:** *Lamar E. Cooper Sr. is director of Denominational Relations, Seminars, and Conferences for the Southern Baptist Christian Life Commission in Nashville, Tennessee.*

Gambling is a phenomenon that has swept the nation in recent years. Its rise has been assisted by state legislators in their scramble to find new sources for declining revenues without increasing taxes. Gambling as an alternate form of taxation has generally been given positive reviews in the media. Legal status has been granted to gambling in some form by every state but Utah and Hawaii.

## Hidden Realities Within Gambling

In spite of the popularity of gambling, public perception has been driven by a number of myths about gambling. The performance of gambling as a generator of revenue has not been consistent with the claims advanced by gambling industry spokesmen. Negative consequences of state-sponsored gambling are rarely presented. The following facts are an attempt to reveal some of the hidden realities about gambling and its impact on people, communities, states and the nation. Here are ten myths which have been used to gain popular support for state-sponsored gambling.

*Myth #1: The Bible has nothing to say against gambling.*

1. Gambling is part of a "get something for nothing," materialistic, get-rich-quick syndrome that has swept our country. It is not simply gaming for fun. Take the potential of winning out of it, and it would be dead. Most people would not gamble if there was no possibility of reward. Exodus 20:15 says, "Thou shalt not steal." Gambling is robbery by mutual consent. A group of people agree to play a game of chance in which one person will take what everyone else has contributed to the pot.

Exodus 20:17 says, "Thou shalt not covet." Gambling is a form of covetous-

Abridged from Lamar E. Cooper Sr., *Critical Issues: Gambling Myths vs. the Hidden Realities.* Nashville: The Christian Life Commission of the Southern Baptist Convention, 1995. Reprinted by permission of the publisher.

ness that encourages greed. In order to gamble you have to want to win the money or possessions of another person. At the root of this is the failure to be satisfied with what God has provided and with the opportunity He has given for us to work. Gambling is particularly insidious since it allows the lottery or casino to hold the winnings. The winner never sees the effect on the lives and families of those who play and those addicted. Gambling promotes disinterested greed with no concern for those who lose.

> *"Gambling is a form of covetousness that encourages greed."*

2. As a form of covetousness and greed, gambling is associated with crime and violence. States that have recently approved gambling have experienced a dramatic increase in all forms of violent crime. After opening casinos in Deadwood, South Dakota, crime rose 250% in the first year [1990–91]. People who are addicted to gambling will commit crimes to get money to gamble just as those who are addicted to drugs or alcohol. . . .

3. Gambling is contrary to the biblical work ethic. The Bible teaches that we are to live by our own work, not by exploitation of others. This ethic does not preclude investments such as stocks or bonds in which a person buys part of a company and allows their money to be used in corporate development. Gambling is not an investment in anything; it is a simple win/lose proposition in which the winner takes all and the loser forfeits all.

4. Gambling violates the law of love which says we are to love our neighbor as ourselves. It also violates the biblical mandate not to tread on or exploit the poor and needy.

5. Gambling sets a stumbling block before those who are weaker and who would easily become addicted. Romans 14:1–21 gives guidelines for deciding about questionable conduct such as drinking and gambling. The rule of faith stated in Romans 14:21 is, "It is good neither to eat meat or drink wine or *to do anything* [including gambling] that will cause your brother to fall." For the same reason we also are to abstain from anything that has the appearance of evil. Gambling takes the possessions of others and contributes to addictive behavior. Especially vulnerable are those in the lower income bracket and also the teenage population. Believers have a responsibility to those weaker and more easily influenced by evil.

## Gambling Is Not Entertainment

*Myth #2: Gambling is a harmless form of family entertainment.*

Within the last ten to fifteen years public perception of gambling has undergone an almost miraculous transformation. Gambling was considered a vice mentioned with drugs, alcohol, prostitution and violent crime. Now it is considered a benign, benevolent and harmless form of family entertainment. What was the basis for this change of attitude? David Johnston, an investigative reporter, has written a history of gambling called *Temples of Chance*, in which he notes that in the early 1980s leaders in corporate gambling enterprises applied mass marketing techniques to transform the image of gambling. They have been highly successful in marketing gambling, especially casinos, as family entertainment. Many casinos have built family-oriented theme parks to attract families. They know if families visit the casino, they get mom and dad now, and the kids when they reach legal gambling age. There has been a dramatic increase in the number of children being taken to Las Vegas since the industry began targeting families in the early 1980s.

Gambling is still a vice today. A vice is any activity which feeds moral depravity and corruption. This vice violates the biblical admonition to do whatever we do, in word or deed, for the glory of God. God gets no glory from gambling. Gambling has no place in church life and consequently it should have no place in the life of God's people, who are the church.

## The State as Con Artist

*Myth #3: Gambling is a sound method for state government to raise revenue.*

The purpose for government as ordained by God is to serve and protect the citizens under its authority. Taxation is a legitimate method for government to raise funds for its operating expenses. When states decide to legalize gambling in order to supplement tax revenue, government is transformed from a benevolent protector

> *"Gambling is contrary to the biblical work ethic."*

of its citizens to a retailer that must convince its customers (citizens) to buy its products (gambling). The nature and extent of this advertisement tends to exploit citizens because it is clear that only an infinitesimal percentage of them will win anything significant.

Misleading advertising which promises players they will get rich quick victimizes the poor. Those who live in states that use this method for raising additional revenue are bombarded with advertisements with the message that all you have to do to win is to play. These ads present a false message that riches are only one lottery ticket away or as near as the closest casino. Those in the lower socioeconomic segment of society are the most susceptible to this kind of advertising. They see gambling as a chance to break their cycle of poverty. Most states have laws to protect citizens against con artists. When the state endorses gambling as a source of revenue and runs misleading ads to encourage citizens to play, it *becomes* the con artist. . . .

## Gambling Is a Regressive Tax

*Myth #4: Gambling provides a "painless" source of new revenue.*

1. State-sponsored gambling is only "painless" for the legislators because it allows government to raise revenue without voting a new tax. Gambling supporters

like to point out that unlike a tax, gambling is voluntary. Due to the aggressiveness and ubiquity of gambling advertisement citizens are assailed by the powerful motivation of an easy money, get-rich-quick message so appealing in our materialistic culture. Young people are especially susceptible to this message. It is difficult to teach young people the value of hard work as the key to success if they are inundated with government-sponsored ads suggesting the road to riches can be achieved by gambling. Teenage gambling has been labeled by experts on compulsive gambling as "the addiction of the 1990s." Of the estimated 8 million compulsive gamblers in America, at least 1 million are teenagers.

2. Gambling is regressive, meaning it preys upon those who can least afford to play. As an example, the state lottery in Texas reports that high school dropouts and those with under $20,000 annual income are the largest segment of lottery players. The second largest lottery outlet in Texas is in the most economically depressed section of the state. This means a larger percentage of their income goes to the state as tax revenue than any other segment of society. . . .

3. There are many other reasons why gambling is not a "painless" venture. These reasons include increased crime, increased police protection, addiction to gambling, increased welfare payments to victims, loss of business income, loss of sales taxes, not to mention the physical, emotional and economic impact on gambling addicts and their families.

## Gambling Revenue Is Unsteady

*Myth #5: Gambling provides a "stable" source of additional revenue.*

1. One of the real problems for states which have sponsored gambling has been the instability of revenues. This especially has been true for state lotteries which start with a euphoric bang but whose revenues decline by the third year as people realize they will never win anything significant. . . . When this happens states usually seek to expand and diversify gambling by adding casinos, video poker or other insidious games to relieve citizens of the needed revenue.

The problem was dramatic in Florida because the legislature placed education totally on lottery funds and reallocated educational tax revenue to other needs. When lottery revenues dropped in the third and fourth years, education funding became a serious problem. Other states such as California, Illinois, Ohio and Virginia have had similar experiences.

> *"[Gambling enterprises] have been highly successful in marketing gambling, especially casinos, as family entertainment."*

2. The gaming industry recognizes the instability of the gaming market. In an article on gaming investment, *Gaming and Wagering Business* recommended that investors get into new markets quickly and remain "light on their feet" so they can exit quickly when revenues begin to decline.

## Gambling Hurts Other Businesses

*Myth #6: Gambling will stimulate other businesses.*

1. One of the prominent myths put forth by the gambling industry as it seeks to move into a state is that money will be stimulated in the larger business community through increased jobs, tourism and other trade. This growth is projected in addition to the hundreds of millions of dollars that the gambling industry predicts as probable revenue from which the

*"Misleading advertising [by states] which promises players they will get rich quick victimizes the poor."*

state will benefit. No one ever asks the question, "From where will these hundreds of millions of dollars come?" The gambling industry is *not* waiting at the border of a state with new money to dump into that state if gambling is approved. Most all the money gambling will make is reallocated from money that otherwise would have been spent in local businesses.

Gambling revenue is reallocated money within the state that will come from what would have been spent on cars, clothes, food, lodging, restaurants, services, home sales, etc., and would have produced sales tax, business taxes, property taxes, etc. Gambling money is not really new money. Much of the revenue which gambling produces would have been received by the state without gambling. When state losses through increased welfare, crime, crime prevention, gambling administration, counseling gambling addicts and their families are subtracted, gambling actually produces negative revenues. Gambling promoters always point to gross revenue projections and never take into account the negative factors of gaming or the factor of reallocated money. . . .

2. Promised gambling revenues are an unreliable source of sound economic development. As an example of what can happen, Fort Madison, Iowa, borrowed $2.6 million to build a ticket center, pedestrian bridge and dock for the Emerald Lady riverboat. After only one year of operation the Emerald Lady and three other Iowa riverboats moved to Mississippi where more liberal gaming laws made their potential profit greater.

## Gambling Hurts Education

*Myth #7: Gambling will provide states with much needed money to support education.*

1. Gambling is presented by promoters as the state's answer for much needed revenue to support education. While it is true that gambling collects billions of dollars annually, especially through state-run lotteries, studies show the actual amount which is provided for education is less than 4% of annual budget needs. In several of those states the figure is 1% or less. . . .

2. Gambling also hurts education in another significant way. Once a commu-

nity or state designates gambling money to education, voters expect that money to pay the bills. States who allot gambling money to education often reallocate education funds for other needs. When gambling revenues decline, people are reluctant to pass any additional taxes or bonds for educational needs.

*Myth #8: Gambling is part of our national heritage.*

1. One tactic used by the gambling industry is to point out that the founding fathers of our country used gambling and lotteries to help defray the expenses of the American Revolution, implying that it is patriotic to gamble. While it is true that lotteries were used to help raise money for the government, gambling advocates do not tell the rest of the story. Because of the widespread vice and corruption that followed in the wake of this decision, gambling was outlawed in all the states. Many states such as Tennessee and North Carolina placed a prohibition in their constitution which made gambling illegal because of the graft and corruption.

2. The logic of this argument is faulty. If government once made a bad choice, we should never want to initiate that bad choice again. Gambling was made illegal in the past because of corruption. This bad choice of a source for revenue should not be repeated.

## Gambling Adds to Law Enforcement Problems

*Myth #9: Gambling will be controlled by the state.*

1. In Tennessee the state authorized charitable bingo in the 1980s in violation of the state's constitution. By 1987 corruption was so bad that seventy legislators were indicted, and a number of them went to prison. The secretary of state committed suicide when he was summoned to testify about his role in gambling corruption. There have been embezzlement scandals in the state gaming commissions of West Virginia and Kentucky. The FBI has raided one casino on the Gulf Coast and identified it as one operated by a crime syndicate. If state legislators could not handle charity bingo without corruption, how will they handle hard-core gaming?

2. Once a state begins to receive gambling revenue it will become dependent on that reallocated money. Whenever gaming revenues decline, legislatures will be open to diversification of gambling. States that begin

> *"Gambling is regressive, meaning it preys upon those who can least afford to play."*

with lotteries inevitably move to casinos, video poker, off-track betting and other forms of gambling to shore up declining revenues. In this way gambling begins to control the state rather than the state to control gambling.

*Myth #10: Compulsive gambling is not a problem in states that have gambling.*

*Gambling*

State-sponsored gambling increases the number of compulsive gamblers. Monsignor Joseph Dunne, former president of the National Council on Compulsive Gambling, states, "All studies show that accessibility to gambling determines the ratio of people who become addicted to it. The more accessible it is, the more people who become involved. That's really the problem with lottery as differentiated from racetrack or casinos."

# Americans Have Historically Considered Gambling Unethical

by Ivan L. Zabilka

**About the author:** *Ivan L. Zabilka is director of the Coalition for Gambling Reform and editor of its newsletter,* Gambling Economics.

All the world religions spend significant space in their sacred writings attempting to define how to live on the edge between selfishness and selflessness. All of them are not, however, equally relevant to where the majority of U.S. citizens are on moral issues. The primary concern here will be the Judeo-Christian heritage that informs so much of American life and relates to the beliefs of the 53 million Catholics, the 10 million or more Jews, and the 60 million or so Protestants. The consideration here is of the more generalized moral and ethical issues that are rooted in that heritage.

## Historical Perspectives

The definition and cataloguing of what is vicious, called a vice, changes over time. The flogging of seamen as a means of discipline was routine in the 1600s and 1700s. Today, litigation would surely follow any captain who attempted it, even on the high seas out of the jurisdiction of the laws of any particular country. Flogging was not a vice in 1650. Now it is. Similarly, it was thought vicious for a woman to smoke a cigarette in 1890. By 1960 most Americans had a difficult time seeing that as a vice. At worst it was a bad habit. Strangely enough, with increased evidence of the clear cause and effect of smoking with cancer, heart disease and birth defects, the habit which harms self and others is once again becoming a vice. Our definitions and acceptance of specific acts as vices are flexible and changing. Yesterday's vice is frequently today's entertainment.

There is a similar ambivalence toward gambling as a vice. Attitudes have changed over time. Archaeologists have found many pair of dice in the ruins of

Abridged from Ivan L. Zabilka, "Morality and Gambling," in *Striving After the Wind*, an unpublished manuscript. Reprinted with permission of the author.

Pompeii in Italy, a city that was suddenly buried by the eruption of Mount Vesuvius. Their presence in numbers implies that playing with them was common. Some of them are loaded, which further implies that there was gambling hinging upon the outcome of the dice. Otherwise, there would be little motive to load them. While we might think that the mere presence of dice does not reveal attitudes toward them, the presence of cheating places them among the less admirable features of the society.

> *"Attitudes [towards gambling] have changed over time."*

We know that in ancient Greek writings some of the philosophers thought that gambling was detrimental to the state. The ancient Egyptians thought that gambling made men effeminate. So, even in the ancient world beyond the influence of the Judeo-Christian ethic, there was uneasiness about gambling, if not clear disapproval.

The early church theologian Tertullian disapproved of gambling. Presumably, others did as well, although no modern scholar seems to have made such a survey. Negative attitudes toward gambling in the medieval period were very mild, and both the rich and the poor gambled, but at different games. The Catholic Church was generally silent upon the issue. With the beginning of the Renaissance gambling began to appear in the popular culture. Jerome Cardano (1501–1576), the Italian philosopher, was known as the gambling scholar. He seems to have initiated some elementary understanding of the probabilities in games of chance. While dice and cards became prominent for gaming during the Renaissance, lotteries also arose just slightly later during the 1600s. Lotteries were conducted both privately and under governmental auspices. With poor communications they were difficult to advertise broadly, and as a consequence, they tended to be local. They were subject to a great deal of manipulation and fraud.

## Gambling in Early America

The frequency of fraud drew the attention of Protestant clergymen, and various of them spoke out against the lotteries. The ambivalent attitudes of the accepting Catholics and the critical Protestants were imported to the colonies on this continent when the great migration to the new world began. As the influence of lotteries grew, some clerics like Cotton Mather spoke against them. The power of gambling became so great that more was spent on lotteries than was spent by the colonial or early federal governments. With only a tiny percent of the population sitting under the teaching of the few well-trained clergy, the influence of Mather and others was limited. His basic argument was that the casting of lots was judged by the Bible to be ". . . used only in weighty cases and as an acknowledgement of God sitting in judgement," and not as ". . . the tools of our common sports." Despite the solemn warning, the lotteries grew until by 1832 the eight eastern states were spending \$55.4 million on lotteries, more than four times the national budget.

Lotteries came under increasing attack during the 1830s and 1840s as a moral blight upon society. In 1827, Governor Dewitt Clinton of New York stated that they were of dubious morality and "pernicious" in their effect upon the people. By 1833 New York outlawed lotteries. Many other states followed suit. During the Civil War lotteries staged a small comeback. They were perceived as useful for revenue. Following the war, however, they were rejected again, except for the Louisiana Lottery in a predominantly Catholic state. The Louisiana Lottery was hardly a paragon of virtue, for the charter was obtained and kept by massive bribery and the corruption of the legislature and judicial system of the state. The Lottery further bribed newspapers to carry the lottery ads by paying up to four times the going rates for advertisements.

The campaign against the Lottery was one of the early victories for the reformers who became known as Progressives in the 20th century. Religiously, the Methodists and Baptists were most prominent in this particular crusade.

This background is necessary to refute the common lottery proponent claim that everybody gambles and they always have. The facts are that most Protestants in the past simply did not gamble. In the last half of the last century, only a tiny fraction of the population, perhaps as low as ten percent, gambled at all, whether religious or not. Gambling was regarded as not respectable and was conducted by those on the fringe of society.

## The Growth of Gambling's Acceptability

After the turn of the century, however, change came rapidly. In the cities, the numbers game replaced the lottery, usually run on the sly at cigar and news stands. Some small merchants also participated to enhance their income, for the numbers games frequently paid out only on the number the fewest picked. There was a similar rise in illegal poker games, which created the image of the well-heeled, polished professional gambler. The reality was often sleazy, for the venue was the riverboat, the backstreet hotel, although poker games were also conducted in private clubs for higher stakes. The alliance with alcohol and prostitution was formed.

The more well-to-do gambled at the few tracks that were scattered around the country, most prominently in Kentucky and New York. Only a fragment of the population gambled on the horses until communications were organized by the Mob in the thirties to provide more sure information to the bookies. In the first half of this century many people played a wide variety of games, and more often than

*"In the last half of the last century, only a tiny fraction of the population . . . gambled at all, whether religious or not."*

not, gambling was NOT part of the fun. For the first two-thirds of this century, gambling was widely disapproved as an immoral activity that caused one to associate with bad characters, frequently from the underworld. Gambling was assumed to have the potential to lead to dissolute character.

During this time the primary arguments of the Protestant leaders were that gambling was an attempt to take the goods that belonged to someone else without working for them or giving something in return. It was viewed as a form of theft, only slightly less repulsive because the element of consent was present. The ministers also pointed to the element of greed present in gambling, a vice clearly condemned in a variety of Old and New Testament passages. The operators of gambling games were regarded as reprehensible for preying upon the innocent. None of these factors has actually gone away, but the attitude toward their validity has changed.

> *"During World War II a major attitudinal change [toward gambling] took place."*

During World War II a major attitudinal change took place. With so many men in uniform with so much time on their hands, gambling became a common form of recreation. There were sharps who abused and accumulated others' money, but mostly the bets were small and the time passed more agreeably. A larger portion of the population, numbering many millions, developed a more ambivalent attitude toward gambling. The nature of gambling as an escape was especially appealing during the stress of war when any moment could be your last. The stress could be controlled in the artificial world of cards and dice. Even more important for the developing of the gambling habit, and the production of pathological gamblers, was that in the service you did not go unfed, or unclothed, or unsheltered or untransported, even if you did lose all your money. Insulated from the consequences of gambling, the military personnel were able to perceive the recreational aspects without recognizing the dangers in a less controlled environment. In the military, while some mobsters were present, the immoral associations were reduced. As a consequence, many adult males learned the thrill or excitement of having an experience heightened by having something at stake, with money riding on it.

## The Campaign to Remove the Stigma from Gambling

After the war, with a vast new audience, illegal gambling boomed. In addition, a much larger part of the population pushed for the legalization of some form of gambling, or the expansion of what was already available. Spearheading the move to legitimize and legalize gambling were such as the author and gambler Jimmy Breslin, who argued that there was a basic right to gamble that was being infringed by outmoded laws designed by little old ladies and other "blue-nosed thinkers." While the basic attitude toward gambling was indeed changing, few bothered to take up the moral issues.

A few writers attempted to deal with the more substantive reasons why gambling was immoral. The association with the underworld and crime was a genuine strike against gambling. If gambling could be detached from the Mob, severed from its evil influences, perhaps it could be sanitized into an appropriate form of recreation. This still failed to deal with the two commandments against theft and covetousness, but it was a start. Of course, there was pulling in both directions. In Minnesota, the clean-up eliminated all the slot machines, of which there were over 8000 around the state, under the leadership of reform governor Luther W. Youngdahl. In most states, however, there were efforts to legalize various forms of gambling in an effort to take it away from the Mob. The Federal Bureau of Investigation and Estes Kefauver, the Senator from Tennessee with presidential ambitions, waged war on the Mob in the early 1950s, trying to detach their interests in Las Vegas.

The argument on the part of gambling proponents was that there should be no moral stigma attached to taking the money of those who are willing and are having fun in the process. This seemed plausible to many because the concept of a pathological gambler was essentially unknown. The impact upon homes was not recognized. The end of expanding legal gambling seemed harmless, and would surely cut into illegal gambling.

## Success for Legalized Gambling

The drive to expand legal gambling has been continuously successful ever since. The number of tracks expanded rapidly in the 1950s. Off-track gambling became legal in a few places. Casino gambling expanded rapidly in Vegas after the war and then, in the 1970s, to Atlantic City. Casino gambling is the hottest expansion area in the mid-1990s, since a 1989 law gave the Indians the right to match any type of gambling allowed in a given state. In the 1970s and 1980s, the lotteries proliferated to 37. Riverboat gambling has been revived, with more boats afloat than was ever the case in the 19th century. The legalization of gambling encouraged millions to gamble who never would have when it was illegal, including approximately four out of five church members. The campaign to make gambling seem to be good clean fun has succeeded, and women have been enticed into the action in nearly the same proportion as men, if, however, their preference is for different kinds of gambling.

The church was co-opted into the campaign to make gambling legal and recreational. Statements by clergymen stating that they could see no

> *"The campaign to make gambling seem to be good clean fun has succeeded."*

problem with an occasional bet on a nag or a friendly low-stakes poker game made the popular newsmagazines. A Cincinnati Catholic bishop received wide publicity in the national press for defending gambling as ". . . a legitimate amusement or recreation because it is intended as a necessary relaxation of the mind." Clergy statements of opposition, if printed by the secular press, were buried deep or confined to the letters to the editor, where they frequently seemed spoil-sport. Extended discussions of the moral issues were confined to religious journals, most of which had very limited circulation.

## Refuting Other Justifications

Gambling as recreation was not the only effort to remove the moral stigma. Other gambling proponents sought to compare gambling to various business activities that had elements of chance or speculation in them. The attempt was to make gambling moral by comparing it to something that was not deemed immoral. The most common comparison was to investment in the stock market. This rather misses the point that most make money in the stock market while only a minute fraction win at gambling. For some the stock market is gambling, which, of course, doesn't make either one moral. Stock speculation has had disastrous results for some, just as gambling has. The comparison ignores the fact that whatever similarity might exist simply points to greed being the common denominator of both activities. Gamblers attempted to ride the reputation of responsible businessmen.

Yet another justification was that gambling was no different from sweepstakes, which most Americans found harmless since they did not have to invest anything other than a stamp. The gamblers reasoned, however, that playing for a prize put up by the participants in gambling was no different than playing for a prize put up by the soap company in a sweepstakes. Such reasoning ignores that the soap company can afford to put up the prize from its advertising budget, whereas the gambler frequently plays his livelihood away. One might as easily argue that both are equally immoral since all customers of the soap company help pay for the sweepstakes, whether they wish to or not. Too many lost track of the fact that the gambler pays for the so-called recreation, and there are many forms of more fruitful recreation than gambling. . . .

> *"From 1950 to 1990 gambling moved from a position of moral condemnation to one of moral acceptance."*

Gambling misses the point of living in civilized society, and exchanges it for selfish individualism. Civilized society has always involved the responsibility to be brotherly, that is to care for one another. That is very far removed from attempting to rip off a person in a gambling game. Society always works better when we observe the Golden Rule. Just because elements of the Judeo-Christian tradition have become unpopular does not mean that they are irrelevant to a functioning society that operates in the best interest of its citizens. Caring and loving have nothing in common with gambling. Gamblers are predators. They do not practice self-denial for the benefit of others, and thus contribute little to the well-being of our society.

From a religious perspective, nothing positive can be said about those individuals or governments that promote gambling. Gambling makes its profit at the expense of those who can be tempted to seek something for nothing. This is immoral, regardless of how many are doing it. The government, in the past, has frequently served to limit the effects of evil upon society through law. Now the government encourages evil effects for its own revenue benefit. From 1950 to 1990 gambling moved from a position of moral condemnation to one of moral acceptance. What has changed is rooted in our ignorance. What is moral has not changed.

# Gambling Does Not Violate Catholic Teaching

## by the Pennsylvania Catholic Conference

**About the author:** *The Pennsylvania Catholic Conference is the official public affairs agency of the Catholic dioceses of Pennsylvania, responsible for promoting the church's views on issues that affect state government.*

The current public discussion of "riverboat gambling" in Pennsylvania has prompted the Pennsylvania Catholic Conference to review the moral and social issues related to the topic of gambling and to offer this statement as a guide to future deliberations on this important issue.

### Considerations Before Legalizing Gambling

There are two major aspects to the consideration of gambling. The first is the theological or moral aspect. From this perspective, we need to consider whether gambling is immoral in itself or whether it is morally neutral, but easily subject to circumstances which can effectively render it immoral.

The second is the public policy and societal aspect. Here the subject becomes more complex, leading us to consider the following questions: Will the expansion of gambling in Pennsylvania enhance the state's revenues without adding to the state's social problems and law enforcement burdens? Will the state be able to regulate gambling so that organized crime will not become involved? Will there be appropriate limits set to protect gamblers from addiction and misuse of personal funds? None of these questions is easy to answer and therefore each piece of proposed legislation will need to be carefully evaluated.

### Theological and Moral Perspectives

We wish to clarify, first of all, that the Catholic Church, according to its traditional theology, does not consider gambling to be intrinsically evil. In fact we recognize that, properly controlled, gambling can have positive aspects such as the provision of legitimate recreation, the generation of funds for acceptable causes and in some cases the enhancement of local economies. There are, how-

The Pennsylvania Catholic Conference, "Criteria for Legislation on Gambling," *Origins*, September 1, 1994.

ever, certain principles governing the intentions of the person who gambles as well as the structure of the activity itself which determine its morality in particular situations.

Traditional Catholic teaching maintains that gambling is morally acceptable when all of the following conditions are met:

1. The money or possessions wagered are not needed to support one's family or to fulfill other just obligations.
2. A person participates freely.
3. The revenues derived from gambling are not used to support any illegal or immoral enterprise.
4. The games of chance are operated fairly and every participant has an equal chance of winning or losing.

The recently published Catechism of the Catholic Church succinctly expresses Catholic teaching as follows:

> Games of chance (card games, etc.) or wagers are not in themselves contrary to justice. They become morally unacceptable when they deprive someone of what is necessary to provide for his needs and those of others. The passion for gambling risks becoming an enslavement. Unfair wagers and cheating at games constitute grave matter, unless the damage inflicted is so slight that the one who suffers it cannot reasonably consider it significant.

## Public Policy and Societal Perspectives

In sharing the Catholic theological perspective on gambling, we are also aware of and very concerned about other important and related aspects of the issue that would serve to make specific pieces of gambling legislation morally unacceptable. We believe that the promotion of the common good of society and the protection of individual rights is always to be the primary goal of public policy. Accordingly, the potential negative consequences of an expanded "culture of gambling" need to be carefully evaluated.

Since gambling is itself morally neutral, but because issues related to gambling can make it morally unacceptable, individuals who participate in gambling are obliged to make conscientious, prudential judgments about their activity. This applies as well to civil governments which sponsor gambling and to the owners of gambling establishments as it does to their patrons. For the same reasons, protective criteria must be considered

*"The Catholic Church, according to its traditional theology, does not consider gambling to be intrinsically evil."*

in the evaluation of gambling-related legislation. Some of these are as follows:

1. The legislation should contain provisions for maintaining the moral and legal integrity of the games. Such provisions should seek to prevent the involvement of organized crime.

2. There should be reasonable and enforceable safeguards in the legislation to discourage the abuse of gambling by individuals. These could include, for example, the placing of reasonable limits on the amounts which can be wagered and the imposition of restrictions on gambling credit.

3. All or a significant portion of the tax revenues resulting from gambling activity should be used for programs that benefit the people of the state or those who reside in the communities where the games are operated. However, civil governments should rely on equitable tax policies and not excessively on tax revenues from gambling.

4. The legislation should contain a local option provision which enables the people to decide through referendum whether gambling should be permitted in their local community.

5. Prohibitions against underage gambling must be clearly stated in the legislation, and such prohibitions must be strictly enforced.

Legalized gambling which is not properly regulated involves considerable risks to individuals and communities with possibly very negative consequences. For this reason, if political leaders legalize riverboat or other forms of gambling in Pennsylvania, they have the obligation to minimize the dangers by safeguards like those recommended above. Otherwise, responsible citizens and organizations should oppose an expansion of legalized gambling in our commonwealth.

# Americans Have Historically Accepted Gambling

## by J.M. Fenster

**About the author:** *J.M. Fenster is a frequent contributor to* American Heritage, *a semimonthly magazine sponsored by the Society of American Historians.*

"I'm dad-gum disgusted at trying to police every half-square and every half-house," Senator Huey Long told a radio audience in Louisiana in May 1935. "You can't close gambling nowhere where people want to gamble."

### "You Can't Close Gambling"

Dozens of casinos in Saint Bernard and Jefferson parishes reopened the next day, after a nearly five-month hiatus.

In California, Santa Anita Race Track was in the midst of its second season in the summer of 1935. As sleek as a luxury ocean liner, it brought horseracing to the West Coast, whereupon a network of bookmakers brought it to the neighborhoods. "I had a wedding at four o'clock yesterday," wrote a minister from Pico Boulevard in Los Angeles. "It was with no little reluctance that the bride's parents turned off the radio which bore the news of their horses."

Back on the East Coast, Harlem ministers reported that gamblers couldn't wait to go to church. Once there they waited anxiously for the hymn to be announced, so that they could bet it, by its numerical designation, in the numbers game. That New York game was controlled by Dutch Schultz, a gangster who feasted upon such superstition, though one day when the winning number in his game came up 0-0-0, he was gunned down by rivals.

Three weeks later the police in Grand Rapids, Michigan, cracked down by putting Mrs. Eleanor Girodat in jail. She had organized a bingo game to raise money for the Catholic Daughters of America.

That one year, 1935, served as a trial for Huey Long's supposition that "you can't close gambling nowhere where people want to gamble." Every other year in American history has tested it as well and, so far, proved it.

The lines were drawn tightest around gambling in America in the nineteenth century, when the betting crowd was small and maverick, pushing around in search of "a place where everybody can do what they please, just so they don't interfere with other people's rights," as a Reno, Nevada, man later said. The best that could be said of professional gamblers in those days was that some of them had nice clothes.

Some of them did not. In 1835 the upstanding citizens of Vicksburg, Missis-sippi, rose up in rage against the gamblers who camped along the river there. They went from shack to shack, chasing the bettors into the swamp, and when they found resis-tance at one dark place, they dragged

> *"You can't close gambling nowhere where people want to gamble."*

five of its denizens out and hanged them from a tree. The incident was widely publicized, and it drew a line between good and bad in the gambling issue, for both sides to see.

Since that eerie night the line has faded. Gambling itself has turned from a so-cial ill to a social remedy; the town today that tried to chase gambling interests out might trip over its own head.

Nothing in gambling has changed as much as have the gambling interests, the people behind it. They create the games, run them, and, in the process, define the bettors. Gambling interests include gangsters and syndicates, but also church groups, charities, corporation stockholders, Indian tribes, and state and local governments. The newcomers are at once part of the tradition of gambling in America and a departure from it. Vicksburg, as a matter of fact, is still chas-ing bettors down to the river—but only as far as the casinos lined up there.

## Gambling in Early America

The Puritans of Massachusetts lost little time in enacting America's first law against gambling in 1638, and in 1682 Quakers in Pennsylvania passed their own law against gambling and "such like enticing, vain, and evil sports and games." Other colonies, especially New York under the Dutch, were not so strict about private games, but all the colonies depended on one public game, the lottery, as a respectable financial tool. At a time when capital was scarce and taxation an extremely sensitive issue, lotteries supported most schools and public works. Harvard College resorted to lotteries for many capital projects until 1793, when the Stoughton Hall lottery didn't raise enough money to pay the grand-prize winner, who was unsympathetic and caused a fracas.

Just before he died, Thomas Jefferson was planning to raise money by staging his own lottery, with most of the Monticello estate as the prize. As heartbreak-ing as Jefferson's situation was (especially since it was brought on in part by gambling debts), the lottery was often used as a means of liquidating property when no single buyer could be found. . . .

During the late eighteenth century, card games were enjoyed as a fashionable after-dinner alternative to music in private homes in the Southern and Middle Atlantic colonies. When Abigail Adams, a New Englander, visited Philadelphia in 1791, she was aghast: "I should have a winter of dissipation indeed, if I accepted all my invitations to routs [big parties] and tea-and-cards." One of the best cardplayers in Philadelphia was Mary Morris, wife of the financier Robert Morris; another was Lucy Knox, whose husband, General Henry Knox, was Washington's chief artillerist. The games of loo and whist were the most common in such circles.

A typical colonist in attitude was the untypical man George Washington, who was content to gamble at cards all day, especially if it was raining out. According to his ledgers—and assuming that in this one specific case a gambler's own records can be trusted—he broke even overall, despite a stinging stretch from January 1768 to April 1769, when he never won once, and lost a total of twelve pounds, ten shillings, and threepence.

As a soldier, however, Washington had far greater problems with gambling, that by the men in the ranks. In 1756, when he was the leader of the Virginia militia, he was warned that he would lose the support of the Virginia House of Burgesses if he could not do a better job of controlling gambling among his men. During the Revolutionary War, as commander in chief of the Continental Army, he issued vehement orders against all "games of chance," but the fact that he had to issue such orders regularly indicates the frustration he faced over the issue. Even at Valley Forge, where men were freezing and going hungry for lack of supplies—

> "A typical colonist in attitude was the untypical man George Washington, who was content to gamble at cards all day."

or, *especially* at Valley Forge, where morale was so low among the troops—gambling was rampant, and it was a keen concern for General Washington.

The favorite game among the soldiers was "toss-up." One player (say, a sergeant) called heads or tails (say, heads) as the other threw a handful of wagered halfpennies in the air. When they landed, the sergeant gathered up the ones facing up heads, and the other player took all the tails. No one could stop a game so simple that it required only spare change and boredom, not where both were in good supply.

## Gambling's Expansion in the Nineteenth Century

As the country expanded, each new advance in transportation brought a new chapter in gambling history. Transportation lines attract professional gamblers because they offer easy avenues of escape, along with a continuing supply of travelers burdened with large amounts of cash. Turnpikes, canal houses, riverboats, Great Lakes ships, and railroads all developed distinct traditions in gambling. The automobile brought a great deal of this to a halt simply because it precluded chance contact, the very elbowing among hundreds of people that brings about the games. Even today, teams of three-card monte players wander through the cars of Chicago el trains, acting out parts written for them a hundred and fifty years ago. . . .

Three inventions developed in the latter part of the nineteenth century allowed gambling in America to expand from a diversion into a major industry. The first one, the telegraph, could have done the job all by itself. The others were the parimutuel system and the slot machine.

> *"Three inventions . . . allowed gambling in America to expand from a diversion into a major industry."*

The telegraph was first exhibited in the United States in 1837 by S.F.B. Morse, but an 1872 refinement called the duplex system allowed more than one message to go through a line at once. Thomas Edison invented the quadruplex system in 1874 that allowed for simultaneous transmission of four messages; through these means, telegraph lines were soon readily available to private concerns. Bookmakers could obtain information on races all over the country, almost immediately. They could also make connections with bookmakers in other cities, forming powerful syndicates for moving around money and bets.

From about 1890 to 1908 the horseracing world was in turmoil. . . . Horseracing was nearly dead, and then, just before the Kentucky Derby in May 1908 the mayor of Louisville served what seemed to be a death stroke by banning bookmaking at the track. The track manager of Churchill Downs, Matt Winn, knew that without betting, racing was not viable. He appealed in court but was offered only a slight concession: bookmaking was outlawed, but not pool betting. Winn accepted the decision and retired to the basement rooms at Churchill Downs, where he rummaged around until he found some parimutuel machines that had been purchased from the French manufacturer about thirty years before. The machines could add each new bet to a general pool and calculate each winner's share of that pool, after overhead expenses had been subtracted. Not only did parimutuel wagering obviate the trackside bookmakers, it also allowed state governments to take a tax on bets. New York State legalized parimutuel betting in 1913, and many other states followed suit. . . .

The modern slot machine was invented by Charles Fey in San Francisco in 1895, but Chicago has been the manufacturing center for them almost ever since. They quickly became commonplace in many drugstores, taverns, gas stations, country clubs, and veterans' and fraternal clubs. Most slot machines paid off in cash, though some of the ones in public places would pay off in gum or cigarettes, which could easily be redeemed for cash. . . .

Even as the telegraph, the parimutuel system, and the slot machine were promising stunning growth for gambling, the frontier was closing, as far as gambling law was concerned. By 1907 Arizona and New Mexico were far more interested in obtaining the respectability of statehood than in continuing to entertain a demimonde. Arizona Territory outlawed gambling that year with a law that inventoried the trade, banning "Faro, monte, roulette, lansquenet, rouge-et-noir, rondo, fan-tan, poker, seven-and-a-half, twenty-one, chuck-a-luck, slot machine or any banking or percentage game, or any other kind of game played with cards, dice or any device." It was a brash move for Arizona, which derived most of its education budget from its tax on casinos. Aside from that, the reform proscribed a certain way of life in both territories. "Oh, this place is dead now," said a young Arizona man in 1908. "Sleeping has become one of our principal industries.". . .

## The Great Moral Debate of the 1920s

At the end of the 1920s, the last great moral debate over gambling erupted when Bishop James Cannon, a Methodist, disclosed in August 1929 that he did speculate actively in the stock market but that since he used careful consideration in making choices, it was not risky, and it was not the same as gambling, which he rejected.

"It seems to me that the Bishop is trying to say that it is sinful to follow a bad tip and virtuous to follow a good one," responded Heywood Broun in *The Nation.* "The late Arnold Rothstein was just as eager as the Methodist leader to eliminate the evil factor of chance from his transactions. . . ." [Rothstein allegedly directed eight Chicago White Sox baseball players to throw the 1919 World Series.—ed.]

*"A 1938 Gallup poll showed that more people gambled at church games than at any other legal or illegal form."*

While Bishop Cannon was trying to explain the difference between speculation and gambling, leaders of the Catholic Church in America were reinforcing a belief that gambling is not a sin but rather, according to the chancellor of the Roman Catholic diocese in Cincinnati, "a legitimate amusement or recreation because it is intended as a necessary relaxation of the mind." Throughout the thirties bingo, raffles, and Monte Carlo casino nights became important sources of fundraising for local Catholic churches; a 1938 Gallup poll showed that more people gambled at church games than at any other legal or illegal form.

The Roman Catholic Church, both the institution and its adherents, was closely aligned with European traditions, including those of gambling games. Because of this and the fact that, as one church representative said, "there is no eleventh commandment against gambling," the church did not fight it as a fundraising activity for local churches, which were sorely burdened during the Great Depression.

Catholic churches undoubtedly used their gambling revenues for good, charitable causes. Conservative Protestants took a dim view of it, however, and they lashed out at church gambling as the thin edge of a wedge that would legitimize gambling and other vices. "I find it impossible even in my weakest moments," wrote Richard Emrich in the *Christian Century*, "when the financial needs of the church are most pressing, to imagine St. John, St. Paul or St. Peter running a bingo party or our Lord sending out his disciples to sell chances. And I shudder at the thought that some young person might say, 'It's all right to gamble. We do it at church.'"

The moral attack on gambling in America became divided among denominations and over which aspects of gambling reflected "legitimate amusement" and which were "evil circumstances." Any prospective gambler could walk through the loopholes that opened up in the argument, and obviously a great many did, without for a minute compromising their religious ideals or their intentions to go to heaven.

## Politicians Attack Gambling

Championed by ambitious politicians and hampered by greedy ones, the legal assault on gambling progressed in fits and starts through the first half of the twentieth century. Among those who leveled broadside attacks were the New York City district attorney William Jerome; the New York governor Charles Evans Hughes; the Illinois governor Adlai Stevenson, and the New York governor Thomas Dewey. And Senator Huey Long (who was alleged to have taken a cut of the illegal slot-machine revenue in Louisiana) used the state police to close down gambling casinos there until two local political bosses visited him at his hotel, according to New Orleans newspapers, and let him know that if he kept the ban on casinos, he would receive no further political support from St. Bernard and Jefferson parishes. Two days later Long went on the radio to reverse his position on casinos. He concluded, "I'll be dad-gum if it ain't a puzzling thing what to do about gambling."

Gambling interests could have said the same thing about politicians. "Those guys want it all," said a casino manager in New York City in 1913. "Last week, on top of the regular $250, they learned I'd trimmed a guy from Atlanta for $2,500 and demanded half of it. How can a fellow be square with them crooks robbing him?"

In 1956, when the mayor of Reading, Pennsylvania, called off his own antigambling drive nineteen days after he took office, federal officials stepped in and forced a major raid on slot-machine operators, one of which, the Reading House tavern, was found to be the property of the mayor's brother. The title had only recently been transferred out of the mayor's name. . . .

*"Throughout the early fifties energetic investigations attacked gambling nests all over the country."*

Throughout the early fifties energetic investigations attacked gambling nests all over the country, along with the police who cooperated with them. The investigators were young and determined, a small army headed in spirit by the freshman senator Estes Kefauver of Tennessee, whose Senate Special Committee to Investigate Organized Crime in Interstate Commerce touched heavily on gambling and showed syndicates a force that would be neither bribed nor beaten. That force was not merely the senator's own sense of integrity but the outrage aroused across America by televised interrogations of gangland figures. Only a few of the major bills written by the Kefauver

> *"By careful design Las Vegas had nothing, but everything, to do with the rest of America."*

Committee passed the U.S. Senate, and it did not eradicate illegal gambling in America, but it did succeed in smothering the momentum that organized crime had been gathering since Prohibition.

The lawyers, district attorneys, reporters, and members of Congress who went to work against illegal gambling were probably less motivated by the morality of gambling itself than by a statement contained in the Kefauver Committee report: "gambling profits are the principal support of big-time racketeering and gangsterism." That feeling was echoed by Willie Moretti, a gambling boss in Bergen County, New Jersey, who was being investigated in 1953 by Nelson Stamler, a deputy attorney general. "Willie Moretti," Stamler wrote, "who was mixed up with Owney Madden, Waxey Gordon, Lucky Luciano and other high-ranking hoodlums during Prohibition, once confided to me that his gambling take always made his rum-running profits look like peanuts."

Under vociferous attack in new holdouts like Bergen County, as well as old ones like Saratoga, Hot Springs, Newport, Florida, and Kentucky, the gambling syndicates looked around for respite. A few of them went to Havana, Cuba, but many never left the country.

## The Birth of Las Vegas

By 1931 Nevada was asking itself the very question it would ask millions of visitors in the future: What have you got to lose? The legislature passed laws that year legalizing gambling and making divorce a relatively simple procedure. The story was big news all over America. "Nevada is tired of cactus, alkali wastes, sparse population, hard times and virtue," reported the Montgomery (Alabama) *Advertiser*. "Hell's hundred thousand acres," spit the Dallas *Morning News*. The Hartford *Times* was equanimous about Nevada: "Perhaps it is merely being honest in writing laws which are hypocritically evaded almost everywhere else."

The first casinos were opened in Reno, and they were owned by Westerners like William Harrah and Raymond Smith, of Harold's Club. By 1945, with relatively minor intervention from outside gambling interests, the Nevada gambling handle was close to a billion dollars. The following ten years witnessed the development of Las Vegas, in the southern part of the state, as a gambling center; much of the capital for that development came from Eastern syndicates. A Los

Angeles gangster named Bugsy Siegel was the visionary behind the personality of Las Vegas, which became a symbol for American gambling as recognizable and as "unspeakably gaudy" as the vest of the riverboat gambler. In 1945 Siegel started to build the Flamingo Hotel on the Los Angeles side of town, the "Strip." Like Wilbur Clark, who followed him with the Desert Inn, Siegel ran out of money halfway into construction. Both men turned to the Cleveland syndicate, one of the toughest and the richest. Siegel was murdered before his hotel was finished, but he had already pushed Nevada gambling forward, far past the days of saloon doors and sawdust.

In the Las Vegas Strip the gambling syndicates had a utopia. Like William Penn creating Philadelphia or Brigham Young arriving at Salt Lake, they had a place in America to make of what they wanted. In it they acknowledged what they knew best by building a series of hotels in the milieu of the forties nightclub: in names, themes, neon signs, muted lighting, entertainment, costume, and even in the roaming cocktail waitresses and cigarette girls. The Strip's founding fathers removed any coherent sense of place. They replaced greenbacks with colorful chips and suspended time, with round-the-clock gambling, a nearly total absence of clocks, and bright lights on the Strip that give to the night the liveliest hours in the day. By careful design Las Vegas had nothing, but everything, to do with the rest of America. After nearly fifty years the Nevada experiment was a sustained success, and it finally took on a competitor in the form of Atlantic City, where gambling was legalized in 1978.

In 1964 New Hampshire conducted a lottery. Tickets cost $3 each, the top prize was $100,000, and the state earned $2.5 million: a success. Tellingly, all but one of the eighteen winners were from out of state. The lottery fever has spread ever since then to thirty-three states, and in most cases the states have imbued their lotteries with benign purpose: education in the cases of New York and New Hampshire, the elderly in Pennsylvania.

In 1980 New York State paid one of its most unsavory elements the compliment of imitation, instituting a numbers game just like "policy." A thousand numbers runners reacted by staging a protest in front of the governor's office. They needn't have worried, however, because most accounts show that the state's games of chance, including Off-Track Betting, have not cut into the illegal business. They have, however, helped bring gambling as a way of life to a greater population than ever before.

About five years ago the example set by Nevada combined with the popularity of state lotteries to obscure gambling's long history of causing problems. A new era began. In the old one gambling was one of the vices, but in the new one it has been recast as "gaming," an amusement, and it doesn't cause problems but solves them: relatively recent problems, like unbalanced state budgets, and long-term ones, like the economic displacement of Indian tribes.

# Americans Approve of Gambling

## by Ellen Donahue

**About the author:** *Ellen Donahue is vice president of marketing for GTECH Corporation, a marketing firm for the gaming industry.*

> It's name is Public Opinion. It is held in reverence. It settles everything. Some think it is the voice of God.
>
> —Mark Twain

Historically, the only "sure bet" in the gaming industry has been uncertainty and controversy. On one hand, state governments increasingly consider the benefits of gaming revenues while opponents voice familiar concerns and maintain a high profile with our elected officials.

## Breadth of Support

Ultimately, however, the true measure of this issue will be taken in the arena of public opinion. As Mark Twain observed, the power of public opinion is enormous. And a new survey among 1,200 U.S. adults from the general population provides us with a concrete foundation—and a consumer "profile"—in support of legalized gaming.

The GTECH Corporation Public Survey, conducted in February 1994 for GTECH by American Viewpoint [a public opinion research firm], showed us that Americans approve of legalized gambling by a margin of two to one (67 percent in favor). And support for expansion of gaming remains high, with 54 percent favoring expanded gaming in their states.

The main reasons for support appear to be economic- and entertainment-oriented. Significant majorities of those surveyed agreed that gaming creates jobs and increases tourism (81 percent). Seventy-four percent said that gaming is an acceptable form of entertainment, and 57 percent reported that legalized gaming helps governments keep taxes lower than they otherwise would be able to.

Members of "the public" are not the only ones aware of the economic bene-

Ellen Donahue, "The Truth About Legalized Gaming," *Public Gaming International*, June 1994. Reprinted with permission.

fits of gaming. When lotteries and casinos are available in neighboring states, public officials often say their states risk losing the economic benefits from legalized gaming. As a result, those states might have to increase taxes to compensate. However, the survey shows that fewer than one person in three (27 percent) would rather have higher taxes than legalized gaming.

*"Americans approve of legalized gambling by a margin of two to one."*

The survey showed that the South, once known as the region most strongly opposed to legalized gaming, has shown a modest short-term increase in support since a baseline survey conducted six months earlier [August 1993]. The South also has registered the greatest level of support for the expansion of legalized gaming in their states.

A longer-term trend is evident when considering a similar survey conducted by Gallup in 1951. It found that of those Americans who favored legalized gaming—only 35 percent nationally at the time—53 percent were in the Northeast and 20 percent were in the South. According to the GTECH survey conducted in February 1994, of the 67 percent of Americans who favor legalized gaming today, 65 percent are from the South. Gary Ferguson, vice president of American Viewpoint, says the consistent growth and acceptance of state lotteries across the country may have contributed to the increase in approval of gaming in general.

Not surprisingly, the East and West—with Atlantic City and Las Vegas, respectively—tend to be the most pro-gaming regions overall (with favorable ratings of 73 and 69 percent, respectively).

The GTECH survey also showed that the most popular forms of gaming are bingo (79 percent) and lotteries (75 percent). Indeed, Americans report high levels of lottery play, with 67 percent playing at least once a year and 23 percent playing at least once a week.

Riverboat gambling (67 percent), slot machines (66 percent), betting on horse races (65 percent) and casino gambling in cities (64 percent) also registered strong levels of approval.

Betting on professional sports (48 percent), video gaming (47 percent) and Jai Alai (36 percent) garnered less than majority support.

## Concern for Regulation, Moderation

This survey clearly demonstrates that the public at large is comfortable with many forms of legalized gaming—and that's good news for an industry that has traditionally had to fight for every inch of acceptance.

At the same time, the research confirms public concern regarding several aspects of gaming. Although 69 percent of those surveyed have no moral reservations about legalized gaming, respondents most often noted the potential for people to "squander" money or become compulsive gamblers, or that gambling would attract undesirable elements to local establishments.

If we indeed believe in the power of public opinion described earlier, then we must treat these concerns as seriously as we do the public support for gaming. It is in our collective interest to promote the public support for legalized gambling, while at the same time continuing to address the perceived gaming risks.

As public policy discussion about legalized gaming—from riverboat and Indian casinos to interactive lottery games—continues, quality data on public opinion will play an increasingly important role. GTECH has commissioned a series of surveys to provide useful insight into the public's perceptions and attitudes toward gaming in our society.

Ferguson suggests that these will be of greatest value to policy makers, however, when validated by similar surveys.

"Methodology and even the wording of questions can affect responses," he notes. "Although our methods and error rate ensure that results accurately reflect the opinions of 95 out of every 100 Americans, we find that policy makers often consider several similar surveys in combination to be convinced that results are reliable and directional."

For example, when American Viewpoint asked Americans on behalf of GTECH to agree or disagree whether gaming is immoral, 69 percent disagreed and 28 percent agreed. When Gallup asked if gaming is immoral, 62 percent of respondents answered no and 35 percent answered yes.

*"The public at large is comfortable with many forms of legalized gambling."*

The consistency of results for both GTECH surveys and the 1993 Gallup survey further suggests that people's attitudes toward legalized gaming are firmly held and not prone to fluctuate, according to Ferguson.

The voice of public opinion expressed in these surveys lays a reliable foundation for continued examination of the issues surrounding legalized gaming. Combined with other pertinent factors, it should help guide our public officials as we consider the role of legalized gaming in our society.

# Gambling Is Entertainment

## by Gerri Hirshey

**About the author:** *Gerri Hirshey is a contributing writer to the* New York Times Magazine.

We are the boat people. That is casino workers' slang for the millions of Americans now arriving at their portals in smelly diesel waves. We come by bus—"motorcoach," if you want to get la-di-da about it. Tonight we have been plucked from rainy parking lots all over the Houston, Texas, area, and we have clambered aboard prepared: pillows, shawls, lucky trolls, full thermoses, white bread, thick stacks of Saran-Wrapped luncheon meat. We're toting worn cotton slot gloves. Intensive Care hand lotion. Insulin. Tylenol. Cash. Doritos.

"We all here? Pedal to the metal, John. Let's git!"

## Average Americans Who Gamble

We are Jeanne's Bingo Buddies of Houston, driving all Friday night in a storm that has already spawned killer tornadoes. We're headed east, into the teeth of it; had prayers before we reached the Interstate. Voices in the dark add a gamblers' homily:

"Gonna leave our worries back in Texas, and our money in Mississippi!"

"Hallelujah."

Out east on the Mississippi Gulf Coast, strung over 30 miles from Bay Saint Louis to Gulfport and Biloxi, beckons a row of floating "dockside" gaming palaces, voted in in the early 90s by Harrison and Hancock counties, some up and running within five months. These are casinos so new that construction workers must weave through gamblers, so busy that some of these $25 million to $50 million investments can pay for themselves in a matter of months.

They'll be waiting for us there in the yawning bus bays, counting heads, papering us with discount coupons. We are low rollers. Slot hogs. And we are part of the great, teeming, itchy-fingered masses that have made legal gambling—now known as "casino entertainment"—America's new national pastime.

Gambling is now bigger than baseball, more powerful than a platoon of Schwarzeneggers, Spielbergs, Madonnas and Oprahs. More Americans went to casinos than to major league ballparks in 1993. *Ninety-two million visits!* Legal gambling revenues reached $30 billion, which is more than the combined take for movies, books, recorded music and park and arcade attractions. Thirty-seven states have lotteries; 23 have sanctioned casinos. More than 60 Indian tribes have gaming compacts with 19 states. As this century turns, it's expected that virtually all Americans will live within a four-hour drive of a casino.

> "Okay, Buddies, sing it *out!*
> *There is a bingo spirit in the air*
> *Cause Jeanne's Bingo Buddies go everywhere*
> *We sit together so that we can share*
> *We're gonna WIN WIN WIN!"*

Rolling toward the Louisiana state line in a big German-made bus, we are the new Gambling Nation, a yammering, munching, snoring aggregate of Italian-, Polish-, German- and African-Americans, tenth-generation Texans, Latinos—and one Comanche. Most of us work; some are retired. Between us we dabble in bingo, the ponies, the dogs, the lottery, keno, cards and the slots. We'd like to win but we sure don't count on it. And if we do hit, our expectations are modest. "Three cherries and you take the family to Red Lobster instead of ever-lovin' Roy Rogers," a gent in a string tie explained to me recently in Las Vegas. "Hell, why *not?*"

*"We are part of the great, teeming, itchy-fingered masses that have made legal gambling . . . America's new national pastime."*

And so we stand in lottery lines and climb aboard buses on the strength of *possibilities*. They're limitless, but with absurdist odds. America has come to count heavily on our cheerful folly. Our modest stakes have become the last best hope for budget-strapped state legislatures, for long-impoverished Indian tribes now permitted to run gaming ventures, for stockbrokers and investment bankers looking to salve the wounds inflicted by 80s excesses. To these grateful constituencies, gambling is no longer a sin, but a saving grace. It can vanquish the ugly specter of raising taxes and shake cash into shambling infrastructures, Head Start programs, fire brigades, tribal medical clinics. It can fatten portfolios with new high-performance issues.

## The Change in Attitudes

On the strength of such boons, Mammon's had a makeover. Much has been made of the new PG Las Vegas, of the theme park hotels, the troops of Dorothys and Totos, buccaneers, knights and hunks in mini-togas who now cavort where made guys and hookers once ruled. Had any of us Buddies brought children along to Biloxi, we could have deposited them in the cheery child-care facility at the Grand Casino.

*It's O.K. now*, say the attitudinal seismologists. According to a national survey conducted by Harrah's, a top-tier casino company, 51 percent of American adults believe "casino entertainment" is "acceptable for anyone." Another 35 percent say it is "acceptable for others, but not for me." Even "gambling," the term that once conjured up green visors, cigar smoke and gumball-size pinky rings, has been buffed with warm fuzzies. We call it *gaming* these days. So Aspen. So Hyannisport. So very . . . *sportif.*

> *"To [some] grateful constituencies, gambling is no longer a sin, but a saving grace."*

Why now? Exactly 100 years ago, Congress banned all state lotteries after a huge corruption scandal in Louisiana. But for the last decade, states couldn't vote them in fast enough or push them harder. The turnabout has to do with exigency, marketing and a mother lode of skepticism afflicting the national mood.

The vision of postwar prosperity that inspired Las Vegas's early gaming entrepreneurs in the late 40s has been inverted in the 90s. Possibility—the cornerstone of this upstart democracy—has rarely been so circumscribed, as the children of baby boomers find themselves competing for low-level "McJobs" and huge companies toss buyouts at once-valued senior staffers. Certainty has eroded, too, as pension plans go bankrupt and one underinsured double bypass can compromise the futures of two or three generations. With fewer and fewer "sure things," the timing is just right for a large-scale flirtation with Lady Luck.

It made all the difference that state and city governments have been her most enthusiastic procurers. Pious and public earmarks for state lottery money—education! senior citizen programs!—helped fade the taint of sin. Further sanitation was provided by the new corporate gleam of casino ownership. As I heard it explained most succinctly in the check-in line of an Atlantic City hotel: "Honey, it's not Don Corleone anymore. It's just Donald Trump."

## Gambling in American History

Industry types like to remind you that gambling has long been the American way. After all, the first Continental Congress helped finance the Revolution with lotteries. Benjamin Franklin, George Washington and Thomas Jefferson each sponsored private lotteries. Our founding fathers were just numbers guys in wigs.

In *Temples of Chance*, his penetrating study of gambling's transformation, David Johnston outlines boom and bust cycles in American history. One telling example: Vicksburg, Mississippi, now supports four riverboat casinos, with four more planned; back in 1835, local citizens, enraged by the proliferation of riverboat cardsharps and gambling dens there, smashed gambling equipment and hanged five professional cheats.

The current gambling boom is unlike any other for its size and for its mainstream status. The big winners are not outlaws, but publicly traded corporations and state and Federal coffers. Never has government been such a devoted book-maker, taking in $25 billion a year on lotteries. The amount Americans spent on all forms of legal wagering in 1993—$330 billion—has set historical precedent of its own. Never has so great a fortune been staked on an itch.

## Casino Excitement

"I just want to see that million-dollar ladies room at the Biloxi Grand," says Maggie Smith, a Buddy. "Everybody comes back talking about that john."

"Honey, those commodes are *red* porcelain."

The Buddies tell me that folks take flash cameras into the third-floor ladies' room at the Grand Casino Biloxi, which features a hand-painted Gibson girl on each stall door and gilt carts laden with gratis cologne, lotions and jumbo cans of Final Net [hair spray]. There are snowy linen towels to help with slot sludge, the shiny grime that blackens hands after twenty minutes of play. Indelicate acoustics are softened by a soundtrack of chirping birds. It's all part of what industry literature calls "feeling casino excitement."

"Some of my hard-core bingo people won't go near casinos," says our leader, Jeanne (pronounced Jeannie) Stewart. "But the ones that come to Mississippi or Las Vegas with us look at it as a mini-vacation. They gawk as much as they gamble, go walking on the beach. Look, I work in a hospital. Of a weekend, I love to see something that's not cinder block."

For more than a decade, Jeanne, a cardiologist's assistant, and her husband, Homer, a former golf pro, have regularly ferried some 500 Houston-area Buddies to the huge, high-stakes Indian bingo halls in Texas, Oklahoma, even as far away as a Cherokee operation in North Carolina, a trip that takes seventeen hours each way.

The Stewarts know all about what investment bankers term "the pent-up consumer demand" to gamble. That mighty urge tops the demand side of an exhaustive report on the gambling industry by Smith Barney Shearson. The report's supply-side forces include the states' need for additional nontax revenue sources, the domino effect when states vote gambling in to prevent an income drain to adjacent gaming states and "high return on investment," at least initially, for new casinos.

> *"It's not Don Corleone anymore. It's just Donald Trump."*

The final supply factor is the proliferation of Indian gaming, which took in approximately $15.2 billion in 1992. Foxwoods, the Mashantucket Pequot casino in Ledyard, Connecticut, is currently the world's largest casino, hauling in more than $600 million in a year. Indian gaming is expected to grow by $500 million a year.

On the demand side, that "pent-up" urge to gamble is measured partly by the estimates of illegal gaming. *Gaming & Wagering Business* magazine, in its most recent survey, figured the aggregate illegal take for horses and sports betting books, cards and numbers to be $43 billion. Also listed in that column: "attitude changes."

## The Stress Reduction Business

Outside Port Arthur, Texas, we're still awake and chatty. Everyone is tired from the week's work—as nurses, administrative assistants, apartment house managers. But all are merry.

"*Gonna win!*" yells Malcolm Peterson, punching his bed pillow. He is the silver-haired, 52-year-old son of Sara Peterson, an elegant, witty, retired businesswoman who describes herself as "only 80." For the last half-century, Malcolm has needed his mother's 24-hour care owing to multiple Down syndrome–related disabilities. They both love the bingo trips and the casino slots. As he will prove with great glee later this morning, Malcolm always wins at the slots.

"You wait," he tells me. "I'll help you win too." Once we pass his favorite part of the drive—the refinery lights of Baytown, Texas—he curls up to nap and reaches back for a reassuring pat from his mother.

"I'm here, Malcolm. Rest now."

She lights a cigarette and leans back, looking very, very tired.

"I'm in the stress reduction business," Jeanne Stewart says. After years working in cardiac units, she can read your blood pressure in your eyes. "I see what they look like when they climb on this bus Friday night. Gray. Tense and pinched."

*"The ones that come to Mississippi or Las Vegas with us look at it as a mini-vacation."*

In workday America, the life of the soul can stagger between exhaustion and escape, with little time for reflection. For many two-career families, single parents and career-driven singles, amusements tend to be compact. Weekend trips. Movies. Fast meals out. Leisure can take on the character of the work it seeks to counterweight. And it is no accident that as jobs creating durable goods give way to the service sector, as work places become more isolationist—setting us in computer stations, telemarketing carrels, home offices—entertainment itself has become less communal, more remote.

In 1993, for the first time, the solitary pursuits of video games outsold movie admissions. Even teen-age bacchanals have been tempered by technology. For most concertgoers of Madonna's "Girlie Show" tour, the Main Dish was just a series of dots on a stadium video screen. Nineteen ninety-four's Woodstock II concert was expected to generate $20 million in pay-per-view revenues from couch potato communards.

How, then, can anyone profess surprise at the casinos' staggering numbers? They're one of the few ways left to experience Saturday night *live*, to get out amid squealing, yee-hawing humans determined to raise a wee tad o' heck.

Call it the Beyond Bugsy Effect. When he built the Flamingo Hotel and casino in 1946, Bugsy Siegel envisioned Las Vegas as an oasis for his kind of people—the restless grifters who couldn't toe that 9-to-5 line. What Bugsy underestimated was that little urge to slip the traces—if only for the duration of a bingo game, a hand of 21—laying nascent in so many of us clock punchers, homemakers and retirees.

## Something for Nothing?

The new casino doges understand. They pack Harvard M.B.A.'s, not heat, provide baby sitters instead of hookers. Of the scores of gamblers I talked to, few voiced resentment at their genial casino hosts. Their greatest contempt was reserved for their elected representatives. Government, they pointed out, is unsurpassed at fostering the great illusion that you can change your life with one bet. Nowhere, particularly in the hyperslick ads that show blue-collar winners cavorting on lavish estates, is it intimated that the state lotteries offer worse sucker odds than any casino or honest bookie. The house edge for slots runs from 10 to 15 percent; the lottery 50 percent.

Recent news magazine stories and television specials have decried this headlong rush toward fool's gold. Thundered Walter Cronkite on a cable special, "Legal Gambling—The Dice Are Loaded": "All this while a nation once built on a work ethic embraces the belief that it's possible to get something for nothing."

Uncle Walter's stentorian moralizing makes very legitimate points about the "hidden" costs of gaming. There *are* plenty of grisly true stories about grannies gambling away pension checks. But ride the buses down here, haunt the Atlantic City bus lounges, the Texas bingo halls, and the majority of seniors will tell you they're spending more time than money. Time is cheap, time is plentiful, and in "golden" America, time can be a dubious kind of wealth. Elder testimony gathered at casinos reads like a wry, cranky litany:

"I cannot tie on those darn Reeboks my kids gave me and mallwalk one more time. I spend more that way than at the casino."

"I *talk* to people on these trips. When I stay home, it's just me and Oprah."

Chapter 2

# Is Compulsive Gambling an Uncontrollable Disease?

# Compulsive Gambling: An Overview

## by Michel Marriott

**About the author:** *Michel Marriott is a writer for the* New York Times.

As Joe S. strained through a lifting fog of anesthesia, his first thought was the realization that he had survived ten hours of heart surgery. His second thought was to summon a relative to his bedside to ask him about a promised $10,000 he needed to settle a gambling debt.

### A Disease or a Moral Weakness?

"I got a tube down my throat and can't talk," said Mr. S., a 45-year-old convicted embezzler who spoke on the condition that his full name not be published. "I asked for his hand and with my finger I traced a question mark in his palm and then I made a dollar sign."

Even as he began recovering from his heart disease, the illness that was still destroying his life, Mr. S. recalled recently, was something else entirely: pathological gambling.

Although Mr. S. and treatment experts describe his addiction as a progressive and debilitating illness, the question of whether pathological gambling should be considered a disease or simply a moral weakness is a matter of much debate in academic and addiction treatment circles these days.

And the answer will likely have major implications for research money into compulsive gambling and for employers and insurers that have resisted paying for intensive inpatient treatment.

Organizations like the American Psychiatric Association, Gamblers Anonymous and the National Council on Problem Gambling have adopted a medical explanation of problem gambling, some describing a physical high and withdrawal that for some bettors is similar to that experienced by drug addicts.

They say it is important that compulsive gambling be recognized as a legitimate disease, arguing that it will spur greater research into the addiction, improve care and treatment and improve the public's perceptions of compulsive gamblers, making it easier for many of them to seek help.

"Because we are the new kids on the block, as yet we do not have that social acceptance," said Mary Ubinas, director of the Gamblers Assistance Program for the State of Iowa. She said that because gamblers often appear to be healthy and functioning, many people feel little sympathy for their plight.

"A big part of our job is education," she said.

Yet other researchers remain skeptical and argue that labeling problem gambling as an illness tends to excuse people who gamble excessively from being responsible for their behavior.

> *"No one truly knows why some gamblers can't control themselves."*

"I don't think it is a disease," said Vicki Abt, a professor of sociology at Pennsylvania State University and an expert on gambling. "I think it is a terrible problem, and it is getting to be more of a problem because we don't know how to help."

Despite the years of research on gambling, she said no one truly knows why some gamblers can't control themselves while the vast majority are able to. She and other experts say that 80 percent of the people who gamble wager less than $400 a year.

"Declaring it a disease is a way of getting money to help these people," Dr. Abt said. She added that treating pathological gamblers could grow into a highly profitable industry if problem gambling was more generally recognized as a true addiction, particularly by health insurance companies that have been reluctant to pay for expensive inpatient care for gambling.

Similarly, Mitchell S. Rosenthal, president of Phoenix House, a national drug-treatment program, said there was a disturbing tendency today for people to excuse troublesome behaviors as a disease.

"It has to do with the whole question of responsibility," he said.

## The American Psychiatric Association's Definition

Such questions are unsettling to many advocates for compulsive gamblers. Officials of Gambling Anonymous and the National Council on Problem Gambling note that since 1980 the *Diagnostic and Statistical Manual of Mental Disorders*, the field's widely accepted guide to mental disorders, has listed pathological gambling as an "impulse control disorder."

The manual, which is published by the American Psychiatric Association, states that pathological gambling is characterized as a "chronic and progressive failure to resist impulses to gamble, a gambling behavior that compromises, disrupts, or damages personal, family, or vocational pursuits."

The manual further describes pathological gambling in terms of its associated features like being overconfident or easily bored and notes that people often develop problems with drug abuse, suicide attempts and nonviolent crimes.

"If this isn't a sickness, it sure mimics all the problems sicknesses have," said Henry R. Lesieur, an expert on compulsive gambling and chairman of the department of criminal justice for Illinois State University.

He said research has shown that pathological gamblers are more likely to go into trance states while gambling, and they are more prone to withdraw when they try to suddenly end their gambling.

Many researchers, Dr. Lesieur said, have found that some compulsive gamblers have abnormally high levels of endorphins in the blood when they gamble, creating a sort of euphoria like that of a runner's. And studies are being conducted to learn whether there is a genetic precondition to problem gambling, much like it is generally believed to exist for alcoholism.

He acknowledged that many people view problem gambling as a bad habit, but said, "You can start out gambling as a bad habit, but there can come a point where the disease process sets in."

## The Insurance Industry's Response

Further complicating the picture for problem gamblers is the response they often get from health insurance companies when they submit claims for their treatment.

Donald R. Thoms, director of the Gamblers' Treatment Center of St. Vincent's North Richmond Community Mental Health Center on Staten Island said: "We are probably where alcoholism was in its development fifteen to twenty years ago when treatment was struggling with insurance reimbursement.

*"If this isn't a sickness, it sure mimics all the problems sicknesses have."*

"We get our fair share of rejections, but I think insurance companies in New York have begun to recognize pathological gambling."

Of his center's weekly caseload of sixty-five to seventy patients about half have insurance that covers the cost of counseling, said Mr. Thoms. His center charges $30 to $35 a session.

Empire Blue Cross and Blue Shield, a major health insurance carrier, does not specifically cover compulsive gambling, a company spokesman said.

"If there are other mental health problems associated with compulsive gambling, for example, severe depression, we would address that," said John Kelly, a spokesman for Empire Blue Cross and Blue Shield.

Other officials noted that while some insurers offer coverage for gambling treatment, many corporations that provide coverage for their employees do not extend the coverage, in an effort to control costs.

Richard Kunnes, chief operating officer of Aetna Life and Casualty, said that some insurers that do cover gambling treatment, including his, favor treatment on an outpatient basis, such as weekly sessions with gambling counselors.

Some treatment centers have resorted to identifying their patients' gambling problems by their related ailments that insurers are more likely to recognize as diseases, said Betty George, executive director of the Minneapolis Council on Compulsive Gambling. "Many professionals are coding compulsive gambling as depression," Ms. George said. "In fact, many are depressed. The reason this is being done is so they will get paid for treating their clients."

## The Numbers on Problem Gambling

Experts say that from 1 to 3 percent of all adult Americans have gambling problems. And they say the numbers are increasing as more and more cities and states turn to legalized gaming, like lotteries and casinos, to fill yawning budget gaps.

People who describe themselves as problem gamblers say they find it hard to resist the allure of the action, of risking a bet and breathlessly hoping against the odds to win and then bet again and again. They often talk about losing homes, dashing careers and even becoming suicidal while chasing the gambler's high.

"I loved the casinos and I loved to play the poker machines," said Sue B., who described herself as a recovering compulsive gambler. In two years, she said, she went from someone who enjoyed an occasional trip to nearby Atlantic City to being obsessed with its casinos' glittery promise of cash and excitement.

Fortunately, Sue B. said, she pays what she can afford for her treatment and her insurance company pays the rest.

For Joe S., the son of an illegal bookmaker who died of a heart attack at 47, he said he had no doubt that gambling for him has been a disease. As proof, he turned to his tortured memories of late 1988.

That was the time he began his final plunge into what he now calls the "desperate stage" of his thirty years of gambling. Convinced that he was dying despite his successful heart bypass operation, Mr. S. went on the worst gambling binge of his life.

In fifteen months, more than a million dollars passed through his stubby, working-class hands and into the clutches of illegal bookmakers, through the parimutuel windows of off-track betting parlors and horse racing tracks and into the bottomless coffers of Atlantic City and Las Vegas casinos. All the while, Mr. S. said he could not manage his family's most basic expenses, such as regularly paying his household's electricity and telephone bills.

> *"People who describe themselves as problem gamblers say they find it hard to resist the allure of the action."*

In many cases, the impulse to wager becomes overwhelming and uncontrollable. And, he said, he would do almost anything, including embezzling from the payroll of the company in which he worked, to get the money to make the next bet on a horse, a football game, a pair of dice, almost anything.

"But I was a big loser," he recalled. In less than two years, Mr. S. was arrested, convicted and sentenced to a New Jersey prison for theft by deception. After serving nine months of his sentence, he was released under a special program that requires him to remain under care for his pathological gambling, he said.

Eileen A. Epstein is part of that care.

"One of the dynamics that all the compulsive gamblers I work with have in common is that there is very early deprivation for these people," said Dr. Epstein, a gambling counselor at the John F. Kennedy Medical Center in Edison, the only gambling treatment center in New Jersey. "There are emotional losses, these voids that go way, way back for them, never really feeling they are as special as they like to show people that they are."

"They want to be big shots," she said.

# Compulsive Gambling Is a Serious Disease

## by Valerie Lorenz

**About the author:** *Valerie Lorenz is executive director of the Compulsive Gambling Center, Inc., in Baltimore, Maryland.*

There were two times in his life when Mike was actively involved with God. "The first time was when I was serving as an acolyte. I did all the weddings and funerals. God was good to me and I always thanked him.

"The second time was when I was gambling. I used to pray to God every time I threw the dice. 'Dear God, let this be a winner.'

"I was on a terrific winning streak for a while. But that ended, and I started losing. That was awful. How do you tell your wife you lost a thousand dollars at a craps table?

"I started chasing my losses, staying at the casino all night, sometimes every night of the week, trying to recoup. Yes, I continued to pray, but the prayers were different then. It was, 'Dear God, just let me win enough to break even.'

"In the end I used to pray for God to end the pain, the torture."

What had started out as innocent recreation and fun became an addiction leading to financial ruin, lying, stealing, and constant emotional pain and turmoil.

"And I still went back for more," Mike says. "Every morning I swore to myself I would not gamble again. Day in and day out I tried to stop.

"Compulsive gambling is like a giant magnet pulling you to the table, and you're there with no brakes, with no way of knowing how to stop.

"The police finally did it for me. They arrested me for stealing from my company. It was such a moment of relief. It's crazy to think of it that way, but it felt like they were taking the monkey off my back. Before that, suicide seemed the only way out."

## A Different Reaction

Mike's wife, Sally, had a different reaction to the gambling. She became angry—with her husband, herself, the casino, and yes, even God.

Valerie Lorenz, "Dear God, Just Let Me Win," *Christian Social Action*, July/August 1994. Reprinted by permission of the Compulsive Gambling Center, 924 E. Baltimore St., Baltimore, MD 21202.

"Why me? What did I do that God would punish me so much? We started out as a happy family. We had our own little house. Mike loved his job and was a terrific salesman. We had enough money for me to stay at home to raise our three children. We had all we ever wanted.

"But then the gambling started. The politicians thought it would raise money for the state budget. And it seemed harmless enough.

> *"Innocent recreation and fun became an addiction leading to financial ruin, lying, stealing, and constant emotional pain."*

"At first Mike went only occasionally, and sometimes I even went with him. But then he went more and more often, and stayed longer, and spent more money. Sure, I would complain about it to him, and he stopped for a while, but then he went back. I felt so betrayed. And then he was gone all the time.

"The bills weren't paid. Day after day I got the calls from the bill collectors, from friends and neighbors Mike had borrowed from. It was so embarrassing.

"Then his boss started calling, wondering if Mike was sick, and I would have to cover for him, so he wouldn't get fired.

"Mike and I could never talk about it, because in the end he was always gone. Night after night I would be home alone, trying to keep the children happy. Do you know what it feels like to lie to your children so they won't learn about their daddy's gambling?

"I did reach out for help, and got nothing that was useful. My doctor put me on pills for my nerves. I became a zombie. My pastor told me to pray. That didn't work with the gas company. One lawyer said to file for divorce to protect myself financially. I love Mike, I didn't want a divorce.

"Life was a nightmare. Physically I was in pain, with constant headaches and stomach problems. Emotionally it was a roller coaster, from loneliness, betrayal and depression, to anger, fear and resentment.

"I turned away from God. I turned away from everyone. Yes, I used to think about suicide."

## Social Gambling vs. Compulsive Gambling

*Social gambling* can be recreational and entertaining. Social gamblers set limits on the frequency of their gambling, in the amount of time spent on gambling, and on how much money they are willing to invest—and lose—to gambling. Today about 80 percent of US adults have participated socially in gambling, gambling without a problem.

*Compulsive gambling*, on the other hand, is very different. What may have started out as social gambling can very quickly turn into pathological gambling for some people. The number of pathological gamblers is rising on a daily basis, as more and more gambling becomes available to everyone.

Compulsive gambling (the lay person's term for pathological gambling) is viewed by mental health professionals as a psychological addiction. Like other addictive behaviors, gambling addiction hurts not only the gambler, but the spouse, the children, other family members, the employer and colleagues, neighbors, and ultimately the entire community.

Compulsive gambling may strike anyone at any time. This psychiatric illness makes no distinction between economic groups, religious beliefs, age, social status, or education. Today, with the vast array of gambling available virtually anywhere, a compulsive gambler may be a teenager or senior citizen, housewife, politician, businessman or preacher, black or white, of any or no religious conviction.

Compulsive gambling's most obvious consequence is financial ruin. Typically, a compulsive gambler with a middle income owes at least one to two years of salary in gambling debts when he or she first goes for treatment. Higher income earners, such as business executives, may owe several million dollars.

Money is the substance of addiction, and compulsive gamblers have a fairly consistent pattern of how they acquire money with which to gamble. First they use money that is readily available from their paychecks or household money. When that is used up, they may dip into a savings account. Loans at this stage are usually paid back promptly.

When losses and debts increase, they will get loans from banks or the company credit union, start selling off jewelry or other valuables, or cash in stock or bonds. Repayments tend to be late.

They usually at this time also acquire a number of credit cards, which are soon charged to the limit with cash advances or with expensive merchandise resold for a fraction of the cost in an effort to get quick cash. Some compulsive gamblers have been known to have dozens of credit cards.

## Resorting to Illegal Activities

When legal acquisition of funds is no longer possible, they will resort to illegal activities. Virtually all research studies show that, minimally, 65 percent of the compulsive gambling population sampled admits to criminal activity. Teenagers tend to steal cash from mom or dad.

*"Compulsive gambling may strike anyone at any time."*

Virtually all of them write bad checks at some time or another. Housewives tend to kite the figures on a spouse's check. People with access to cash at their place of employment often embezzle funds from their company. The higher the income, the more they gamble, lose, and steal.

Besides the criminal violations, compulsive gamblers also commit civil violations, most often those related to motor vehicles.

Speeding tickets, parking tickets, no insurance, and outdated tags are common offenses among compulsive gamblers. They drive like drunk drivers. They are a menace on the highway. They also have many accidents, often totalling their cars. These accidents occur most often on the way home after a long day of gambling at the casino or race track. Often these accidents are not accidents; instead they are deliberate suicide attempts.

"I used to think that if I crashed the car, the insurance money would pay the bills and my family would have money to live on," one compulsive gambler says.

Twelve percent of compulsive gamblers become physically abusive. Also, almost all the spouses admit to becoming verbally abusive to the gambler and to their children as a means of coping with the constant state of fear and stress.

Both the compulsive gambler and the spouse tend to suffer from a multitude of psychosomatic stress-related symptoms, such as chronic headaches or migraines, cardiac complications, stomach problems, and insomnia. Video machine and slot machine players especially complain of stiff necks and shoulder, arm, elbow, and lower back pain.

Gamblers often feel, one explains, "like my head is going to explode or like my stomach is tied in knots. Sometimes you can't breathe, or you hyperventilate, or you feel like you're in a different time zone, a grey zone where nothing is real. It is not fun; it is hell."

*"Besides the criminal violations, compulsive gamblers also commit civil violations."*

Alcohol and drug abuse at this time is not unusual although more often compulsive gamblers with an alcohol problem tend to have maintained sobriety for a number of years and then crossed over into the gambling addiction. Others abuse alcohol or drugs during the losing phase of their gambling.

"You do it to numb out, to kill the pain," a pathological gambler says. "And the whole time you're trying to act normal so no one will discover your gambling. You lie to people you love. You withhold information. You wear a mask." That's why compulsive gamblers are described as Dr. Jekyll and Mr. Hyde.

While regional differences exist, current research shows an ongoing increase of compulsive gambling. In the 1980s teenage compulsive gamblers were unheard of. In the 1990s many chapters of Gamblers Anonymous and professional gambling treatment centers regularly see teenagers.

In the 1970s virtually all members of Gamblers Anonymous were white, middle-aged, middle-class males who went to casinos and race tracks to gamble. In the 1990s more than half of the members of a chapter might be women, who tend to be addicted to playing the lottery, bingo, poker or slot machines. Lower income people in general tend to prefer the state lotteries and poker machines.

## Factors in Compulsive Gambling

A number of factors lead to compulsive gambling. Invariably compulsive gamblers come from a dysfunctional family of origin, where there may be alcoholism, abuse (physical, verbal, or sexual), or an absent parent. These homes offer little nurture, and the parents do not teach effective communication or coping skills. There is a strong emphasis on money in these families, although, ironically, these parents do not teach the children how to save money or how to spend it wisely.

Personality characteristics—such as being very competitive, athletic, above average in intelligence, and motivated to achieve—are universal among compulsive gamblers, at least to date. This may change as compul-

> *"Compulsive gambling today is not only 'the addiction of the Nineties,' but has also become a major public health problem."*

sive gambling becomes a more democratic illness affecting a more diverse group of people.

Peer pressure and social pressure to gamble, such as through lottery advertisements, and the availability of gambling by phone, on credit, or at the nearest supermarket, are other factors.

Most often, though, what "pushes" the gambler from social gambling to addictive gambling are a number of losses and traumas over an extended period of time, which result in loss of self-esteem, depression, and anxiety. Repetition of those losses or traumas also tend to result in relapses.

Where can compulsive gamblers and their families go for help? The first option is that of the support group Gamblers Anonymous, which has about 800 chapters in the United States. There are also about 300 chapters of Gam-Anon, a support group for family members of the compulsive gambler.

A few professional treatment programs exist. Unfortunately, few compulsive gamblers have health insurance or money to pay for treatment.

Compulsive gambling today is not only "the addiction of the Nineties," but has also become a major public health problem. It costs the state of Maryland $1.5 billion in lost work productivity, stolen or embezzled monies, or state taxes not paid. The national costs have yet to be computed and would quickly become dated as the legalization of gambling increases.

Compulsive gambling is a public health problem of such proportion, with ongoing growth, that it can ultimately destroy the social fabric of our families and communities and the economic balance of our budgets. It is a problem that merits the concern and action of all citizens.

# Pathological Gambling Is a Psychological Addiction

by Richard J. Rosenthal

**About the author:** *Richard J. Rosenthal is a doctor and assistant clinical professor of psychiatry at the UCLA School of Medicine.*

Why does anyone gamble? Predicting the outcome of some future event, even if it is only the turn of a card or the winner of a football game, gives us an illusion that we possess greater power and control than we really have. *People gamble to control the uncontrollable.* At a time when they are feeling helpless or overwhelmed, they turn to just such solutions.

## Social Causes of Gambling

There is a big increase in gambling today. Some of the reasons might include the break-up of the nuclear family, the loss of familiar and established values, the threats of destruction to society and to our planet, uncertainty about our economic futures and, at least for those of us in the United States, uncertainty about our role as a nation. Of course, we cannot ignore the impact of new technologies, and the acceleration of change. We now have a generation raised entirely upon television. Gambling caters to a need for immediate relief and gratification, a preoccupation with material success, and a kind of action without involvement—very much the mind-set inculcated by television.

Thus, the increase in legalized gambling may be not so much a cause as a consequence of the problems. The validity of this opinion is supported by supply and demand patterns in the drug trade. As Norman E. Zinberg observed:

> . . . availability is always intertwined with the social and psychological factors that create demand. . . . For example, when the morale of U.S. troops in Germany declined in 1972, large quantities of various drugs, including heroin, became readily available, even though Germany is far from opium-growing areas.

A more recent example is the use of cocaine in the 1980s.

There is no doubt that, when it comes to gambling, greater legalization brings about greater accessibility. Particularly when coupled with aggressive marketing, this produces an increase in the number of gamblers, as well as the number of compulsive gamblers. However, rather than blame the lotteries or the other forms of commercial gaming which have proliferated, we might consider them as a reflection of the deeper changes which are taking place in society.

## Gambling and Psychological Addiction

What about compulsive or pathological gambling? I have gradually come to believe that pathological gambling is indeed an addiction. There is a great deal that we do not know about addiction, but I am convinced that whatever we will learn about neurotransmitters—about endorphins, and noradrenalin, and serotonin and dopamine—that addiction is not just a chemical reaction in the brain, and that we will still need to talk about the experience produced by the drug. Some drugs create feelings of exhilaration or euphoria. Gambling produces a sense of power.

This is an oversimplification. Gambling is more complex than that. In fact, its complexity adds to its attraction. Usually thought of as a stimulant, it is just as capable of functioning as a relaxant or tranquilizer—for many it is the numbing effect that is important—while for others it is disinhibiting. These occur in various combinations.

> *"Pathological gambling is indeed an addiction."*

Gambling can be used to regulate affect, arousal, or self-esteem. But in every case, it is the feeling, or more accurately, the state of mind, to which the person becomes addicted.

I consider *omnipotence* the central concept for an understanding of pathological gambling. I define omnipotence as an illusion of power and control which defends against intolerable feelings of helplessness, depression, or guilt. To feel omni-potent (literally meaning all-powerful) is the most basic of the self-deceptions, since it is experienced precisely at the moment one is most helpless and out of control. Omnipotence is borne out of desperation. There is *omnipotence of thought*, in which one's thoughts are regarded as all-powerful (wishing will make it so), *omnipotent action*, in which doing something, anything, even if it is something destructive, is felt to be better than doing nothing; and *omnipotent provocation*, in which one flirts with danger, and the risk of great loss, in order to prove oneself powerful and in control. *Pathological gambling is basically an addiction to a false state of mind*

## Causes of Pathological Gambling

So what causes pathological gambling? There appear to be at least three components:

1. *An intolerable feeling state—helplessness, depression, or guilt.* Specifically, the individual may feel pulled equally in two directions at once, so that

there is a sense of futility about doing anything. They may feel they can never do enough, or that they can never be good enough. Or they may feel unlovable. For some, there is a sense of irreparable guilt. I have never seen a pathological gambler who did not have significant problems in self-esteem prior to the onset of his or her gambling.

2. *A highly developed capacity for self-deception.* In addition to the omnipotence, there are other types of magical and primitive superstitious thinking, a belief that problems can be avoided, and frequently, an early pattern of lying. Again, these precede the gambling.

> *"Pathological gambling is basically an addiction to a false state of mind."*

3. *Exposure to gambling under circumstances in which it is valued.* Compulsive gambling seems to run in families. Many gamblers are initiated into gambling by a parent, the experience providing the only closeness between them, or perhaps that and sports. For some, there was a family poker game, where to be allowed a seat was a sign of acceptance, either as a family member or adult. Others gambled away from home where, through luck or skill—and many were initially skillful gamblers—their early winnings brought recognition and status.

## Signs of a Gambling Problem

It is not the length of time spent gambling, or the amount of money lost, nor is it bad luck, or poor money management, that makes a pathological gambler. In fact, it may surprise some people to learn that there are pathological gamblers who come for treatment while they are still winning! Not many certainly, but a few. Some recognize their over-involvement with gambling; their preoccupation with it while at work, or when they should be concentrating on other things. They notice that they are escalating their bets, or taking greater risks than they should. Or perhaps they are concerned about the sweaty palms, rapid heartbeat, or that feeling in the pit of their stomach. Maybe winning, or just not losing, has become too important.

Just as some people can recognize an early gambling problem, researchers are beginning to identify those who are at risk of becoming pathological gamblers. Possible predisposing factors include:

1. *A family history of compulsive gambling.* As many as one third of compulsive gamblers have a biological relative with the disorder. It is not unusual to find such a history extending through two and three generations.

2. *Growing up in a family with an extremely critical, or rejecting, or emotionally unavailable parent.* For men, this is usually the father, and there is a lifelong campaign to please that parent and win their approval. This is generalized onto others as a need to impress, and an over-concern with being appreciated. There may be a rebellion against this—a kind of pseudo-independence—as well as a great deal of destructive anger.

Many pathological gamblers grow up believing they can never be good enough, or they can never do enough. They develop compensatory fantasies of some spectacular success, like a "big win," which will show others just how good they are. Such a win, they believe, will also bring them financial (i.e., emotional) independence.

3. *An emphasis in the family on status—or an overvaluing of money.* Many pathological gamblers were taught at an early age to equate money with self-worth—or with power, control, or security. For example, I have seen a number of pathological gamblers among the children of holocaust survivors who grew up with fathers who were not only angry, depressed, or emotionally unavailable, but who believed that the only way to achieve security was to have enough money. This was their only way to counter a profound sense of helplessness, and to assure themselves that what happened to them could not happen again. It is what they transmitted to their children, who then became pathological gamblers.

4. *Men, in particular, brought up to be extremely competitive.* Pathological gamblers are, typically, extremely competitive. Many were deliberately raised that way, usually by their fathers. Winning became everything. Initially essential for parental approval, it was soon the basis of their self-esteem. For many, there is a kind of "all-or-nothing" thinking, in which one is good or bad, perfect or worthless, a super-hero or a piece of garbage. In other words, a winner or a loser.

5. *The existence of an early physical or developmental problem.* Also at risk seem to be those who are compensating for some physical or developmental problem which caused them great shame and humiliation early in life. This might include some congenital abnormality, speech defect, a problem with bed-wetting, obesity, short stature, or delayed puberty. This seems to be a factor for addictions in general.

6. *Hyperactivity.* For many with Attention Deficit Hyperactivity Disorder, gambling initially serves as a rather specific way to medicate oneself. Just as they discover with video games, or with certain drugs such as cocaine or the amphetamines, gambling has a paradoxical effect on them—it slows them down, calms them, allows them to concentrate. However, when there are other factors present, it gets out of hand. This is a subtype of pathological gambler we are only just beginning to recognize.

> *"Researchers are beginning to identify those who are at risk of becoming pathological gamblers."*

71

# State Governments Should Provide Treatment for Compulsive Gamblers

by Henry R. Lesieur

**About the author:** *Henry R. Lesieur is a professor of sociology at St. John's University in New York and a member of the board of the National Council on Problem Gambling. He is the author of* The Chase: Career of the Compulsive Gambler.

In 1974, the number of Americans who gambled was 61 percent of the total population. They wagered 17.4 billion dollars legally. In 1989, the Gallup organization reported that 71 percent of the public gambled, while the gross legal gaming handle was 246.9 billion dollars for the year. This represents a 1,400 percent increase in dollar volume in just fifteen years. Currently, forty-eight states (all but Utah and Hawaii) have some form of legalized gambling. The California lottery alone is a 2.5-billion-dollar-a-year operation.

## A Rise in Pathological Gambling

Not only did the number of states involved increase, but the variety of gaming offered has moved up as well. In addition to the state of Nevada and Atlantic City, New Jersey, local casinos have opened in Deadwood, South Dakota, in three mining towns in Colorado, and on the Mashantucket Pequot Reservation in Connecticut. Iowa, Illinois, and Mississippi authorized riverboat or dockside casinos; Video Lottery Terminals (VLTs), similar to slot machines, have been approved for Iowa, South Dakota, and West Virginia; charitable gambling has increased at a similar rate. For example, Minnesota with bingo run by charities and recently legalized pull tabs (called "paper slot machines") had gross sales of 1.2 billion dollars a year in charitable gaming in 1989.

Evidence suggests that in areas where more forms of gambling are legal, the incidence of problem and pathological (compulsive) gambling is also higher. In

1974, fewer than 1 percent of the adult population in the United States were recognized as compulsive gamblers while the comparable rate for Nevada was 2.5 percent. Recent surveys done in New York, New Jersey, Maryland, and Iowa and in Quebec, Canada, revealed that problem and pathological gambling in Iowa, where there is less legalized gambling, was about half that in the other states and Quebec, where the studies were made.

Given the recent increase in legalized gambling, it is important to determine the potential impact of such legalization on the segment of the population prone to developing problems. So far, no systematic analysis of the costs of pathological gambling has been made.

## Pathological Gambling Defined

What is pathological gambling? The American Psychiatric Association defines it as chronic and progressive failure to resist impulses to gamble, and gambling behavior that compromises, disrupts, or damages personal, family, or vocational pursuits. While the terms *pathological* and *compulsive* are technically not synonymous—for psychiatrists a compulsion is a behavior that is involuntary and in gambling this does not occur until quite late in the problem gambler's career—professionals and lay persons use them interchangeably.

While pathological gambling does not involve the use of a substance, research conducted by numerous scholars has noted similarity with other addictive behaviors. For example, pathological gamblers state that they seek "action" as well as money or a means of escaping from problems—an aroused, euphoric state comparable to the "high" derived from cocaine or other drugs. Action means excitement, thrills and tension—"when the adrenaline is flowing." The desire to remain in action is so intense that many gamblers will go for days without sleep, without eating, and even without going to the bathroom. Being in action pushes out all other concerns. During the period of anticipation, there is also a "rush," usually characterized by sweaty palms, rapid heartbeat, and nausea.

Pathological gamblers, like alcoholics and drug addicts, are preoccupied with seeking out gambling; they gamble longer than intended and with more money than intended. There is also the equivalent of "tolerance" when gamblers have to increase the size of their bets or the odds against them in order to create the desired amount of excitement.

> *"In areas where more forms of gambling are legal, the incidence of problem . . . gambling is also higher."*

Researchers in Australia, Germany and the United States have noted "withdrawal-like symptoms" in pathological gamblers who stop gambling. Hence, while not physiologically addicting, gambling has addictive qualities. Because of this, excessive dependence on gambling is often called an "addiction." Like substance abusers, pathological gamblers make frequent unsuccessful attempts at cutting down and quitting. While gambling does not produce intoxication or physical impairment and consequently does not have an impact on social, educational or occupational obligations in that way, the obsession with gambling has been noted to impair performance in these spheres.

The American Psychiatric Association is proposing new diagnostic criteria for pathological gambling for inclusion in its *Diagnostic and Statistical Manual*. Maladaptive behavior is indicated by at least five of the following: (1) preoccupied with gambling—preoccupied with reliving past gambling experiences, handicapping or planning the next venture, or thinking of ways to get money with which to gamble; (2) needs to gamble with increasing amounts of money in order to achieve the desired excitement; (3) is restless or irritable when attempting to cut down or stop gambling; (4) gambles as a way of escaping from problems or relieving dysphoric mood—feelings of helplessness, guilt, anxiety, depression; (5) often returns another day in order to get even ("chasing" one's money) after losing; (6) lies to family or others to conceal the extent of involvement with gambling; (7) engages in illegal acts such as forgery, fraud, theft, or embezzlement, committed in order to finance gambling; (8) has jeopardized or lost a significant relationship, job, educational or career opportunity because of gambling; (9) relies on others to provide money to relieve a desperate financial situation caused by gambling (a "bailout"); (10) repeats unsuccessful efforts to control, cut back, or stop gambling. "Dimensions" for each of the criteria are: preoccupation, tolerance, withdrawal, escape, chasing, lies/deception, illegal acts, relationship/job disruption, financial bailout, and loss of control.

> *"While not physiologically addicting, gambling has addictive qualities."*

## Costs of Pathological Gambling

Most gambling is merely a reshuffling of resources from one player to another with no net loss to the system as a whole. However, there is a redistribution of resources from losers to winners and from losers to the operators of the gambling activities. In some instances the operators are illegal bookmakers, people who run card rooms illegally, and so on. More recently, with the increasing legalization of gambling, the operator has been the state. State (as well as charity or corporate) profits therefore represent player losses.

Some people gamble more than others. These people, including pathological gamblers, account for a greater share of the state profits than the typical player. Most of this money comes out of paychecks and savings and is difficult to measure, particularly since the average gambler does not always lose but experiences a roller-coaster relationship with wins, losses and breaking even. Because losses outweigh wins in the long run for pathological gamblers, they typically borrow in order to finance continued play or to recover past losses. This debt can be examined.

Researchers have reported on different rates of indebtedness of pathological gamblers in treatment. The mean gambling-related debt (excluding auto loans, mortgages, and other "legitimate" debts) of individuals in treatment ranges from 53 thousand dollars to 92 thousand dollars. Female Gamblers Anonymous (GA) members have a lower level of gambling-related debt, averaging almost 15 thousand dollars. This is only the debt they accumulate and does not include the debt they pay off. For an estimated 18 percent of males and 8 percent of females in studies of treatment samples and members of Gamblers Anonymous, this eventually led to bankruptcy. Other defaults on indebtedness and civil suits also need to be added to the costs.

Since the data are limited, it is not possible to estimate the total debt, bankruptcy, and other civil problems produced by pathological gambling in the United States per year. Using a twenty-year gambling history and estimates of the number of probable pathological gamblers in New Jersey, I estimate that over 514 million dollars are accumulated in debt by compulsive gamblers in that state alone per year. This, however, is based on the assumption that pathological gamblers not in treatment are similar to those in treatment. Yet, it does not include the costs of bankruptcy proceedings, attempts to garnish paychecks, and other civil actions related to indebtedness.

> *"State (as well as charity or corporate) [gambling] profits . . . represent player losses."*

Gambling-related debts appear to be a reflection of easy credit and check cashing policies of the casino and the racing industry in New Jersey. Based on a review of the literature as well as discussions with members of Gamblers Anonymous, the following policies by gambling establishments appear to exacerbate the debt of pathological gamblers: (1) check cashing services at gambling facilities; (2) holding a check for months or allowing gamblers to "buy back" their checks at a later date rather than cashing them right away; (3) cash machines at the gambling location or within easy walking distance from the casinos; (4) credit in any form associated with gambling; (5) one-time credit checks on the gamblers rather than a periodic review of credit required; (6) no total review of credit when a payment for a [credit] marker has "bounced" or is overdue; (7) loan sharks operating in or near the gambling facility; (8) drinking in association with gambling, which produces irrational play and increases debt. This is based on overall assessments of debt-related problems of GA members and those in treatment. A review of the interaction of these policies in other states and the gambling patterns of the broader gambling public would prove useful in guiding public policy. . . .

## Gambling and Crime

Ultimately, pathological gambling results in crime. Studies conducted to date uncovered a wide variety of illegal behaviors among compulsive gamblers interviewed. Jay Livingston found compulsive gamblers involved in check forgery, embezzlement, theft, larceny, armed robbery, bookmaking, hustling, running con games, and fencing stolen goods. My research uncovered similar patterns. In addition, I found gamblers engaged in systematic loan fraud, tax evasion, burglary, pimping, prostitution, selling drugs, and hustling at pool, golf, bowling, cards, and dice. Compulsive gamblers are engaged in a spiral of options and involvements wherein legal

> *"Ultimately, pathological gambling results in crime."*

avenues for funding are utilized until they are closed off. Dependent on personal value systems, legitimate and illegitimate opportunity, perceptions of risk, the existence of threats (for example, loan sharks) and chance, gamblers become involved in more and more serious illegal activity. For some, the amount of money involved runs into the millions of dollars.

Studies of prisoners, alcohol and drug abusing inpatients, female members of Gamblers Anonymous, and a study of Veterans Administration inpatients and Gamblers Anonymous members provide useful comparative information. In all four studies, the subjects were asked if they had engaged in a range of financially motivated crimes in order to gamble or to pay gambling debts.

Approximately two-thirds of non-incarcerated and 97 percent of incarcerated pathological gamblers admit engaging in illegal behavior to finance gambling or pay gambling-related debts. White collar crimes predominate among treatment samples while street crimes and drug sales are more frequent among imprisoned compulsive gamblers. The total cost of this crime is unknown at present. An estimated 10 to 30 percent of prisoners are probable pathological gamblers. Most are also addicted to alcohol and/or other drugs. We need to find out what percent of their drug-related crimes are actually produced by gambling in combination with drug use. Treatment programs that address multiple dependencies are vitally needed in prisons and diversion programs, and halfway houses are needed for individuals on probation and parole.

Given the high level of property crime among pathological gamblers, to what extent do they engage in violent behavior? In a study examining nonviolence among pathological gamblers, Iain Brown surveyed 107 Gamblers Anonymous members in England and Scotland and found that thirty-five of them (33 percent) had criminal convictions. He examined these convictions to find out whether pathological gamblers had patterns of crime which were more similar to alcoholics (with a mix of violence and property offenses) or drug addicts (primarily property offenders). Theft and fraud offenses accounted for 94 percent of all criminal convictions. An additional 4 percent of convictions were for armed robbery. Fewer than 1 percent of convictions were for non-property violence offenses. Brown concluded that pathological gamblers are primarily nonviolent and their crime patterns are closer to those of heroin addicts who exhibit primarily property-oriented crimes than to alcoholics who have high rates of violent crime.

Estimates of the percentage of probationers and inmates who are pathological gamblers range from 14 to 30 percent. There is no accurate estimate of how many got there as a result of gambling-related offenses. In one study, 13 percent of both male and female prisoners stated they were in prison as a result of gambling-related debt. The cost of arrest, prosecution, probation, parole, and imprisonment must also be figured into the total cost of pathological gambling to the general society.

The relatively high rate of illegal activity among pathological gamblers and its obvious social cost makes it imperative that probationers, parolees, and inmates be screened. Treatment for gambling should be provided along with treatment for alcoholism and for drug addiction.

## Cost Assessment

How does one measure the cost of pathological gambling? The financial costs seem fairly straightforward. If the 514-million-dollars-a-year figure for New Jersey can be believed, even one-third of this figure extrapolated to the [entire] United States would mean billions of dollars in loans every year. . . . The cost to employers is also immense and has not yet been measured. Similarly, the expense of prosecution, probation, prison, and parole for pathological gamblers driven to crime to support their obsession has not been studied. However, if the 13 percent figure arrived at in New Jersey (or even half of it) is accurate, these costs are enormous as well.

> *"The cost of . . . prosecution . . . must also be figured into the total cost of pathological gambling to the general society."*

While financial costs can be assessed, how does one measure the cost of a suicide attempt, an ulcer, a child filled with anger and hatred for a parent or using drugs to obliterate painful memories? We could conceivably measure these in terms of cost of medical care, psychiatric care, marriage counseling, suicide prevention, drug prevention and other counseling. The greatest difficulty lies in measuring the intangible. Loss of trust in a marriage, divorce and separation, heart-wrenching tears, burning anger, shame, resentment and guilt, all leave emotional scars wrought by gambling-related problems.

No statistical evidence exists that confirms that the legalization of gambling increases the rate of pathological gambling. However, as noted above, there is an association between legalization and the extent of gambling problems. Calls to hotlines in Maryland, New Jersey, and New York reveal that the majority of callers are dependent on legalized forms of gambling. In New Jersey, for example, 62 percent of the callers mention problems with casino gambling, 33 percent with horse racing, 38 percent with state-run lotteries, 10 percent with bingo, and 8 percent with stocks and commodities. (These figures add up to more than 100 percent because many pathological gamblers have problems with more than one type of gambling.)

## State Responsibility

Gambling problems are not evenly distributed across the general population. Epidemiological surveys indicate that the problem is greater among the poor and minorities than other segments of the population. There is also evidence that the poor, minorities, and women are grossly underserved by available treatment resources. There are long waiting lists (up to six months) in states with some treatment services to pathological gamblers and their families. In spite of enormous gaming revenues the states receive and the enormous expenditures for advertising to attract new customers or repeat business, these same states devote nothing or only meager resources to the education and training of professionals and the general public about problem gambling.

At present, only [a few states] parcel out money to deal with problem gambling. . . . Massachusetts and Iowa cut the budget devoted to the issue and the governor of New York proposed wiping it out altogether while floating plans to legalize sports gambling to ease the fiscal crisis. In the 1990/91 fiscal year, the New Jersey state treasury took in a net sum of 783 million dollars from various sources (after winners were paid out and other expenses), yet the state spent only 260 thousand dollars for all compulsive gambling-related programs combined—in other words, only 3/100 of a percent of its gambling revenues—this in a state where compulsive gamblers accumulate an estimated 514 million dollars in gambling-related debts per year. The irony is that New Jersey is one of the most generous states. Nevada, for example, contributes nothing to education, training, research, or treatment of problem gambling.

Surveys indicate that approximately 1 to 2 percent of the adult population are probably pathological gamblers and 2 to 3 percent are problem gamblers. We have *no* estimates of what percentage of total gaming revenues are produced by problem gamblers. Given that they expend much more money than the typical player, it would not be unreasonable to estimate that at least 10 percent (and possibly as much as 50 percent) of gaming revenues are produced by problem gamblers.

Given this simple reality, I propose the following steps to be taken:

(1) No new forms of gambling should be legalized without first providing treatment on demand for gambling-related problems in all localities of a state. A no-waiting-list policy should be adopted whereby all costs of treatment should be derived from gambling revenues. This does not mean that the state should be responsible for the gamblers' debts, but it should be responsible for providing adequate treatment programs for the gamblers and their families.

> *"There is an association between legalization and the extent of gambling problems."*

(2) No promotion of gambling should be allowed without a warning label and an 800 (toll-free) helpline number to call for those with gambling problems. The full cost of the helpline would be derived from gaming revenues or specific gambling fees (possible sources include but are not limited to unclaimed prizes, taxes on gaming machines, entree fees, and so on).

(3) Careful epidemiological studies of all gamblers should be conducted to gain an estimate of what percentage of the money wagered is being wagered by problem gamblers.

(4) A percentage of the revenues lost by problem gamblers (and hence, added to state coffers through state gambling taxes) should be devoted to education, treatment, and research.

# The Federal Government Should Address Compulsive Gambling

## by the National Council on Problem Gambling, Inc.

**About the author:** *The National Council on Problem Gambling, Inc., is a non-profit organization that seeks to develop public awareness of pathological and problem gambling as a public health issue.*

In 1976 when the Commission on the Review of the National Policy Toward Gambling issued its final report, only thirteen states had lotteries, only one state had approved off-track wagering, and there were no casinos outside of Nevada. The Commission estimated that the total volume of money legally wagered on gambling in 1974 was $17.3 billion.

### The Spread of Legal Gambling

By 1993, the amount had reached $394.3 billion—a 2300% increase in just nineteen years. Today a person can make a legal wager of some sort in every state except Utah and Hawaii. Over thirty states and the District of Columbia operate lotteries, so that the majority of states not only actively promote gambling, but have become dependent on it for essential revenues. There is an increasing urgency by state lotteries to go beyond scratch-off tickets and weekly drawings to faster and more exciting games. Lottery keno offers a new game every five minutes. By 1993, eight states already had lottery keno in operation; twenty others had bills to introduce it. Right behind lottery keno are video lottery terminals (VLTs) and video poker machines. These are already allowed in four states in 1993, and others are very interested in legalizing them. . . .

On the horizon are technological innovations that will make gambling even more accessible, while speeding up games to make them more involving for the participant and the exchange of money more efficient. Soon there will be "cashless" gambling in which wagering is done by insertion of a credit or debit card,

Excerpted from *The Need for a National Policy on Problem and Pathological Gambling in America*, November 1, 1993, by permission of the National Council on Problem Gambling, Inc., (800) 522-4700.

home access in which cable television will bring satellite wagering into the home, and interactive television in which one can stop the action of a sporting event and wager on each aspect of the game. A cable television company has proposed televising gaming events twenty-four hours a day so that at-home participants can wager on gaming events around the world. Airlines have plans to offer interactive gambling during international flights.

> *"At what point will the American public have enough gambling?"*

To date, the innovation with the greatest impact has been the video gaming machine, commonly known as video poker. Like other technological advances in this field, video poker was introduced without any attempt to assess potential harm on the lives of participants. Widely publicized remarks by one clinician calling video gaming the "crack cocaine" of gambling and observations by hotline counselors who report an increasing frequency of calls from video poker players underscore the need for systematic impact studies of this form of gambling.

At what point will the American public have enough gambling? Comparisons with other countries suggest that saturation is a long way off. In the United States, expenditure per capita on legal gambling in 1991 was $200 compared to $400 in Australia. Some American states have already equaled or exceeded Australia, most notably Minnesota with $500 per capita and Nevada with $1,000.

## Defining Problem and Pathological Gambling

Most Americans are social gamblers. They gamble for entertainment and typically do not risk more than they can afford to lose. If they should "chase" their losses [continue to gamble at increased levels] to get even, they do so briefly; there is none of the long-term chasing or progression of the pathological (compulsive) gambler.

Clinicians tend to use the terms "pathological" and "compulsive" gambling interchangeably. This goes back to 1980 when the American Psychiatric Association first recognized compulsive gambling as a bonafide mental disorder and included it in its *Diagnostic and Statistical Manual (DSM-III)*. However, they changed its name. Compulsive gambling was thought a misnomer, since in the language of psychiatry, compulsive behavior is involuntary and "ego-dystonic" (externally derived or foreign to the self). Examples of a compulsion would include repetitive hand washing or the irresistible urge to shout an obscenity. Pathological gambling is more like an addiction. It is typically experienced in its early states as pleasurable.

*The essential features of the disorder (according to the American Psychiatric Association) are a continuous or periodic loss of control over gambling; a progression, in frequency and in amount wagered, in the preoccupation with gam-*

*bling and in obtaining monies with which to gamble; and a continuation of the behavior despite adverse consequences.* This is essentially the definition of an addiction.

Other similarities with alcohol and substance dependence have been noted. While money is important, most pathological gamblers say they are seeking "action," an aroused, euphoric state comparable to the "high" derived from cocaine or other drugs. Many will go for days without sleep and for extended periods without eating or relieving themselves. Clinicians have noted the presence of cravings, the development of tolerance (increasingly larger bets or the taking of greater risks to produce a desired level of excitement), and the experience of withdrawal symptoms. Some gamblers report a "rush," characterized by sweaty palms and rapid heart beat experienced during the period of anticipation of gambling. Other gamblers may exhibit different symptoms. For example, because many women gamblers gamble as an escape mechanism and are more passive in their gambling behavior, their physical reactions may differ from those of the action-seeking male gambler.

For both male and female gamblers there are distortions in thinking—notably denial, various superstitions and fixed beliefs, and an illusion of power and control. This latter sense of certainty or conviction about the future is born out of desperation. Trance-like or dissociative states have also been reported.

## Diagnosing Pathological Gamblers

In order to be diagnosed as a pathological gambler, an individual must meet at least five out of ten diagnostic criteria established by the American Psychiatric Association. These criteria are based on solid research and have been shown to be highly reliable and valid. The ten criteria include loss of control; tolerance; withdrawal; increasing preoccupation; gambling to escape problems and dysphoric feelings; chasing one's losses in an effort to get even; lying about one's gambling; jeopardizing family, education, job or career; serious financial difficulties requiring a bailout; and illegal activities to finance gambling or pay gambling debts.

It is not poor luck or the loss of money that makes one a pathological gambler. Some individuals have sought help in the early stages of their gambling careers, when they were still winning. They were astute enough to become concerned about their intense physical reactions or the preoccupation with gambling, which created problems at home or work. Others experience gambling problems without developing all the signs of pathological gambling, most notably the lack of progression or preoccupation with long term chasing. The term "problem gambling" has been introduced to describe this group, which may represent an early stage of pathological gambling. The term is also used as a more inclusive category that

*"Pathological gambling is more like an addiction."*

encompasses pathological or compulsive gambling as one end of a continuum of problematic gambling involvement.

## The Number of Problem Gamblers in Society

The only national prevalence study to date was conducted by the University of Michigan's Institute for Social Research under the auspices of the Commission on the Review of the National Policy Toward Gambling. The results were published by the Commission in 1976 and as a separate report by the Survey Research Center. The authors concluded that, in the year of their inquiry (1974), there was a prevalence rate of 0.77% or 1.1 million probable pathological gamblers in the United States.

While most researchers contend this rate is low, only Lawrence B. Nadler has published an extended critique of the study. He ends his analysis with what he considers to be three undeniable conclusions: (1) the methodology of the Michigan study renders its prevalence estimate equivocal, (2) many social and clinical changes have occurred since the national study was completed, and (3) a "national study is badly needed . . . to generate a valid and reliable estimate of pathological gambling which can serve as the basis for decision making in all affected realms of society." As of 1993, there is still no national study of the prevalence of pathological gambling.

*"The term 'problem gambling' has been introduced to describe . . . an early stage of pathological gambling."*

Although there has been no recent national study, prevalence studies have recently been conducted in thirteen states. While the results cannot be generalized into a national prevalence rate, some important conclusions can be drawn. Prevalence rates for probable pathological gambling range from 0.1% to 2.7%. Prevalence rates for problem gambling range from 0.6% to 3.6%. Combined rates range from 1.7% in Iowa to 6.3% in Connecticut. The data seem to cluster into two groups. States with fewer problem and probable pathological gamblers tend to be those, like Iowa prior to the beginning of riverboat gambling, with more homogeneous populations and less legalized gambling. At the higher end of the spectrum are states like Connecticut with heterogeneous populations and greater accessibility to legalized gambling.

## Legalized Gambling Creates Problem Gambling

In general, in states with more legalized gambling, the prevalence of problem and pathological gambling is about double what it is in states that have less legalized gambling. These cross-jurisdictional results support the finding of the Commission that increases in legalized gambling create new gamblers and ultimately larger numbers of pathological gamblers.

Demographically, males, non-whites, younger individuals, and those with lower education appear to be at greater risk for developing gambling problems. However, females, non-whites, lower income individuals and those under the age of thirty are underrepresented in treatment programs. They are also less likely to attend Gamblers Anonymous or to call gambling hotlines for help.

There is some evidence that gambling problems are more common among high school and college students than among the older adult population. They are also more likely to be victims of child abuse than the general population. Surveys among adolescents and young adults find rates that are three times higher than for adults. As with adult surveys, rates are higher for males and non-whites than for other demographic groups. . . .

## The Lack of Treatment and Public Education Programs

Less than one hundred outpatient and a dozen inpatient treatment centers provide treatment for pathological gamblers in the United States. In contrast, there are over 13,000 treatment programs for alcohol or other drug problems. Most mental health and substance abuse treatment professionals have not been exposed to the subject of pathological gambling in their professional training and thus know little or nothing about treating clients with a gambling problem.

In some states that have funded treatment services for pathological gamblers and their families, there are long waiting lists—up to six months. There is also evidence that the medically indigent, ethnic minorities and women are underrepresented in treatment programs. Only thirteen states provide any financial support for education or research for pathological gambling, and the federal government provides none. . . .

A preliminary comparison of the prevalence data reported earlier and the resources available for treatment and/or participation in Gamblers Anonymous leaves one with the sad conclusion that only about one in a hundred pathological gamblers is currently receiving help.

## The Need for Involvement by the Federal Government

Because of the rapid expansion of gambling activity in the United States and the problems that pathological gambling creates for society, there are a number of compelling reasons why the federal government should become involved in addressing pathological gambling issues:

(1) When the Commission on the Review of the National Policy Toward Gambling issued its Final Report (in 1976), no one could envision the new technologies that would

> *"States with fewer problem and probable pathological gamblers tend to be those . . . [with] less legalized gambling."*

bring about a qualitative change in gambling or the sheer amount of gambling and of problem and pathological gambling that exists today. The Commission report has long been outdated and there is presently no coherent national policy toward problem and pathological gambling.

(2) Gambling has become national in scope. While state governments have the primary responsibility of regulating gambling, much of the gaming industry is managed and/or conducted by large-scale interstate companies and thus falls under the jurisdiction of federal agencies. Players, meanwhile, win money in one state only to lose it in another. Cash is transferred from home state to host state. While the benefits of gambling (economic development, tourism, increased jobs and tax revenues) are local, the problems (criminal acts, family disruption, financial difficulties, etc.) are often exported to another state.

(3) The Indian Gaming Regulatory Act of 1988 has directly and indirectly caused casino gambling to spread across the country. [The law allowed Native Americans to negotiate compacts with states for legalized gambling on reservations.] With this single act of the Congress, the federal government involved itself in the consequences.

(4) Congress has also interjected itself into the gambling debate by its enactment of laws banning certain gambling games (sports betting in 1992), permitting certain gambling activities (gambling ships) or making changes in existing games (interstate simulcasting of horse races). Even the idea of a national lottery is frequently raised on Capitol Hill.

> *"Less than one hundred outpatient and a dozen inpatient treatment centers provide treatment for pathological gamblers in the United States."*

Federal commissions also interject themselves into gambling issues, such as Federal Communications Commission (FCC) rules on advertisements of gambling activities and Internal Revenue Service (IRS) rulings on gambling wins/losses.

(5) The impact of problem gambling, and more especially pathological gambling, on the federal criminal justice system is severe. Yet treatment of underlying pathological gambling that leads to gamblers' crimes and subsequent imprisonment is ignored or neglected. While federal dollars are allocated for the education and rehabilitation of alcohol and drug offenders, nothing has been done for the person with gambling problems. There are virtually no Gamblers Anonymous meetings in the federal prison setting, and while prison rules prohibit on-site gambling, many observers believe prison officials often ignore the activity if it keeps inmates occupied.

(6) Gambling can also be a problem for the armed services. A 1992 study of military personnel found 2.1% of respondents scored as lifetime problem or probable pathological gamblers and suggested the need for further study of gambling problems among military personnel.

While the treatment of pathological gambling was first begun in a Veterans Administration hospital, the lack of any federal policy toward pathological gambling, combined with the operation of video gaming machines on U.S.

bases in foreign countries, suggests the need for education, intervention and treatment of pathological gambling in the military.

(7) While the federal government has traditionally provided leadership in research on issues of health and public safety through agencies like the National Institute of Mental Health, the National Institute on Drug Abuse and the National Institute on Alcohol Abuse and Alcoholism, there is no agency mandated to research gambling problems, nor has there been any recommendation from existing agencies to fund programs in public education of problem and pathological gambling.

> *"There are a number of compelling reasons why the federal government should become involved in addressing pathological gambling issues."*

(8) Ignoring the effects of pathological gambling serves as a barrier to the rehabilitation of substance abusers. There is solid evidence of overlap between pathological gambling and other addictive and mental disorders in professional treatment programs as well as Gamblers Anonymous. Substance abusers are also at risk of relapse as a result of gambling problems.

A 1992 survey of mental health and substance abuse treatment professionals in Montana found that 60% had treated one or more clients in the past year whose gambling problems coincided with other addictive disorders or with a mental illness. Other estimates of the number of substance abusers who are problem or pathological gamblers range from 10% to 30%.

The federal government has taken a leading role in addressing the prevention and treatment of chemical dependency. The federal government could potentially improve the effectiveness of prevention and treatment efforts for substance abusers if it took a similar leading role in relation to problem and pathological gamblers.

(9) In part, the states' need to raise revenues from gambling has been a response to the dramatic drop in program dollars available from the federal government. Thus, the federal government has played a role in the rapid spread of legalized gambling by state governments.

In short, pathological gambling is national in scope and should be addressed on the national level by the federal government.

## Recommendations

Some experts have called for a moratorium on the further legalization of gambling. Others advocate a national initiative to address the issue of pathological gambling, such as a National Institute on Problem Gambling or another national commission to review policies toward gambling.

The recommendations of the Public Policy Committee of the National Council on Problem Gambling are a variety of cost-efficient and easy-to-implement steps:

1. Recognition of the severity of pathological gambling by the adoption of a national policy statement about problem and pathological gambling.
2. Inclusion of pathological gambling and substance abuse in the national health care plan.
3. A national prevalence survey of problem and pathological gambling to develop prevalence rates of problem and pathological gambling, a social impact study to determine the costs and benefits of legalized gambling, and an assessment of the impact of pathological gambling on at-risk populations: youth, women, minorities and the medically indigent.
4. Funding of the National Council on Problem Gambling to provide public education, training, prevention and early intervention services.
5. Development of policies to address pathological gambling in the federal criminal justice system, including federal sentencing guidelines, treatment of pathological gamblers in the federal probation and/or prison system and continuing education for judges, prosecutors, probation officers, prison officials and others involved in the federal criminal justice system for identification, education and treatment of pathological gamblers.
6. Ending the discrimination against pathological gamblers through exclusion from protection afforded to disabilities. Pathological gamblers should also be afforded the same inclusion in insurance coverage and all relevant federal legislation as are the chemically dependent.

*"The impact of problem gambling . . . on the federal criminal justice system is severe."*

A priority of a national initiative on problem and pathological gambling should be the development of funding mechanisms to support programs. These revenues would provide the needed services of prevention, early intervention, treatment and research, including but not limited to public education, toll-free hotlines, outreach to the medically indigent and those at special risk, and ongoing epidemiological studies.

# Casinos Should Address Compulsive Gambling

**by Harrah's Casinos Task Force on Compulsive Gambling**

**About the author:** *Harrah's Task Force on Compulsive Gambling, composed of employees of Harrah's Casinos, was formed in 1987 to study problems caused by compulsive gamblers and underage gamblers and to recommend steps for the casino to take to combat these problems.*

*In the six years since Harrah's Task Force on Compulsive Gambling reported these findings in 1989, the company has led the casino industry on the responsible gaming front. Harrah's Casinos founded two responsible gaming programs—Operation Bet Smart and Project 21—which tackle the issues of problem and underage gambling. These education and awareness programs have been adopted by other casinos in some states, and in a few cases by the states themselves, as the official program to inform guests and employees about the consequences of underage gambling and where to find help for a gambling problem. Harrah's Casinos have provided funding for a national problem gambling hotline. They have funded state councils on problem gambling, produced public service announcements, implemented employee assistance programs and awarded scholarships to winners of Project 21 poster contests.*

Below are the major findings from which Harrah's Task Force on Compulsive Gambling drew its recommendations. They came from work experience, interviews with experts, reading, and much discussion. We have presented these findings in a question and answer format to highlight the major issues and the Task Force's varied conclusions related to the questions.

*Are Harrah's employees presently concerned about problem gambling?*

Yes, very much so. Problem gamblers cause business problems in daily operations.

Most employees and managers are aware that problem gambling does exist. We were surprised by the frequency of comments welcoming the existence of an employee task force on problem gambling.

Some departments already respond to the problem gamblers among cus-

From the "Findings" section of the *Task Force Report on Compulsive Gambling* of Harrah's Casinos, 1989, including a 1995 update. Reprinted by permission of Harrah's Casinos, Memphis, Tennessee.

tomers. Some policies (e.g., in the Credit Department) are intended to deal with them. Despite lack of direction from policies or senior managers, many line employees and managers lightly intervene with distressed customers.

At the individual level, problem gambling is a very sensitive topic. To comment openly on anyone's problem gambling behavior is to intrude deeply into his or her personality. Many employees know a problem gambler personally as a customer, family member, fellow employee, or supervisor. Although there is no uniform approach, many line employees, supervisors, and managers discreetly intervene with customers in various situations.

> *"Problem gamblers cause business problems in daily operations."*

## Problem Gambling's Effect on Casinos

*Do problem gamblers presently affect Harrah's business?*

Yes, but we don't know how much; and we need to know how much. Hard cost data are entirely lacking; no studies exist of problem gambling in casinos. Our conservative estimate is that 1 percent to 5 percent of casino customers and up to 10 percent of casino employees may be identifiable as problem gamblers. The real percentages are more likely to be higher than lower, but not greatly so.

Casinos may attract fewer problem gamblers than do lotteries. Most customers and employees are normal adults enjoying recreation. However, informal reports from employees and study of formal procedures (e.g., in Credit) suggest that problem gamblers affect all areas of our business to some degree, especially collection operations, security, legal, and floor operations. Control is easier over credit customers than cash customers.

*Does Harrah's already acknowledge problem gambling?*

Yes, but not officially, except in New Jersey signage. [The state of New Jersey requires Atlantic City casinos to post signs advertising the hotline number of the Council on Compulsive Gambling of New Jersey.] The official policy implementing New Jersey signage has had a considerable impact on the public, with benefits to Harrah's. Other effects are as yet unknown.

Individual employees acknowledge the existence of problem gambling, and so do some departmental policies, but companywide policies and procedures and attitudes do not. Encouragement by supervisors of existing employee behavior in this area would be a major change. So would acknowledgment by the Human Resources Department, etc., that the problem exists among employees.

If we're talking about making a change in the casinos' culture, corporate-wide acknowledgment of problem gambling is crucial. Management must set the example.

*What is problem gambling?*

Problem gambling is a broad part of the spectrum of gaming behavior. At one end is unwise social gaming. At the other is compulsive gambling. The latter is a medically recognized psychiatric disorder of impulse control; a disease. Acknowledgment of problem gambling, its symptoms, and cure is very new in the psychological professions [as of 1989]. Current definitions are likely to change.

Harrah's needs a very practical definition of problem gambling: Does it harm our operations? Can it be easily described? Obviously, we are not diagnostic experts. We don't need to do so, especially if proper business procedures are in place. We don't want to interfere impertinently with customers.

We see problem gambling as one of several problem behaviors among employees and customers. It is the behavior, not the cause, that should interest Harrah's.

We also see problem gambling as a possible CAUSE of other problems which seem to have other sources (e.g. poor employee performance, theft, turnover of employees). In that area it can be precisely defined.

We've therefore defined problem gambling as that casino gaming behavior which *both* (a) has elements of compulsiveness *and* (b) interferes with business operations or employee performance.

## Drawing Attention to Problem Gambling

*Why hasn't the gaming industry long since admitted the existence of problem gamblers?*

Like the liquor and tobacco industries, it's been thought wiser not to draw attention to the subject. Also, casinos could be charged with hypocrisy. Further, some employees believe that we make our income from the problem. Additionally, many casino operations and employees are oriented only to the short term.

The industry as a whole is likely to take the initiative only if regulations require it, but times are changing swiftly. Nevada's casinos are the least-regulated in the world and are unlikely to be a model for elsewhere.

*Should Harrah's take the lead in acknowledging the existence of problem gambling?*

Yes. Taking the lead would be precisely in line with Harrah's role as the corporate good citizen and the responsible member of the industry.

Taking the lead could give Harrah's a lasting image in the industry as the most responsible casino group. This image is vital to likely developments nationally and internationally in the next twenty years. Licensing authorities will normally choose the most "respectable" corporation, other things being equal.

> *"If we're talking about making a change in the casinos' culture, corporate-wide acknowledgment of problem gambling is crucial."*

Harrah's attitude to problem gambling could prove very, very important to our position in the long-term and international market.

Following others' leads (e.g. because of regulation) would have no benefits to our image.

*What would be the effect on the bottom line?*

Any reduction of problem gambling would be profitable. Problem gamblers at present cause unknown amounts of loss in terms of employee turnover, in failures to collect, and in other ways. Their behavior makes them undesirable. We can't attach dollar figures without research.

Getting rid of identified problem gamblers is not the most profitable approach. Firing some employees would send the problem underground, lower morale, and raise accusations of hypocrisy. We see no way of "firing" customers except by refusing credit. We already consider written requests by customers to refuse them credit.

> *"Problem gambling [is] that . . . behavior which both (a) has elements of compulsiveness and (b) interferes with business operations or employee performance."*

After any change of corporate attitude, loss could come from driving away profitable customers by insensitive handling or procedures, especially moralistic labeling. That loss would be unmeasurable but probably small. We believe counterbalancing profits would be substantial.

Profits would come first from improved employee performance and reduced turnover. In conjunction with a Wellness Program, those profits would start to show within two years and increase steadily. Other profits from a reduction of employee misconduct are unmeasurable but could show up quickly.

Further long-term profits would come from Harrah's positioning in the market, especially internationally, as the responsible corporation.

Finally, recognition of problem gambling will help in our credit and collection procedures. Also, this would assist in the legal and liability aspects of the problem.

## What Casinos Can Do

*Should Harrah's do something now?*

Yes. Couldn't be more timely.

The late 1980s saw a dramatic speed-up in national recognition of problem gambling. Because of lotteries, gambling looks likely to become the next behavioral problem to be focused upon (compare smoking, drinking, drugs).

Recent developments include formation of a National Council on Problem Gambling; creation of a national hotline; lead stories on television news and in major newspapers; signage in New Jersey casinos; and new prevalence studies showing increases in problem gambling.

*Should we single out problem gambling?*

On the whole, no.

We should include it in the corporate response to undesirable behavior of all kinds. This is especially true when it impairs employee performance. The idea of a Wellness Program for employees needs management support and would be very timely.

Harrah's could usefully expand attention to problem gambling in its own community-oriented programs (e.g., for schools, treatment programs, courts). Experts agree that there are more problem gamblers residing in casino communities than elsewhere.

*Should we do something short term or long term, quickly or slowly?*

Certain positive steps can be taken quickly (e.g., signage, research choices, funding support). Most, however, require a cautious and thorough response. Most involve cooperation between departments, some between [corporate-owned] properties. Some involve major changes (e.g., employee training). Others require a new positioning of existing programs (e.g., marketing). All should be supported by information campaigns.

Regarding customers, signage can be done without commitment to anything, except funding for a hotline for Nevada. Other short-term steps (e.g., funding support) can be taken with maximal press relations benefits and no promises.

Acquiring adequate knowledge of the effects of problem gambling on our business will take longer.

Among employees, we should do something short term and long term. Employee programs should be carefully planned. Certain ill-planned programs among employees have caused employee skepticism about Harrah's.

A true new positioning of the corporation should be a permanent and institutionally formalized commitment to the subject (similar to the watch we keep on legal developments now). Harrah's should start now to acquire ongoing professional knowledge in the area.

## Gauging Public Reaction

*How would customers and employees and the public react to a change of Harrah's attitude in this area?*

We can see no downside with these groups except being seen as hypocritical.

The "public" in this case is (a) the vocal groups with a special interest in compulsive gambling; (b) legislators, regulators, and licensers; and (c) stockholders and financiers. From the public relations viewpoint, anything we do would have very positive benefits if done correctly.

Customers should not be interfered with except both positively and cautiously. Passive information or education is probably safe. Any em-

> *"Problem gamblers at present cause unknown amounts of loss in terms of employee turnover, in failures to collect, and in other ways."*

ployee training on how to intervene with customers would have to be very carefully developed and implemented.

Employee response would be favorable if the commitment is genuine and long term and it becomes recognized as part of an overall approach to problem behavior. That is, it should be a genuine wellness approach. . . .

*What's a reasonable summary of the new attitude?*

For customers, a slightly more formalized recognition and approach to problems and the addition of signage.

For employees, a long-term investment in their well-being for the sake of our well-being.

*Any special advice?*

We cannot emphasize strongly enough the need to keep what we do in line with what we say in this subject area. Anything we do would set a new norm for the Harrah's culture and the gaming culture, as has the signage program. We would be sending out a new message. We would be saying, "Gaming is fun but some people have problems with it. We don't want problem gaming to harm our customers, our employees, our communities, our industry, or our operations, so we're proactive. We take many positive steps to see that any harm is minimal."

The Task Force believes that the steps are all positive and that many should be taken as part of an overall, managed strategy. This approach by Harrah's is reasonable, prudent, responsible, humane, and profitable.

# Gambling Makes Life Exciting

## by Robert Altman

**About the author:** *Robert Altman is a film director, writer, and producer.*

There were these two musicians. They got a gig in London and they decided to take the *Queen Elizabeth* over. About three days out, they were sitting on the top deck, smoking a joint. It's a real quiet night, and it's ocean 360 degrees around—it's all just ocean. Very still, like a lake. The moon is reflecting very brightly off it. This one guy takes a hit and looks around, and he says, "Jesus, look at all that fucking water!" And the other guy looks around and says, "Yeah, and that's only the top!"

### A Gamble Pays Off

Isn't that great? I know exactly what that guy is talking about. There was this one weekend about twenty, twenty-five years ago, and it was my wife's birthday or our anniversary, some special day, but I wanted to go out to Hollywood Park, and I couldn't figure out how to get out of keeping her happy. So I made this plan. I said, "For your birthday we're flying to Las Vegas and we're going to spend the weekend there, and that's going to be your birthday celebration." I said, "Get ready. I'm just going to run out to the racetrack"—I said this real fast—"and I'll meet you at the airport at about 6:00."

She said, "Can we afford this?"

And I said, "Absolutely." So I went to the track and I lost every race into the last one. I'd blown the money for the weekend. I had just enough left—$200 or so—for the final race. I'm sitting there, I've got maybe four horses I want to bet on. Martha Raye came by and said, "Here's a tip, I don't know if it's any good but there's a horse called Pal Fast." I looked up and saw that Pal Fast was going off at thirty to one. "Thanks a lot," I said.

I walked up to the window, deliberating between my four horses. They were about to ring the bell, and I couldn't decide, and I'm thinking, *What the fuck am I going to do? I can't cover a check for Las Vegas and I can't lose face.* Finally

Robert Altman, "A Long Shot Pays More Than the Odds," *Esquire*, October 1993. Reprinted with permission.

I said, *Oh, what the hell*, and I bet $150 across the board on Pal Fast. I won close to $3,000. I went to the airport and I was king of the hill. When I got off the plane, I went immediately to the crap table, and I won $6,000 more right away. It was quite a weekend, which was a fluke because it could just as easily have been a disaster. That's junkie gambling when you do that. But that's the best win I've ever had.

## Playing the Odds Is Boring

I've gambled all my life, but I've managed to gamble within my loss range. I've been lucky, because I haven't always been careful. My attitude is, why not? Professional gamblers are the most uninteresting gamblers of all because they're like the banks. They play the odds and cut it right out of the middle. They don't even *think* about the long shot. Absolutely boring.

I used to go to the racetrack with a guy named Little C. We'd sit in the box and he'd tell us, "Don't bother going to the window, I'll book your bets. What do you want?" We'd just sit there. He was taking the track odds because he knew he had a 20 percent edge on those things. But he had no fun. And I had no fun. I would much rather play the fantasy and stand in line and buy the ticket.

What I'm talking about is the individual nature of gambling. Just you and the odds. And not knowing whether it's going to work. In my business, in writing, when you do your cover, you're gambling. So when I go to make a picture and people say, "Oh, this is very dicey, you're taking a big gamble here," I say, "What's my gamble? There's no gamble." Not making it would be more of a gamble. I mean, I remember days when I was living in Kansas City and going out to California and failing and being absolutely dead-ass broke and trying to sell the television set out of my car for fifty bucks just to keep going. But it can pay to follow a hunch. We don't rely enough on instinct in this culture. Sometimes you just feel the heat and you know the fucking number is going to come out and finally it does. Waiting for it is part of the joy.

> *"It was quite a weekend, which was a fluke because it could just as easily have been a disaster."*

# Compulsive Gambling Is Not a Disease

## by Richard E. Vatz and Lee S. Weinberg

**About the author:** *Richard E. Vatz is a professor of rhetoric and communication at Towson State University in Baltimore, Maryland. Lee S. Weinberg is a professor of public and international affairs at the University of Pittsburgh in Pennsylvania.*

Robert Terry, the *Philadelphia Inquirer*'s chief police reporter, borrowed money from that city's police commissioner and other department officials. Despite the fact that such borrowing creates a blatant conflict of interest, Terry was suspended *with pay*, with no decision made on a final disciplinary action. His managing editor, James Naughton, accepted Terry's explanation that it was a "disease" of gambling that put him in such dire straits. Naughton stated that he would await the outcome of a therapy program intended to cure Terry's "disease" before rendering final judgment.

### Miscreants or Courageous Victims?

In 1992, former *ABC Monday Night Football* producer Chet Forte was given a suspended sentence for bank fraud and income tax irregularities after Gamblers Anonymous testified at his sentencing hearing.

Former Baltimore Colt quarterback Art Schlichter went from object of scorn to one of pity in 1983 when it was claimed that his wagering, which had cost him hundreds of thousands of dollars, was the result of the "disease of compulsive gambling" (sometimes called "pathological gambling"). The late psychiatrist Robert Custer, often referred to as the father of compulsive gambling, stated, "Art has suffered the full effects of his disease."

In mid-1989, it was revealed that baseball hero Pete Rose had dropped more than $500,000 through heavy gambling. It also was reported that he had had to sell treasured memorabilia because of his debts. After weeks of bad press following a denial that he had a problem with gambling, Rose made a public statement that he had what his recently acquired psychiatrist called "a clinically significant

Richard E. Vatz and Lee S. Weinberg, "Refuting the Myths of Compulsive Gambling." Reprinted, by permission, from *USA Today*, November 1993. Copyright by The Society for the Advancement of Education.

gambling disorder" that rendered him powerless over his gambling. He then went on a media tour, during which he was greeted by a lengthy standing ovation from Phil Donahue's television audience and congratulations for his "admission" from Barbara Walters. Rose had gone from miscreant to courageous victim.

Since then, press attention to compulsive gambling—with uncritical acceptance of its being an illness and uncontrollable—has abounded. It has been heralded as the "Addiction of the 1990s." In the *Journal of Gambling Studies (JGS)*, the major academic journal on gambling and social issues, editor Henry Lesieur wrote quite accurately in 1992 that "Not a day goes by . . . without something appearing in the professional literature or mass media about compulsive gambling."

## Establishing Heavy Gambling as a Disease

The groundwork for the successful promotion of the disease model for heavy gambling was laid firmly more than a decade ago. After years of what *JGS* called his "unflagging advocacy," Custer persuaded the American Psychiatric Association in its 1980 update of the *Diagnostic and Statistical Manual (DSM-III)* to elevate gambling to one of its categories of impulse disorders or, more specifically, a "Disorder of Impulse Control not Elsewhere Classified." This act was heralded in articles and media appearances by prominent gambling researchers as establishing that heavy, self-destructive gambling was a disease, the medical identity that was seen as necessary for sympathy for heavy bettors, and status and financial support (third-party payments, grants, etc.) for the researchers themselves, of whom few were—or are—medical doctors. If such gambling were a disease (the manual uses the term *disorder*, but its "nomenclature" specialist, Robert Spitzer, claims that it may be considered the same as disease), it was axiomatic that it was beyond the individual's control.

The problem is that there is no evidence that compulsive gambling is a disease (a point psychiatrist Thomas Szasz has made for decades) or uncontrollable. Revealingly, there are indications that, at least as far as the disease claim is concerned, many gambling researchers don't believe it either. Moreover, the consequences of accepting compulsive gambling as addictive or uncontrollable may be to hinder efforts of heavy gamblers to resist their urges.

Psychiatry's diagnostic manual lists no medical criteria in its "diagnostic criteria" for pathological gambling, only those referring to frequency of wagering and its social, financial, and legal consequences. Put

> *"[Compulsive gambling] has been heralded as the 'Addiction of the 1990s.'"*

simply, heavy gambling is not an illness in the sense that most people think of one. There is no credible evidence whatsoever of any neurochemical or neurophysiological status causally linked to heavy gambling, only changes such as increased adrenaline or palpitations caused by the excitement of the action. No study has found any neurobiological status specific to compulsive gamblers as contrasted with other excitable people. Yet, the finding of neurobiological correlates—especially if they were specific to heavy gambling—would constitute a Holy Grail for researchers, providing a basis for maintaining that it is a disease and uncontrollable.

## A Lack of Biological "Proof"

Thus, it was discouraging to gambling researchers in the late 1980s (and confirmed in recent follow-ups) when a year-long study at the National Institute of Alcohol Abuse and Alcoholism showed no differences in serotonin levels between compulsive gamblers and normal men. A positive finding could have been used to argue that such gamblers lacked impulse control.

In 1989, however, gambling researchers argued that they finally had their "proof." A study published in the *Archives of General Psychiatry* found that 17 heavy gamblers had neurochemical elevations correlated with their "extroversion." The article was—and continues to be—heralded by gambling researchers and the popular press as evidence that gamblers' biology is destiny. The *New York Times* headline read: "Gambling: Biology May Hold Key," and a piece in the February, 1992, *Harvard Mental Health Letter* argued that the 1989 study demonstrates that "the gambling addiction may even have a physiological basis."

*"Put simply, heavy gambling is not an illness in the sense that most people think of one."*

Even this study, the gambling researchers' best evidence that chronic gambling is compulsive and a disease, proved little beyond what one would expect—namely, that gamblers are excitable personalities who evidence heightened neurological measures of excitement. It demonstrates neither that such biological differences are causal nor that they are specific to compulsive gamblers or even gamblers at all. As the study's senior researcher, psychiatrist Alec Roy, concedes, the gamblers "were not compared to other groups, so we cannot answer the question with regard to specificity." He adds that no follow-up studies have been done or currently are being done to his knowledge.

Responsible gambling researchers do not maintain that there is any proof of biological causation in compulsive gambling. Sirgay Sanger, president of the National Council on Problem Gambling, admits in the *Journal of the American Medical Association* what one rarely, if ever, reads in gambling researchers' quotes in the popular press: Pathological gambling "has the smell of a biochemical addiction in it," but, he admits, "there is no research proof."

The most prominent medical doctor promoting the gambling-as-disease concept is psychiatrist Sheila Blume, the medical director for the alcoholism, chemical-dependency, and compulsive gambling programs at South Oaks Hospital, Amityville, N.Y. She often talks about heavy gambling as an illness, but there is reason to believe she doubts the claim herself and uses medical language only for strategic purposes.

In an article in *JGS*, Blume makes a remarkably frank recommendation that, regardless of objections to the medical model, heavy gambling should be considered an illness for practical benefits for gamblers and their doctors: "It is concluded that the many individual and social advantages of the medical model make it the preferred conceptualization of our present state of knowledge." Lesieur also has cited the strategic importance of public acceptance of pathological gambling as an illness, arguing that, without it, the gamblers themselves are less likely to accept the disease model, an acceptance he views as crucial to successful treatment.

> *"Responsible gambling researchers do not maintain that there is any proof of biological causation in compulsive gambling."*

## The Strategic Importance of the "Illness" Definition

Valerie Lorenz is executive director of the National Center for Pathological Gambling and one of the most vocal promoters of the illness model for gambling in her constant beseechings for governmental and other source funding. She sees the acceptance of gambling-as-illness as critical to legal exculpation and counsels that "the expert witness for the compulsive gambler facing legal charges" must "educate" judges and others as to the "illness" of the "compulsive gambler" in legal trouble, in order to avoid the unfair punishing of those who are "seriously disturbed" and "out of control."

Significantly, I. Nelson Rose, a professor of law and vice-president of the California Council on Compulsive Gambling, who, according to *JGS*, is the "nation's leading authority on gambling and the law," disputes the medical model for compulsive gambling. In an interview, he expressed skepticism regarding the notion that heavy gambling can be a disease: "I have a lot of trouble with that idea, especially within the law, where it is used as an excuse." In terms of insanity-like defenses, wherein people are found not guilty of crimes by virtue of suffering from pathological gambling, Rose says, "It just doesn't work anymore," even though the plea still is attempted. What does work to some degree—and probably is increasing in usage—is its employment in criminal cases to provide alternative sentencing programs comparable to alcohol treatment programs, as well as in divorces, tax problems, and bankruptcy.

Regardless of questions of validity, the public appears conditioned to call any deviant behavior disease if the situation entails sufficient poignancy. In an article in *Good Housekeeping* titled "When Gambling Becomes a Disease," the magazine asserts that "it is only when gambling overtakes a person's life that it moves from recreation to an illness." However, does gambling *really* overtake people's lives?

## Is Compulsive Gambling Treatable?

In the wake of the claim of the astronomical prevalence (almost six percent of all adults in Maryland—more than one in every twenty) of problem or pathological gambling, legislation was passed in Maryland to require all state lottery tickets to carry the following warning: "Compulsive gambling is a treatable illness." Those six words concede all three of the major disputable claims of the gambling researchers: that heavy, self-destructive gambling is an illness, is uncontrollable, and is treatable, which implies that treatment programs have been shown to be significantly helpful to those who seek aid to resist the urges.

Researchers who argue that compulsive gambling is beyond control believe the proof to be self-evident by virtue of the devastating consequences of such activity and confirmed by the participants' claims that they cannot stop. How, they wonder, could people willfully gamble themselves into such financial, legal, and family problems, consequences that define for the most part gamblers' "chronic and progressive failure to resist impulses to gamble" as required for psychiatry's current diagnostic manual (*DSM-III-R*)? This is, of course, a circular definition, as no one can verify a person's ability to control his or her behavior. Let us look at that assertion with reason as a guide.

When we wrote an article several years ago that "control" is not accessible or measurable except through the potentially self-serving claims of gamblers, Blume responded by accusing us of saying that gamblers could not be believed. Leaving aside that researchers invariably insist that lying is one of the cardinal signs of the compulsive gambler, the point is that a claim of inability to control one's gambling—even if made sincerely—cannot logically confirm such inability. At most, the statement might reveal the gambler's honest belief.

Chet Forte, who gambled himself into millions of dollars of losses, has asked rhetorically how anyone could think he willfully would have "gone through the money" or "destroyed my family"? The answer is twofold. First, his stated concern for his family notwithstanding, many heavy gamblers—including, perhaps, Forte, according to a letter written to us by his first cousin, Anne Perrin, and her husband—simply don't care so much about their families.

> *"The public appears conditioned to call any deviant behavior disease if the situation entails sufficient poignancy."*

Gambling researchers themselves are aware that the image of the heavy gambler whose actions destroy what otherwise would be a great family man (most heavy gamblers are men) is simply a myth. Most compulsive gamblers are not committed family men, with or without their gambling. Perrin stated that Forte defrauded her family, despite his being "someone my mother helped put through college and whose parents were constantly helped financially by my parents!" She adds that Forte has no real remorse and quotes him as saying that he learned that, "when you are stealing, steal big." Along a similar line, gambling researchers who attribute great social costs to gambling, such as those to businesses due to lost productivity, do not consider the possibility that a compulsive gambler who wasn't gambling would not be very productive or might have high absenteeism regardless.

## Are Treatment Programs Successful?

Second, gambling is exciting for many reasons, including the risks and opportunities it provides for "big wins," as well as extensive losses. Heavy gamblers often engage in "chasing," which involves a type of exponentially increasing betting that can win back losses quickly, even substantial ones. Gamblers don't expect to lose.

The assumption that they cannot control their urges figures largely in gambling treatment programs, as it does with those for other behavioral "addictions." In fact, the first in the well-known Twelve Steps of Recovery common to such programs is that the addict must admit that he or she has a problem (or illness) and is powerless to resist it. Despite the exaggerated claims of the promoters of groups like Gamblers Anonymous (GA) and Alcoholics Anonymous, there is little or no evidence of their widespread success. With respect to compulsive gamblers, anecdotes exist in abundance, but there are few studies available on the outcomes of such group-oriented treatment.

> *"A claim of inability to control one's gambling—even if made sincerely—cannot logically confirm such inability."*

What studies there are reveal very limited success in achieving gambling abstinence. The astronomical dropout rate of 70 percent and more in GA and other groups makes it appear that whatever success there is—and sometimes high rates are claimed—is due largely to the high level of commitment of those who stay in the program, rather than the program itself. Neither is abstinence verifiable.

It is time for at least some skepticism regarding the unquestioned need for addicts to admit powerlessness over their own behavior. It is worth considering whether such admissions constitute a self-fulfilling prophesy—that is to say, the belief that a habit is uncontrollable actually may discourage people from trying to stop behaving in a self-destructive manner since it is beyond their control.

## Should the "Illness" Become an Excuse?

Assertions that heavy, destructive gambling is a disease, uncontrollable, and treatable simply do not withstand close scrutiny. Questionable research, reasoning, and evidence are used to criticize the existence of state lotteries, exculpate irresponsible behavior of heavy gamblers, and, in the case of treatment, perhaps undermine efforts to help people resist the urge to gamble. That the unique excitement and risk-taking motivates some people to neglect many important aspects of their lives is intriguing, but not overly surprising. It is the medicalizing of heavy gambling that makes it seem so utterly mysterious.

The debate about compulsive gambling, like that about other self-destructive or socially unacceptable behaviors ranging from compulsive drinking to com-

> *"The assumption that [gamblers] cannot control their urges figures largely in gambling treatment programs."*

pulsive shopping (a supposed new disorder whose advocates urge its inclusion in the next revision of psychiatry's diagnostic manual), ultimately comes down to a single question: Should individuals who engage in these behaviors be excused on the grounds that they suffer from a disorder that produces urges they are unable to resist? Without further evidence, we believe the answer to be no.

Whether talking about newspaper employees who have a conflict of interest due to borrowing to pay off gambling debts, people who defraud banks and associates, or athletes who bet on games in violation of league rules, there should be no general moral or legal recognition of compulsive gambling disorder as a valid reason for such behavior. The practical effect of recognizing disorders is to make these excuses significant because they are alleged disorders while rejecting other exculpatory claims.

The implication of this position, however, is not that no differences exist among individual cases of misconduct or self-destructive conduct. Quite the contrary. For instance, the employee who embezzles money to pay for a child's medical care may be entitled to more consideration than the one who pleads compulsive gambling. While both should be made to repay the stolen money, perhaps the former, not the latter, is entitled to a second chance. This much is clear: it is time to stop all special consideration for those whose excuses are sympathy-provoking only because they bear the unscientific "disorder" imprimatur of psychiatry.

# Casino Tricks Encourage Heavy Gambling

## by James Popkin

**About the author:** *James Popkin is a senior editor for* U.S. News & World Report.

At precisely midnight on October 11, 1991, an obscure Chicago neurologist slipped behind a row of quarter slot machines at the Las Vegas Hilton and switched on a homemade contraption of cardboard, black metal and old fan parts. For the next forty-eight hours, the hidden device pumped a pleasant-smelling vapor into the stale casino air.

### Getting Gamblers to Gamble Longer

The neurologist was not an intruder but a scent expert invited to the Hilton by casino manager Lee Skelley to test whether certain smells can subtly influence slot machine players to wager more. Over the next two days, Hilton gamblers poured thousands of quarters into the eighteen nearby slot machines—45 percent more than usual for an October weekend.

> "Our goal is not to get more out of a customer in three hours but to get him to stay for four hours."
>
> —Bob Renneisen, President and CEO
> Claridge's Casino, Atlantic City

The days of shaved dice, missing face cards and rigged roulette wheels are long gone. But the pursuit of profitability in the corporate era of gambling has turned the average casino into a financially hazardous place for bettors. In Nevada and Atlantic City, for example, confidential documents reveal that five casinos now pump Chicago neurologist Alan Hirsch's secret scent—Odorant 1—into the slot machine pits twenty-four hours a day. (The Las Vegas Hilton never took the idea beyond the testing stage.) Some casinos have even studied how the controversial psychologist B. F. Skinner altered the behavior of rats and pigeons. But of all the tricks in the casino manager's Psych 101 handbook, the subtle manipulation of time is by far the most common.

In 1980, a math whiz named Jess Marcum spelled out exactly how time affects a gambler's odds. Marcum, who helped to develop radar and the neutron bomb before becoming a casino consultant, figured that a craps player who wagered just $1 every bet for two months straight would have only one chance in 2 trillion to win $1,000 before he lost $1,000. On the other hand, by decreasing his exposure at the craps table to just 25 minutes and wagering $200 every bet, that same gambler would increase his odds to 1.15 to 1. Even the lowest-ranking casino official knows the concept: Since all casino games give the house a mathematical edge, the longer a player gambles, the greater the house's chance of winning.

That helps explain why gamblers frequently get lost in a maze of slot machines and why down-home gambling halls offer free "Ladies Breakfasts" at 6 a.m., a slow point in the casino day. Over a year, a special promotion or interior-design element that somehow keeps gamblers at play for just five more minutes a night can add millions to a casino's gross, or "hold." The Harrah's Casino spends tens of thousands of dollars a year studying whether fresher air, wider aisles and even back supports on slot-pit stools will make customers comfortable. And slog it out longer, too. "We're now developing technology that's just lighting the felt" on blackjack tables, says Harrah's president, Phil Satre. "We're trying to keep [light] off the forehead of the customers, which is draining on them from an energy standpoint."

Such sensitivity to customer comfort abounds. For example, nearly all new slot machines sold in the United States have built-in bill acceptors. Gamblers like the devices because they no longer have to wait in line for change, and casino managers love them because they keep slot hounds glued to their stools.

## Casinos Stress "Productivity"

Like car plants, casinos also stress productivity. The hidden cameras above the casino floor scan for fast-fingered dealers and card cheats. But the ubiquitous "eye in the sky" also enables casino officials to conduct regular "game-pace audits." At the Aladdin Casino in Las Vegas, blackjack dealers are instructed to deal at least 75 to 80 hands per hour. They are also supposed to shuffle six decks of cards in less than 80 seconds. The reason: Shuffles can eat up eight rounds of playing time an hour. In a year, the Aladdin could earn an extra $1.2 million if its blackjack dealers never had to shuffle.

*"The longer a player gambles, the greater the house's chance of winning."*

Penny-pinching casinos set faster production schedules, especially when the nightly cash hold tumbles. "We don't instruct people to deal faster," says Bob Stupak, owner of the Vegas World Casino in Las Vegas. "They better deal as fast as they [expletive] can or they're gonna work someplace else."

"If you give a guy a $100 bill he looks at it like a round of golf, a golf cart, two beers and a hot dog. But if you give him chips, it's just betting units and it loses its value."

—Bill Zender, Operations Chief
Aladdin Casino, Las Vegas

Casinos have become pop-psych laboratories. When a player at a low-limit blackjack table flashes a $100 bill and asks for chips, for example, dealers at many casinos are under orders to dole out chips of the lowest-possible denomination. Partly a convenience for gamblers, the practice also is meant to discourage low bettors from pocketing higher value chips when they leave the table. Such players are likely to blow all twenty of their $5 chips one at a time, the thinking goes, but might hold onto a $25 chip and never gamble it away. "Psychologically, casinos don't want gamblers to realize how much they're losing," explains one Atlantic City dealer.

But slot pits are the true training grounds for casino mind games. Deep, dark colors like black, red, purple and blue trigger a strong response in slot players, research shows. So, slot machine manufacturers like International Game Technology (IGT), based in Reno, Nevada, prominently feature those hues. IGT North American President Bob Bittman says research also shows that gamblers no longer associate winning with the cherry and plum symbols on many slot machine reels. Poof, they're gone. "Fruit is a dinosaur. Ninety-nine percent of the machines we sell now will not have fruit." Bittman says.

> *"Slot pits are the true training grounds for casino mind games."*

Some casinos go to even greater lengths to exploit gamblers' subconscious preferences. Casino consultant David Britton says that after surveying dozens of Nevada-based slot players he confirmed a hunch that they are drawn to bright-red machines. But after several minutes, the players subconsciously tire of red and seek softer hues. Since casinos want to avoid "transitional periods," when players leave one machine in search of another, Britton devised a new system where players are now lured to the brightly colored machines at the end of a long row of slots. But the machines closer to the middle of the row feature softer colors, like blues and greens.

"What is gambling? It's really just a hype on emotion."

—Jack Binion, owner
Horseshoe Casino, Las Vegas

Sometimes casino operators look to actual psychology for inspiration. In 1966, University of Nevada undergrad Larry Andreotti was studying Skinner, one of the first scientists to demonstrate how positive reinforcement can influence animal behavior. Andreotti told his father, the late Rome Andreotti, who at the time was one of the rising stars on the operations side of the growing Harrah's chain. "A lot of the behavior I saw in the lab seemed comparable to the control one has over behavior in casinos," explains Larry Andreotti, who today is a college psychology professor and Skinner specialist in Canada.

In 1937, Skinner taught a white lab rat named Pliny to operate a rudimentary slot machine. After Pliny pulled a chain with its teeth, a marble would fall. The rat would then drop the marble in a slot and receive its reward, 1/20 of a gram of a dog biscuit. By tracking Pliny's reactions over time, Skinner learned that the rat became more motivated when he got a biscuit only occasionally, and randomly. Pliny would drop even more marbles into the slot, in other words, when he was not sure when the biscuit would fall next.

> *"Modern slots reward players with frequent, small payoffs . . . that entice gamblers to keep chasing their dream."*

Rome Andreotti applied Skinner's findings to the casino. If most slots were set at about the same payout rate, recalls a former Harrah's president, Richard Goeglein, Andreotti would slip in a few machines with a much more generous jackpot percentage. The casino wouldn't indicate which machines offered better odds, but gamblers soon learned that there were a few ringers in the crowd. And the search for those machines sent gamblers into a Pliny-like, quarter-dropping frenzy. "Rome knew how to reward people for continual, consistent play," says Goeglein.

Coincidentally, slot machine makers have also put Skinner's theories into practice. Modern slots reward players with frequent, small payoffs—often as inconsequential as one quarter—that entice gamblers to keep chasing their dream. Thirty years ago, by contrast, small, frequent payoffs were unheard of, says slot machine historian Marshall Fey. The new payout system works. "It's like eating popcorn. It's very hard to stop playing," says Jeffrey Lowenhar, senior management consultant with the Resorts casino in Atlantic City.

One firm took gambler manipulation too far. In 1986, Universal Distributing began selling slots that produced "near miss" combinations. Instead of running randomly, the slot reels often stopped so that players could see the symbols of a payout just above or below the pay line, giving the false impression that gamblers had missed a massive jackpot. Although the machines quickly became a hit with customers and slot managers, Nevada gaming authorities outlawed the near-miss illusion in 1989.

## Profiling Gamblers

"Push a button and they can find out everything about you. Sometimes it's scary."

—Gambler Sam Roberts

It was a Sunday afternoon, and Pennsylvania jewelry salesman Sam Roberts was bellied up to a roulette table at his favorite Las Vegas casino. Dressed in what he described as his "Mr. T starter set"—three gold necklaces, four gold bracelets, a gold watch and four gold rings—Roberts seemed to epitomize the successful Vegas man about town. When asked whether he was ahead after three days of roulette, Roberts said he wasn't "paying any attention."

But the casino certainly was. On a computer screen just off the casino floor, the file on Sam Roberts (not his real name) was extensive. Not only did it reveal his exact losses on his current trip ($2,092) but it had already figured his average bet ($20.88), time spent gambling (11 hours and 39 minutes) and "average worth," or how much Roberts should lose ($528) based on time and the house's 5.26 percent edge at roulette. It also contained personal data like Sam's height (5'10"), weight (300) hair color (brown)—even whether he needed corrective eyewear (yes).

Casinos amass personal information to enhance customer service and reward steady players with "comps"—complimentary meals, show tickets and hotel stays. (They never reveal internal data, although Roberts agreed to for this article.) But there's a hidden agenda. Casino marketers need detailed histories to keep old customers loyal and, more important, to "capture" new ones.

If marketers learn, for instance, that divorced slot players from Cleveland who love boxing lose big and often, the casino will buy mailing lists and try to find sucker clones. Gamblers who can be lured to the hotel are especially prized. "If we can get you to stay in our hotel, we can bump up your average trip worth," one marketer says. Everyone gets in on the hustle. When a casino hotel is nearly full, reservationists will scan the computer and open remaining rooms only to known gamblers with a high trip worth.

## Targeting the Meat-and-Potatoes Gambler

A decade ago, most casinos bothered to gather data only on high rollers. Now they use slot-club cards to snare the meat-and-potatoes guy, too. After filling out a survey and receiving an ATM-like card, slot junkies insert them into a "reader" built into almost all slot machines. In a distant computer room, casinos track the action twenty-four hours a day down to the last quarter.

Players who use the cards the longest get the most comps, somewhat like a frequent-flier giveback. At the Trump Castle in Atlantic City, an internal document shows that 64 percent of all slot players now use the Castle slot card. The cardholders lost $109 million to the slots last fiscal year, or about $101 per player per trip. Slot players who never bothered with the card, by contrast, lost $31 per trip on average.

> "A decade ago, most casinos bothered to gather data only on high rollers. Now they . . . snare the meat-and-potatoes guy, too."

"The stickman controls the pace of the crap game like a barker at a carnival. He pushes the 'proposition' bets, which have a much greater house advantage."

—Al Glasgow, consultant and editor
*Atlantic City Action* newsletter

Chapter 2

For an industry governed by odds, casinos leave little to chance. To line their pockets just a wee bit more, they've added games with stunning house odds. Many casinos now offer "double-exposure blackjack," for example, in which the dealers reveal all their cards; players keep trying to top the dealer's hand without going over 21. Novices fall for the ruse, overlooking the rule allowing the house to win all ties. "That one rule change is worth about 8 or 9 percent in favor of the house," explains Arnold Snyder, editor of the *Blackjack Forum* newsletter.

Many riverboat casinos also offer "multiple-action blackjack," with complex rules that encourage gamblers to place three bets on every hand. "It causes players to play dumb and put more money on the table," Snyder says. If gambling critics can be believed, that neatly sums up the danger of America's latest entertainment craze. As any old Vegas hand will tell you, "If you wanna make money in a casino, own one."

# Chapter 3

# Does Gambling Benefit State and Local Economies?

# Casino Gambling and Local Economies: An Overview

by Kathleen Sylvester

**About the author:** *Kathleen Sylvester, a former senior writer for* Governing *magazine, is vice president of domestic policy for the Progressive Policy Institute, a Washington, D.C., think tank.*

Gambling is on a roll in America. With a total take exceeding $200 billion [annually], it is the nation's most conspicuous and fastest growing brand of entrepreneurial government. And many states and localities are getting hooked.

It has been a remarkable turnaround. Just a decade ago, casino gambling in the United States was limited to two isolated spots—Nevada and Atlantic City. Not a single state opened up a casino in the 1980s, and a dozen states rejected the idea. Ten years after the tables in Atlantic City first opened, it was hard to find a community anywhere that wanted to repeat the experiment.

Today, all that has changed. There is casino gambling in one form or another [as of the end of 1992] in Arizona, California, Colorado, Connecticut, Illinois, Iowa, Michigan, Minnesota, Mississippi, Montana, Nebraska, Nevada, New Jersey, South Dakota, Washington State and Wisconsin. Louisiana and Missouri soon followed suit. The moral misgivings that once prevailed in debates about casinos have faded into the background.

## Public Attitudes

"The public attitude has shifted in the past five years from prohibition to permissiveness," says William Eadington of the University of Nevada's Institute for the Study of Gambling. As he sees it, the only serious questions government is asking these days are who gets to benefit by running the casinos and how gambling should be regulated.

"The wraps are off the issue," agrees William N. Thompson, a gambling expert at the University of Nevada-Las Vegas. "The morality question is discredited because government is sponsoring it, and there is a perceived economic crisis. So politicians think of it as free money, and they think it's a tax people endorse."

Abridged from Kathleen Sylvester, "Casinomania," *Governing*, December 1992. Reprinted with permission of *Governing* magazine, ©1992.

How did it all happen? In tiny but quick steps. With large-scale, high-stakes casinos perceived as dangerous, most states began small in the 1970s and 1980s, instituting lotteries whose funds were usually earmarked for education and other good causes. Lotteries—now legal in [at least] 36 states and the District of Columbia—escalated into higher-stakes lotto games and into video poker. Eventually, a few states moved modestly into the casino business by permitting small-stakes gambling in relative isolation on riverboats and in remote mountain towns.

> *"For most [states], the selling point has been the lure of more jobs and more tourist spending."*

In the meantime, Native Americans upped the ante by opening casinos on reservations. When the profitability of those operations became obvious, many more states decided to play the game.

For most of them, the selling point has been the lure of more jobs and more tourist spending. Louisiana Governor Edwin W. Edwards, a lifelong crapshooter himself, maneuvered the legislature into approving a New Orleans casino by one vote with the promise that it would bring back the good times. His prediction: the creation of 15,000 new jobs and the addition of $25 million in city taxes and $67 million in state taxes each year.

In neighboring Mississippi, both riverboat casinos and land-based casinos won legislative approval in 1990. Legislators were swayed by the argument that it might help the struggling Gulf Coast. In Chicago, Mayor Richard M. Daley hopes for similar success with his argument that a downtown casino complex will create 36,000 new jobs and bring $82 million in new state taxes the first year alone.

## Colorado's Experience

It all sounds very promising. There are a few things, however, that the politicians in Louisiana, Mississippi and Illinois could learn from Jack Hidahl.

Hidahl is the city manager of tiny Central City, Colorado, one of two mountain towns an hour northwest of Denver that legalized low-stakes gambling in 1991. Gambling has created the town's third economic boom.

Central City and nearby Black Hawk were boom towns created by the gold rush of the 1850s. After the mines had played out, the revival of the local opera house in the 1930s helped create a new tourist economy and a second boom that lasted into the mid-1970s. But then Central City and Black Hawk lost out to the competition—a fast growing ski industry that had moved into year-round tourism with horseback riding and biking and summer music and wine festivals. Gold mines and cowboy-style saloons could not compete with that, and tourism fell off badly.

By the end of the 1980s, the two towns had dwindled to a few hundred people each, the historic buildings were on the verge of collapse, and the owners had no money to repair them. When Central City needed $400,000 to replace water lines and another $50,000 to shore up a failing wall on the reservoir, there was no tax base to provide the money. Local officials, looking to the Old West town of Deadwood, South Dakota, where low-stakes gambling had begun in September 1989, decided that might be their solution.

In November 1990, 57 percent of the Colorado voters approved the idea of gambling in Central City and Black Hawk, as well as in Cripple Creek, an old silver mining town about 70 miles to the south. On October 1, 1991, the games began.

What the local backers had envisioned was something rather simple: a few slot machines in the back of the local T-shirt shop and the ice cream parlor, a novelty that would bring the tourists back to town. They felt they could keep gambling manageable—and under local control—by limiting bets to $5 and restricting the casinos to 35 percent of the floor space in buildings in the new gaming districts.

## Effects of a Full-Blown Industry

That is not how it has played out. "Our original intent was to create an attraction," says Hidahl. "What we got was an industry."

In the first year, Central City and Black Hawk experienced a boom as dramatic as the gold rush of 1859. The rush was due in part to a decision by the newly created state gaming commission to interpret the 35 percent rule liberally. The commission allowed gaming licensees to use 35 percent of the total floor space—including bathrooms, kitchens, storage areas, stairways, hallways and attics—not just 35 percent of the public space. The practical effect was to allow casinos to squeeze large numbers of slot machines into very small spaces. And while locals had urged the state to set the tax rate on gambling proceeds as high as 40 percent, the commission set the ceiling at 15 percent.

So, contrary to local expectations, low-stakes gambling quickly drew outside investors. Some of the big-time players in the gaming industry bought in, including Resorts International and Hawaiian resort developer Christopher Hemmeter. Mona Dawkins, the Black Hawk city administrator, says simply, "I don't think anybody had any idea how attractive gambling was, and with that kind of demand, somebody was going to supply it." Within one year, Central City and Black Hawk had 7,000 gaming devices and 41 casinos—triple the number that anyone had predicted.

*"Our original intent was to create an attraction. . . . What we got was an industry."*

Central City still has its T-shirt shop and ice cream store. But virtually every other square foot of space in the gambling districts there and in Black Hawk has been turned into a casino. What businesses did it drive out? "All of them," answers Dawkins. "We don't have a grocery store, we don't have a laundromat, we don't have a filling station anymore." Even the Central City coffee shop, where locals used to congregate, is a casino now.

Government had to grow quickly to keep up. In 1990, Jack Hidahl's budget for Central City was $350,000; in 1992, he proposed $6.5 million. In the pre-gambling era, a staff of three ran the city, aided by two police officers and two public works officers. Now the number of employees is 34 and still growing. Meanwhile, the city's $400,000 water problem has become a $10 million problem. The casino industry created demand for more infrastructure. The city just put $3 million into the water system, and passed another water bond issue for $7.7 million. There was a $6.5 million transportation bond proposal to build new parking lots to handle the traffic.

*"Within one year, Central City and Black Hawk [Colorado] had 7,000 gaming devices and 41 casinos—triple the number that anyone had predicted."*

But the biggest source of stress has come from the casino owners who have spent millions of dollars on high-priced real estate and now want to make millions of dollars from their investments. Almost as quickly as competition in Central City increased and the revenues of the first few months began to level off, the owners began to seek concessions.

"There's going to be people dropping like flies in this industry unless taxes are lowered," warned Joe Behm, director of the Central City casino owners' association. "We're putting together a study showing that this industry isn't as profitable as you might think."

## Concerns for Larger Cities

Is that any reason for Edwin Edwards or Richard Daley to pay attention? Do the troubles of a remote little town in the Colorado mountains have any relation to the future of gambling in a city like New Orleans or Chicago? Well, maybe not. But experts on the subject aren't so sure. In their view, there are certain problems that a casino-seeking government should look out for whether the community in question is small, medium or large.

One is that the size and scope of the operation are very hard to keep under control. Another is that the casino operators never stop trying to rewrite the rules. A third is that it can be just as hard to keep a casino in town as it was to lure it there in the first place.

I. Nelson Rose, an expert on gaming law who teaches at the Whittier School of Law in Los Angeles, says the behavior of the gambling industry follows a predictable pattern. Once it gets a foothold in a local economy, it starts asking for concessions. In 1991, for example, the 12 Atlantic City casinos persuaded the New Jersey legislature to extend gambling hours from 20 to 24 a day on weekends, pointing out that they could hire more employees and put more tax dollars into state coffers. In 1992, they asked for and received an extension from 18 to 24 hours a day on weekdays.

In New Orleans, the casino deal was approved with an understanding that the owners would pay the state $100 million a year or 18.5 percent of adjusted gross revenues, whichever was greater. Before the contract was even awarded, however, Mirage Resorts, one of the bidders on the project, was suggesting that the tax rate of 18.5 percent was too high. Other bidders have echoed that sentiment. There is speculation that one of the first things the winner will do is ask regulators to change their minds about limiting food and beverage sales on the casino premises. When one of those bidders finally wins—and holds 15,000 jobs in New Orleans hostage—it may have the leverage to get those concessions.

"The spread of gaming in America," says William Thompson, of the University of Nevada-Las Vegas, "is being pushed by an industry that sees tremendous opportunities for profits." Gaming entrepreneurs are constantly seeking new territories "where they have monopoly windows." And while governments have not yet reached a saturation point in their interest in gaming, he suggests that "they may be reaching a saturation point as far as making money for government is concerned."

## Success Comes Early

There is a rule of diminishing returns. The first player in wins big; the last player in may fail. The first casino in Atlantic City made billions; the twelfth went bankrupt. The rule applies to governments as well as to the casinos themselves. Some of the first states and localities to get into the gambling business have done well. As the pie is cut into smaller pieces, however, the later experiments are riskier. It becomes harder and harder to bring in the dollars from outside the community.

"What governments have to learn," says Thompson, "is that gambling is good for economic development only if you can import the gamblers." Otherwise, government is fostering a system that merely redistributes income from the local citizens to the people who own the machines and the tables. . . .

*"Do [small town] troubles . . . have any relation to the future of gambling in a city like New Orleans or Chicago? Well, maybe not."*

The picture is somewhat brighter in Deadwood, the South Dakota mining town that launched the current wave of gambling fever with its bold move into the casino business in 1989. Three years after low-stakes gambling began in Deadwood, local officials declared the venture a tentative success. The town has taken in more than $5 million in taxes and accomplished its goal of restoring many of its old buildings. But, says Mayor Bruce Oberlander, "the pressure has been tremendous."

Deadwood has done better than the Colorado towns at keeping the scale of the operation under control. It has only about 2,000 slot machines (compared with 11,000 in the three Colorado casino towns), mainly because it allows only 30 machines per building. That restriction has limited the interest of outsiders. . . .

If neither states nor localities can count on casino gambling as an easy windfall, however, there is one group in America that is emerging as a clear winner: Native Americans. Just over half of America's 280 Indian reservations now have casinos of some sort, and nationally, Indian gaming revenues are close to $1.4 billion a year. . . .

> *"The spread of gaming in America . . . is being pushed by an industry that sees tremendous opportunities for profits."*

Minnesota, which has 14 Indian casinos, has become a lure for out-of-state tourists, creating a boom that has produced about 6,000 new jobs and greatly reduced unemployment on reservations and surrounding communities. The Grand Casino Mille Lacs, for instance, has brought virtually full employment to Mille Lacs County, where the jobless rate in pre-gambling days was as high as 45 percent. . . .

The question remains, though, whether much larger communities, counting on gambling to help them solve much more complicated economic problems, are not setting themselves up for a disappointment as great as the optimism many of them now express. I. Nelson Rose offers them Atlantic City as a precedent to think about.

"Gambling did what it was supposed to do," says Rose. "It created 43,000 jobs. But it didn't change the character of Atlantic City. It used to be a slum by the sea; now it's a slum by the sea with casinos. And it couldn't solve the economic problems of the region. It isn't that big."

# Gambling Will Continue to Benefit Nevada's Economy

by William N. Thompson

About the author: *William N. Thompson is a public administration professor at the University of Nevada in Las Vegas.*

The automotive industry came to Detroit by accidents of history and geography. The industry could have been located in a number of places. But Henry Ford as a young man set up shop in Detroit. There he applied the ideas of mass assembly and economies of large scale to the construction and distribution of automobiles. Detroit was centrally located with railroad lines and Great Lakes transportation channels. It attracted the best labor from eastern and midwestern populations that were freshly stocked with waves of European immigrants.

Ford's early successes attracted other automobile industry innovators and leaders. With his leadership, Detroit came to hold undisputed leadership in the auto industry that lasted into the 1960s.

But today when we think of quality, we do not think of the American "Big Three" automakers—General Motors, Ford, and Chrysler. Instead, we look to the Japanese who have cornered the market by making a third of the automobiles purchased in our country. At the same time automakers such as G.M. lose $15 million a day.

## Another Detroit?

Just twenty years ago Detroit was on a roll. Now it seems the only thing rolling is an eight ball. This raises a question: Where will Nevada be in twenty years?

Just as the automobile industry of Detroit was at a pinnacle in 1970, so it is that the Nevada gaming industry is similarly positioned as we entered the 1990s. For sixty years, when anyone thought of casinos—anyone in the entire world—they thought of Nevada—Reno and Las Vegas.

Gaming came to Nevada much as automobiles came to Michigan—by geographical accident. In 1931, an economic vacuum in the Desert Southwest de-

William N. Thompson, "Is Las Vegas Doomed to Become Another Detroit?" *Las Vegas Metropolitan Economic Indicators*, vol. 5, no. 1 (Spring 1992). Reprinted by permission of The Center for Business and Economic Research, University of Nevada, Las Vegas.

manded that any industry, any enterprise, enter. The state legalized casino gambling. Then in the 1940s gaming personalities such as Bugsy Siegel, Meyer Lansky, and Moe Dalitz played roles similar to that played by Henry Ford: they made their product—glamorous gaming halls—accessible to ordinary people.

In the world market, the ravishing effects of war and the politics of morality kept other countries from embracing the concept of mass-oriented casinos. On our shores, other American jurisdictions were happy that Nevada was attracting illegal gaming operators away from their territories and supportive of its monopoly on the casino industry.

> *"The new competition is not confined to a single location 2,500 miles away. The competition is coming from all directions."*

In the 1970s, for the first time, Detroit seriously faced national and world competition in automobile production. Since then they have suffered from the rigors of the free-market system. Both an American auto industry and a regional economy have been commercially devastated. Similarly, although Nevada quickly overcame an earlier scare with competition from Atlantic City in the early 1980s, for the first time it faces serious national and world competition in gaming production in the 1990s.

The new competition is not confined to a single location 2,500 miles away. The competition is coming from all directions, and several potentially competitive gaming states are less than a one-day drive from the Silver State. Surrounded by potential competitors, we are confronted with new questions. Will the Nevada casinos survive the rigors of the free-market system? Will the Nevada gaming industry and the Nevada economy be commercially devastated in the face of the open free-market competition? Are we doomed to become another Detroit?

Several factors have been cited as explanations for the decline of the Detroit automobile industry. As we examine these factors, we should juxtapose the conditions in the gaming industry to see if they fit the same model.

## Examining New Ideas

*Factor 1: The Close Circle of Leadership: Synergy or Group Think?* When entrepreneurs are located close to one another, they may enhance mutual opportunities for success by exchanging information and by seeking to out-compete one another. This powerful interchange—called synergy—was in force in the early Detroit car industry. However, over time success led a closed circle of manufacturers to fall into a trap. They engaged in an entropic process called "group think" in which they came to believe that they had all the knowledge necessary for success. When outsiders suggested that cars should be smaller, more fuel efficient and safer, they said, "No, we know best. The public wants big cars."

117

Is "group think" present in Nevada? A close circle of operators have been very successful in Nevada. Casino managers may feel they "know it all." Yet if we are to adjust thinking in order to maintain a dominant market position, we must accept new ideas whatever their source. We must examine successful operations on riverboats, in South Dakota, and on Indian reservations and learn from these ventures. Fortunately, Nevada's larger and more fluid leadership is reaching out in a quest for new knowledge.

*Factor 2: Innovations and Marketing Philosophies.* Henry Ford achieved abundant profits by marketing a basic product to the masses. The notion of making a few models in order to realize economies of scale became part of management thinking. Year-to-year model changes were essentially cosmetic ones. When customers indicated they wanted variety, Detroit was not ready to change. Japan was. They weren't burdened with thoughts that all production had to be on a mass level. They also demonstrated an ability to quickly introduce new models by taking only three years to produce a new product line. Detroit took five years.

In the gaming field, Nevada may still view production as Detroit did—as a massive operation allowing for cosmetic changes only. However, the new operators on the rivers and on the reservations, many of whom are Nevadans, are showing they can put new approaches into place quickly, aimed at completely different markets. One reaction of the state has been to oppose legalization of gaming in other jurisdictions. Instead, the state must meet the new competition head-on with changes that will keep customers coming to the Silver State.

## Consumer Demand

*Factor 3: Listening to the Consumer.* Detroit would not listen to the customer. The "Big Three"—General Motors, Ford, and Chrysler—kept making big cars. They were the last to hear the cry for quality. Any problems with cars were dealt with as engineering problems. "Recall" became the industry byword. However, competitors came to understand that problems with cars were customer problems.

Many Nevadans have been slow to realize that customers want a "total product." They want more than just the opportunity to gamble. This is Nevada's strength. The state is not unique in having gaming products. And Nevada can't claim that it is the only place offering tourist attractions. However, Nevada has a unique advantage in that the state offers both tourism and gaming. If the customer wants both, Nevada can and should deliver.

> *"Nevada . . . offers both tourism and gaming. If the customer wants both, Nevada can and should deliver."*

One example of how not to offer total product was provided by a Las Vegas Strip property that catered mostly to high rollers. A tourist group asked how they could visit Death Valley. The management balked at the suggestion—they were a gambling house and couldn't make any money if their guests were at Death Valley. They refused to help the tour director find a means to take his group to Death Valley, hoping, of course, that the group would decide instead to remain in the city. But the determined group encouraged its tour director to independently locate a bus company that would transport them. They were given a very complete all-day tour, and they returned to Las Vegas with one thought on their minds—sleep.

> *"Nevada need not fear that foreign operators, either within or outside the United States, will soon be competitive forces of concern."*

If the casino had catered to these guests, they could have organized a more relaxing four-hour tour of Death Valley that included slot play beforehand and, afterwards, a dinner and a show, followed by more gaming. Tourism and gaming could have been linked together.

Casino management should capitalize more on the tourism value of the state by working closely with those marketing the natural scenery of Nevada and surrounding areas to assure that the customer base remains strong. They need to work a lot more on listening skills if they hope to avoid a Detroit-like fate in the future.

## Not Easily Replicated

*Factor 4: Capital for Replicating an Industry.* The automobile industry symbolized America's world economic dominance. The dominance continued as long as other nations lacked the capital resources to duplicate our factories. But prosperity came to mean cars, and as soon as other nations found the resources to invest in manufacturing, they sought to replicate our auto industries. With new facilities, they realized that they could make cars as efficiently as we did and that they could meet the needs of American consumers as well.

Fortunately, while a car factory can be rather easily replicated, a gaming environment such as Nevada's cannot. Its industry is built upon an infrastructure of variety, entertainment choice, inexpensive hotel accommodations (rooms and meals), an ambience of good weather, and constant offerings of many special events. And those high capital investors with major investments already established in Nevada will not be eager, and may not even be able, to assist in duplicating the ambience elsewhere.

*Factor 5: Economic Development and Industrial Duplication.* Automobile manufacturing is considered desirable because the factory jobs involved have a very high multiplier effect; that is, as many as six residents can be supported from the activity of a single autoworker. As autoworkers are laid off, many other jobs are also lost. The demise of the Detroit industry has also been quickened by this negative multiplier.

The multiplier effect in the casino industry is less pervasive. It is greatly influenced by the residence of its gamers. In Nevada, most are outsiders. However, in many new gaming jurisdictions, the players are local residents. If these new jursidictions cannot offer gaming to patrons who come from outside the region, economic growth will be illusive at best. As future experiences are analyzed, there will be less pressure on other jurisdictions to seek to replicate the Nevada gaming scene.

*Factor 6: The Expertise of Foreign Players.* Japanese car manufacturers demonstrated an ability to quickly learn the American market and to deliver products which met demands of Americans. They were good competitors.

However, such cannot be said for many non-Nevada gaming operators. Las Vegas has witnessed the experiences of four Japanese-owned casino operations: the Aladdin, the Park, the Dunes, and the San Remo. The first three failed while only the last has prevailed. Also, in foreign arenas, casino gaming is not conducted in a manner that will lure Nevada customers. Often foreign casinos cannot advertise, offer complimentary services, or offer credit play. Casinos have dress codes, entrance fees, and a very restricted offering of games. Nevada need not fear that foreign operators, either within or outside the United States, will soon be competitive forces of concern. Nevadans clearly do gaming best. It is not an easy industry to learn. The experts are in Nevada.

## Economic Incentives

*Factor 7: Labor Costs and Union Practices.* Labor costs and union contract provisions provided tremendous disincentives for automobile manufacturers to remain in Michigan.

The Nevada casino scene, however, is quite different. Gaming employees are not unionized, and wages are standardized at lower levels. There is a recognition that tips provide the largest share of a dealer's compensation package. In contrast, most other gaming jurisdictions find wages either higher as tips are low or find dealers organized into strong unions.

*Factor 8: Taxation.* Government taxation—both national and local—has driven the cost of automobile production to uncompetitive levels for Detroit automakers. The taxation situation has been a major incentive for plants to relocate to other jurisdictions, both domestic and foreign.

*"The challenges of competition can be met. Certainly Nevada is not doomed to become another Detroit."*

Gaming operations will not relocate outside Nevada for taxation reasons. Nevada casino taxation is the lowest of any jurisdiction—just over 6 percent. New Jersey has a gross win tax of 8 percent, Iowa's is 20 percent, while most European casinos assess win taxes in excess of 50 percent. Taxation is a positive for Nevada, and state policymakers should keep it that way.

*Factor 9: Government Policy.* The national government had seen Detroit as a vulnerable military target. Therefore, defense policymakers encouraged automakers to disperse their production facilities. On top of this incentive to move factories out of the Detroit area was a non-incentive provided by urban renewal policymakers. National housing policy supported by local officials found land clearance projects devoted almost exclusively to low-income housing at a time when the automakers needed new space for factory modernization. Residential groups, forgetting the source of their economic livelihood, cried out "Not in my backyard" as they pointed out the pollution, traffic, and aesthetic disadvantages of having to live near factories.

No such government pressures exist for the Nevada gaming industry. Indeed, there are zoning pressures against casinos in residential areas; however, considerable space for casino development remains within the Las Vegas area and throughout the state. Contrary to federal desires for a dispersed automobile industry, federal policy regarding gaming, minimal as it is, encourages the concentration of casino facilities in remote areas such as Nevada.

*Factor 10: Trade Barriers.* Foreign trade barriers have restricted the ability of Detroit automobile makers to compete. However, trade barriers would be totally ineffective as a deterrent to those players from foreign jurisdictions who come to Nevada for gaming recreation. Indeed, while the United States has experienced a major growth in trade deficits in the manufacturing sectors, there is no deficit in the service areas. The Japanese are among the best customers in Nevada casinos. They will continue to be.

The ten factors above suggest that Nevada need not fear a fate such as fell upon the Detroit and American automobile industry. However, the state cannot simply stand back and let events take their natural course and still expect to enjoy the prosperity realized in recent decades. We do have competition today, and a determined state policy should be put into place to deal with emerging trends.

The policy need not be one of total opposition to the legalization of casino gaming in other jurisdictions. Nevada should realize that casinos elsewhere can generate players for Nevada casinos.

Exterior gaming will also add to the export strength of the state's economy. Much gaming equipment is made in Nevada. Also the expertise of the local gaming industry can be packaged for export. Nevada can become a training center for gaming operatives throughout the world. Competitive taxation advantages should not be altered.

Also our gaming industry leaders need to work together with state tourism officials to develop joint marketing programs that will capitalize upon the state's unique position as the only tourism destination with complete gaming opportunities.

The challenges of competition can be met. Certainly Nevada is not doomed to become another Detroit.

# Riverboat Casinos Help Local Economies

**by Janice C. Hernon and James R. Appel**

*About the authors: Janice C. Hernon is a former planner/analyst for the city of St. Louis, Missouri. James R. Appel is chairman of Real Estate Analysts Limited, a St. Louis real estate appraisal firm.*

In 1951, U.S. Senator Estes M. Kefauver, chairman of the Senate Crime Investigating Committee, said that "big time gambling is amoral . . . and legalizing it will not make it less so. . . . America will be in a bad way if we ever have to resort to taxing crime and immorality for the purpose of raising revenue to operate our institutions."

That statement reflected the attitude of the country at the time when the national gambling "take" was estimated at $15 to $28 billion. Today "gaming" is no longer a blight on the nation's morals, but a respectable form of entertainment competing with baseball games and movies for the family's leisure time and budget.

## Rise in Popularity of Legalized Gambling

In this century, Americans carried on a love-hate relationship with gambling. Popular during the period between World Wars I and II, gambling was largely outlawed after the Kefauver Committee hearings in the early 1950s. At that time, the public believed that gambling was always intimately associated with organized crime even when the activity was sanctioned by the local community.

The moral dilemma of legalized gambling troubled state and local governments much less during the 1980s. Midwest areas, already stung by the decline in manufacturing and the middle-class population exodus, faced severe cuts in revenues from such sources as federal revenue sharing and community development block grants. The ability of state lawmakers to raise taxes to make up for the loss and provide essential services was curtailed by the popularity of "Proposition 13"-type [tax-cutting] amendments that required voter approval for virtually all tax and fee increases.

Janice C. Hernon and James R. Appel, "Riverboat Gaming Bonanza," *Appraisal View*, Summer 1994.
Reprinted by permission of the publisher, Arthur Gimmy International, San Francisco.

By 1990, state and local governments could no longer ignore the potential of a large source of revenue favored by a seemingly infinite supply of willing participants. Many states already allowed dog and horse racing, bingo, jai alai, and state-sponsored lotteries. The rush to embrace casino gambling on riverboats began in Iowa in 1991. Illinois and Mississippi followed in 1992. By the end of 1993, 20 states had passed legislation allowing casino gambling. Most of these states required proximity to water, but some, like Colorado, allow land-based casinos.

> *"A lively debate has occurred in Chicago concerning the benefits of casinos . . . on the city's lakefront."*

The Federal Indian Gaming Regulatory Act of 1988 authorized casinos on tribal lands, and gaming on Indian reservations is now a multi-billion-dollar industry in 17 states. Significantly, the Gaming Act allows states to receive only sufficient funds to reimburse them for the cost of overseeing gaming operations. Although almost all Native American casinos are located on tribal lands, it is likely that future facilities will be located on other property through mutual agreements with state and local governments.

## State Legislative Issues

The diversity of the enabling legislation passed by various states reflects their differing attitudes toward casino gambling. Iowa, the first state to open its borders to riverboat gambling, showed ambivalence by imposing a $5 per bet wagering limit and a $200 per excursion betting loss limit. It also specified that boats must cruise, adding to operating costs; a maximum of 30% of the vessel's square footage may be devoted to gaming. Gaming licenses were awarded to not-for-profit corporations that made whatever agreement they could negotiate with gaming boat operators. When Iowa was the only state with riverboat gambling, it was home to five boats. Three relocated to Mississippi shortly after that state voted to allow gaming; two remained in Clinton and Davenport, and a third started cruising in Sioux City.

With a more relaxed attitude, the Illinois legislature enacted a law that does not include a betting loss limit. Competition is managed by restricting gaming franchises to 10 throughout the state. Cruise requirements do exist. A lively debate has occurred in Chicago concerning the benefits of casinos versus the perceived aesthetic blight of gaming facilities on the city's lakefront. The casinos in Joliet, Illinois, benefit from the absence of gaming in Chicago, and are among the highest revenue-generators in the industry. The state of Illinois imposes the highest taxes on waterfront gaming of any state: a 20% tax on adjusted gross proceeds (defined as the house win, or what each gaming patron loses), of which one-fourth is sent back to the local jurisdiction.

Mississippi appears to have the most lenient gaming environment. Facilities must float, but they're often located in ponds and do not have to cruise or con-

123

tend with the problems of being on a navigable waterway. There are no wagering limits, and no restrictions on the number of licenses. Finally, taxes on adjusted gross revenue and machine fees are the lowest of any state. Eleven boats opened in little more than a year, and the state has received license applications from dozens more.

The Missouri legislature approved gaming regulations following passage of a referendum in late 1992, and imposed a $500 per day wagering limit. The facility may devote a maximum of 50% of space to gaming, and some boats do not have to cruise. (Others have the option of proving that cruising is not economically feasible.) However, the Missouri Supreme Court raised serious objections to the initiative petition and subsequent regulations.

In 1994, Missouri voters reauthorized gaming via a statewide vote.

The impact of state legislation on gambling operators' profitability will be demonstrated again as boats on the western side of the Mississippi River in Missouri are allowed to compete with those on the Illinois side of the river for the same market.

## Local Government Issues

At the municipal and county government levels, a variety of issues are generating attention. Very small towns and gulfside resort communities, with tiny governments and few or no staff, confront problems similar to those posed in larger metropolitan areas. Local attitudes toward casino operators vary, but they share concerns about matters that affect the successful balance of gaming operator interests and those of the general public.

*"Many localities see gaming as an opportunity to invigorate deteriorated waterfront commercial areas."*

Most localities employ a request for proposal (RFP) process in selecting one or more gaming operators. The RFP document is crucial in describing how the casino operation is viewed and what goals are expected to be accomplished. Some of the more routine requirements include plans and specifications for exterior and interior design; ingress, egress, and parking plans; details of sanitary and solid waste disposal; and public safety and security matters. Other jurisdictions require, or at least give added weight to, plans to train and hire local residents. Some localities encourage additional investment in their community and links with community-based organizations.

Significantly, the Mississippi State Port Authority at Gulfport required a performance bond of $125,000, to be used in the event the boat operator failed to maintain the boat properly, installed objects without Port Authority approval, or, in a worst-case scenario, ceased operations and needed to be towed away.

Many localities see gaming as an opportunity to invigorate deteriorated waterfront commercial areas, either through spin-off development or direct invest-

124

ment on the part of the casino owners. Some operators have agreed to contribute to infrastructure improvements that are not closely related to demand created by the casino. For example, Kansas City has enlisted Hilton Hotels, operator of Missouri's first casino boat, to construct a $14 million Grand Avenue viaduct and a 1,500-space parking garage. The operator will also make a lease payment to Kansas City of 3% of gross gaming revenues, or $2 million, whichever is greater.

The prospect of jobs and job training for unemployed residents is especially important in cities hit hard by the shift from manufacturing to a service economy. The East St. Louis, Illinois, proposal process gave strong weight to the Casino Queen operator's efforts to hire unemployed local residents. When details were finalized and a formal announcement made, the boat's telephone lines were jammed for days by job seekers. Meanwhile, the Empress, in Joliet, employs 1,100 people, with an estimated 880 gaming positions. (Many of the jobs pay above-minimum wages, and salaries of dealers and other managers can exceed $30,000.) On average, it is estimated that the ratio of new local employment to gaming positions on gaming boats is in excess of one to one (1:1).

## Revenue Generation—Direct and Indirect Impact

The above-mentioned benefits pale in comparison to the actual fiscal return to municipal and county coffers. Money may be collected by the state as gross revenue tax, and the state sometimes remits a portion of the revenue to the city. Some localities collect a per-person gate fee or head tax; others tax slot machines. When the city controls the waterfront property, it can earn additional revenues by leasing mooring or berthing rights, or occupancy of publicly held property. In one year, a lease for one berthing space and attendant access areas generated $800,000 in revenue to the Mississippi Port Authority.

Several not-for-profit licensees in Iowa collected substantial revenues, generally used for historic preservation and public improvements; some licensees received a per-person fee, others received a percentage of gross revenues. In Dubuque, Iowa, it was reported that the licensee received 15% of gross revenues, which was a factor in the boat's relocation.

The impact of gaming as a windfall source of revenue has been profound.

*"During the brief existence of legal riverfront gaming, the visitor industry has benefited most."*

The Joliet Empress reported a casino win, or adjusted gross receipts, of $14.05 million for May 1993 alone. The city of Joliet received $702,500 for that month. An additional $1.00 per-person fee remitted approximately $84,000 to that city for the same month. Joliet now has four operating casinos, but it is unlikely that all will generate that level of revenue in the future.

Towns that become gaming destinations should feel the ripple effect of increased revenues from hotel and motel taxes, restaurant taxes, sales taxes, business license fees, and, in larger cities (where they exist), earning taxes. This indirect impact is especially important in larger population centers with healthy convention and tourism industries, where gaming is one more inducement to lure meetings and events. However, few groups would cite gaming as a critical factor in selecting a conference location.

> *"The selection of a locality for riverboat gambling is a symbolic statement of confidence in the community."*

Local government is not the only beneficiary of the gaming industry's multiple effects. Many businesses, especially service firms, can expect increased traffic, particularly in areas that are already tourist destinations, in which visitors might extend a trip for gaming purposes. Taxes on restaurant, sales, amusement, transportation, and business licenses in a major metropolitan area with an anticipated gaming market of $240 million might easily approach $4 million annually. The direct impact of this level of activity, measured in terms of a 2% tax on gross gaming receipts remitted to local government, could approach $4.75 million. Many localities receive more than that.

## Related Development

Spin-off development is more likely to occur when gaming establishments have enjoyed a sustained period of success. During the brief existence of legal riverfront gaming, the visitor industry has benefited most.

The President Riverboat Cruises promised to buy and renovate a downtown Davenport hotel, build a new $30 million hotel, and purchase and renovate a vacant downtown department store. It has not delivered on the new hotel, it removed the restaurant boat and planned to substitute a "service barge," and it failed to renovate the historic department store. But, renewed interest in the riverfront did lead to a 33,000-square-foot addition to the existing exhibition hall, a 775-car parking ramp, and negotiations with Embassy Suites to build a hotel in the area.

In Rock Island, Illinois, an existing hotel was purchased and extensively renovated. Several restaurants were renovated and two new ones opened. The riverboat operator, the city, and a development authority plan a downtown arts and entertainment district encompassing the riverfront site. In Metropolis, two downtown buildings were renovated for retail shops, and three new restaurants emerged from two vacant buildings and a vacant caboose; a 120-room hotel has opened. Alton is considering several waterfront projects. Unincorporated Jo Daviess County, near Galena, used gaming revenue to construct water and sewer lines to a development site that recently landed American Freezer Service, employing 140 people. St. Louis, Missouri, is using the sudden interest in riverboat gambling as a springboard for developing a new central riverfront plan.

As the industry matures, it will be easier to see if gaming patrons can be encouraged to combine their riverboat trips with other tourism activities, such as visiting amusement parks, shopping, and sightseeing, that would spread economic ripples throughout the community. For now, it appears that gaming customers tend to be more singularly motivated, and that convenience is the major factor in casino selection.

The most intangible impact of gaming may be the most important. The selection of a locality for riverboat gambling is a symbolic statement of confidence in the community. When a riverfront environment that has languished for decades receives a jolt of activity from gaming, a contagious energy can spread to surrounding business and institutions. One expert in Davenport felt that despite lagging time frames for development and diminishing expectations from the city's riverboat industry, the resurgence of pride in its downtown has made gaming a worthwhile experience.

## Potential for Market Saturation and Volatility

The number of potential gaming customers and the dollars they can afford to spend on gaming will reach its limit at some point, adding turmoil to an already volatile activity. Signs of saturation may already have appeared. In 1992, *Forbes* magazine reported that 33 of Colorado's 100 casinos had been purchased by competitors or closed down, and it estimated that half of the remaining casinos were losing money. The Iowa-to-Mississippi relocations show the dramatic consequences of casinos chasing what they consider to be more attractive locations.

*"Casinos can be counted on to take aggressive measures to thrive in a market threatened with saturation."*

St. Louis took this possibility into account when planners discussed relocating gaming boats away from the central riverfront area because the activity might be "transitory."

Riverfront properties once considered worthless skyrocket in value when they are designated as sites for casino gambling. Of course, the value can also plummet if the casino relocates and no other use can match it in revenue-producing intensity. The arrival (and departure) of gaming businesses affects the values of tourism-related properties, as well, and real estate appraisals for any property relating to gaming in any way would need to take this volatility into account.

## Casino Operators' Responses

Casinos can be counted on to take aggressive measures to thrive in a market threatened with saturation. For marketers, the situation offers a choice of targeting a niche market or attempting to expand the potential market. Where a locality contains several operations, it is likely that consumers will be offered targeted incentives, as occurred in land-based areas such as Nevada and New Jersey.

Nevada, once the nation's only mecca for legalized gambling, now uses food, drink, and lodging incentives more selectively than it did years ago, targeting groups most likely to frequent its gaming operations and encouraging repeat visits in an attempt to maximize the use of local gaming facilities by a finite but reliable user market.

The Grand Casino on the Mille Lacs Band of Ojibwe tribal lands in Hinckley, Minnesota, provides a video arcade for teenagers and an 8,000-square-foot day care center to attract whole families to the facility. A similar development opened in January 1994 in Biloxi, Mississippi.

So far, the strategy seems to be working. In Illinois, adjusted gross proceeds, figured on a per-person basis, are about $75; for the St. Louis area the per-person expenditure is forecast at about $55. These figures indicate the presence of consumers who equate casino expenditures (losses) with the cost of a four-star restaurant dinner or a night at the theater; the figures do not indicate a dominance of "high rollers."

## Future Prospects

It is risky to predict the future of such a volatile activity with a short history. State and local governments, and casino operators, can expect an extended period of being buffeted about in a changing competitive climate. Beyond that, the legalization of casino gaming has created, and will create, a number of issues.

1. Disappointed government officials and residents of Iowa have discovered that gaming is no substitute for consistent investment in a solid public education system, job training, and other economic development programs. However, gaming revenues could be targeted for these purposes. In St. Louis, for instance, the mayor has proposed linking the selection of riverboat gambling operators with the financing and development of a convention hotel.

2. In the matter of tax and revenues, gaming offers elected officials an option they can extend to a frequently cynical and disaffected electorate. But significant compromises may need to be made to maintain profitable, competitive gaming operations. Loss limits may need to be increased and cruise requirements eliminated. Ultimately, land-based casinos may be unavoidable. If the community is unwilling to make concessions, gaming operations—and revenues—will relocate, and the underlying local fiscal problems will be exacerbated.

   *"In the context of a strong planning environment, . . . casino gaming can be a potent development tool."*

3. If casino marketers continue their success at mainstreaming the casino experience, then local tourism, visitor, and recreation industries may need to examine the possible ramifications. For example, will casino patrons spread their money around town,

or, if casino gaming attracts the couple who would otherwise go to the baseball game, can there be an adverse effect on visitor attendance at the ball park? If patrons are singularly motivated, and the gaming operators build an on-site restaurant, will its presence negatively affect other area restaurants?

4. Casino gaming comes with the highest of opportunity costs. It requires untold energy from officials at all levels of government. Much of a state legislature's time can be devoted to enabling legislation. Substantial staff time is needed to develop ensuing regulations. Those rules require enforcement, background checks, and other ongoing duties. Local governments must select operators, inspect facilities, and perform other oversight duties. In the meantime, attention to other important issues is diverted while energy is expended on the single issue of casino gaming. Must "other issues" be, in effect, victimized by the lure of potential benefits created by casino operations? It is up to the community and its elected officials to assign priorities and target resources. In the context of a strong planning environment, one that understands the high costs as well as the fiscal benefits, casino gaming can be a potent development tool, if perhaps a temporary one.

# Gambling Revitalizes Poor Communities

**by Alan Salomon**

**About the author:** *Alan Salomon is a reporter for* Advertising Age, *a weekly publication covering the advertising industry.*

In 1982, the U.S. Department of Commerce called Mississippi's Tunica County the poorest in the nation, with a per capita income of $5,868.

But in 1994, that number has nearly doubled to $10,575, the jobless rate for the county's 9,400 residents has plunged to 4.9% and retail sales are way up.

The reason? Tunica County, thirty miles south of Memphis, Tennessee, has become "Little Las Vegas."

No fewer than twenty-five casinos line the Mississippi River from the Gulf Coast to the doorstep of Memphis. Seven call Tunica County home, four more were expected to open in 1994 and a total of twenty have been proposed for the county in northwestern Mississippi.

## Business Is Booming

"Everything is up, and business is booming," said Wiley Chambers, owner of the new Grease Rack Lounge in the Blue & White Restaurant in Tunica. "And when more casinos come, everything will be up even more."

The recent additions in Tunica have allowed Mississippi to surpass New Jersey in casino square footage. As of April 1, 1994, Atlantic City had 802,000 square feet of casino space and Mississippi, 860,132.

"It is hard to say casino gaming in Mississippi is simply a phenomenon," said Danny Mitchell, chief operating officer of the Godwin Group, a Jackson [advertising] agency whose clients include Tunica's Hollywood Casino. "It is here to stay. It certainly has helped our business—not to mention the [outdoor billboard] industry in the state and the TV stations. You can see [outdoor boards] for Mississippi casinos an hour into Louisiana."

That's not surprising since two of three customers are from outside the state.

Statewide, casinos took in $428 million in revenue in fiscal 1993, their first full calendar year of operation. That number was expected to jump to $1 billion in fiscal 1994.

Money from the casinos, which by mid-1994 had paid the county more than $12 million in boarding and gaming fees since Splash Casino opened in October 1992, will help upgrade roads and schools, county officials say.

The state's share of boarding fees and taxes was $128 million from 1992 to 1994.

## New Jobs, New Revenue

Mississippi's economic outlook is among the sunniest in the Sun Belt, according to the Federal Reserve Bank of Atlanta. "Mississippi is No. 2 in economic outlook, and that's a change," said Robert Forrestal, president-CEO of the Fed. Mr. Forrestal cited gaming as the biggest factor in the state's economic showing.

"During 1993, gaming represented 25% to 33% of the new jobs created in the state," said Denton Gibbs, public relations director for the Mississippi Department of Economic & Community Development.

Casinos employed 10,000 people in 1993, a number that more than doubled to 28,000 in 1994.

"And for the second consecutive year, the state budget surplus in state government was increased," Mr. Gibbs said. "It was in excess of $300 million in 1993, and we figure gaming contributed to probably 35% of that."

*"Mississippi's economic outlook is among the sunniest in the Sun Belt."*

State officials say because of that windfall, Mississippi can now address infrastructure enhancement projects. "We can repair bridges and improve and enlarge highways, such as what we are doing now on Highway 61 from Memphis to Tunica and Highway 90 on the Gulf Coast," Mr. Gibbs said.

"It's no doubt we had an image problem, and casinos have helped Mississippi's image perception," said George Smith, director of tourism for the state.

He said casinos statewide have a combined marketing budget of $100 million, adding, "Put that with the state's $10 million, plus $7.5 million for direct marketing, and we have the ability to run an effective marketing campaign."

Mr. Smith, whose department didn't have a marketing budget in 1992, said he will get out Mississippi's tourism message with ads in 36 national and regional publications. And for the first time, Mississippi is able to use the electronic media and will air commercials on the Nashville Network, one national TV network and some spot markets. The Ramey Agency, Jackson, handled Mississippi's 1994 tourism campaign, which carried the theme, "The South's warmest welcome."

The media are also benefiting. "We have seen growth and casinos have had much to do with it," said Frankie Thomas, VP-general sales manager at WLBT-

TV in Jackson. "We have five casinos advertising with us now and could have more, but we have a limit to what we will accept."

Paul Gartland, general manager of Lamar Outdoor Advertising in Gulfport, said an outdoor salesman in Mississippi today would do very well.

"If I were one, I would think I had died and gone to heaven," said Lance Hopkins, account supervisor for the Godwin Group.

Mr. Gartland said revenue from gaming has been great but casinos have also created spin-offs for other businesses coming in and using outdoor advertising.

> *"Even the [spread of casinos] in Louisiana can't shake the spirit of Mississippi casino operators."*

"That has resulted in more hotel business, and they use [outdoor boards]," said Mr. Gartland, noting his office has added 50 [billboard] faces on the Gulf Coast alone. "We could do more if we weren't so regulated."

The casinos have also been good for retail growth. Sales in 1993 were up statewide—a 15% increase on the Gulf Coast and 13% in northwestern Mississippi. In the northeastern corner of the state, where there's no gaming, sales were up 11%.

On the Gulf Coast, the economy can be summed up in one word—gambling.

A report from the Harrison County Development Commission for fiscal year 1993 noted gambling has provided economic stimulus "unequaled in modern times."

"It is expected that the casino industry will produce more than $500 million in total capital investments in the Gulf Coast economy [in 1994]," the report said.

It has already produced a 10% increase in the number of jobs there and a 28% increase in gross sales tax, Harrison County officials say.

## Tunica County's Edge

Even though the Gulf Coast had about a year jump on casinos, many feel Tunica County has the most development potential.

"One thing that Tunica has that the coast doesn't is abundant land," Mr. Mitchell said. "And they don't have hurricanes up there."

Two land developers who are taking advantage of those facts are Dick Flowers and Dutch Parker, who are partners in the Mhoon Landing Casino Resort in Tunica County. They announced plans for a 300-acre development to include hotels, apartments, recreational vehicle park, clubs, theaters, restaurants, shopping center, tennis and fitness center, airport and golf course. Major hotel chains such as Choice International, Hampton Inn and Holiday Inn have said they will build there.

The fact that there are more than fifty applications on the desk of the Mississippi Gaming Commission doesn't bother those already in the game.

"The market [in Tunica] is big enough for a number of successful competitors," said Mike Rose, chairman of the Promus Cos. in Memphis, owners of Harrah's casinos in Tunica County and Vicksburg.

Things are going so well in the state now that even the prospect of a giant land-based casino in New Orleans and fifteen new riverboats in Louisiana can't shake the spirit of Mississippi casino operators.

"We don't take it for granted," Mr. Mitchell said. "I believe the state has approached it with a jaundiced eye because they aren't sure it's going to last."

# Gambling Is Economically Harmful

by John Warren Kindt

**About the author:** *John Warren Kindt teaches courses on commerce and legal policy at the University of Illinois in Urbana-Champaign.*

> "[G]ambling itself . . . is probably the biggest producer of money for the American La Cosa Nostra [that] there is."
> —James Moody, chief of the Organized Crime Section of the FBI

Critics of expanded legalized gambling activities argue that if the U.S. public has been satisfied with the progress in the "War on Drugs," that public is going to be ecstatic about the forthcoming "War on Gambling." There are some obvious parallels. Arguably, the war on drugs was not even necessary until the widespread use of illegal drugs during the 1960s when such use came under the rubric of social acceptability. A recognized addictive activity similar to illegal drug use, gambling was not just becoming sociologically acceptable, but as of the 1980s, it was being "legalized"—unlike harmful drugs. Sociologists recognize that this "acceptability factor" combined with an "accessibility factor" will increase the number of compulsive gamblers in society. The "legalization" of gambling activities means that society can anticipate that the number of compulsive gamblers will increase from .77 percent of the overall population to between 1.5 and 5 percent of the population—with a total of 10 percent of the population constituting problem economic gamblers. Historical trends and conditioning factors indicate that the war on gambling will be the added sociological war of the 1990s—financed by society in general and by the taxpayers in particular.

## A Warning Against Gambling

In 1976, the definitive U.S. Commission on the Review of the National Policy Toward Gambling cautioned against the trends toward legalizing and expanding legalized gambling activities and anticipated the increased socio-economic costs and costs to the criminal justice system of ignoring these warnings.

John Warren Kindt, "Increased Crime and Legalizing Gambling Operations: The Impact on the Socio-Economics of Business and Government." Reprinted with permission from the *Criminal Law Bulletin*, vol. 30, no. 6, ©1994 Research Institute of America, Inc., Warren Gorham Lamont Professional Publishing Division, 210 South St., Boston, MA 02111. 800 999-9336. All rights reserved.

Among other findings, the Commission concluded "[i]t is axiomatic that the two principal goals of legalized gambling—revenue raising and crime control—are incompatible." Another conclusion was that gambling activities "contribute[d] more than any other single enterprise to police corruption in . . . [U.S.] cities and towns and to the well-being of the Nation's criminals." Furthermore, the Commission reported that there was "some evidence that the existence of gambling sanctioned, licensed, or run by the various states—and the attendant publicity—tends to increase citizen participation in *illegal* as well as legal gambling." In 1988, this observation received more conclusive support from the New Jersey Governor's Advisory Commission on Gambling. However, in the years since these Commissions, these *caveats* have slowly eroded from the public memory, and the aforementioned trends have apparently intensified.

> *"Gambling sanctioned, licensed, or run by the various states . . . tends to increase citizen participation in* illegal *as well as legal gambling."*

## Tax Revenues and Jobs

Proponents of increased legalized gambling activities counter that these social negatives are more than offset by the increased tax revenues and new jobs created by legalizing gambling activities. Increased tax revenues and jobs are definitely created by the initial increases in legalized gambling activities. However, critics argue that the increased social-welfare costs dwarf the benefits and that preexisting businesses are "economically cannibalized" by legalized gambling enterprises. To investigate these claims, the Ford Foundation and the Aspen Institute funded a study by the Center for Economic Development at the University of Massachusetts. This study analyzed fourteen major reports prepared to evaluate increased legalized gambling activities. Only one report was considered balanced and the reports advocating increased legalized gambling activities were tagged as "often done by the industry itself" and as "hiding the costs," including increased costs to the criminal justice system.

This debate is far-reaching and beyond the scope of this discussion, but the gravamen [substantial part of a complaint] of the present analysis is that as the University of Massachusetts report concluded "[t]here are no *state* gambling plans" and "[t]he research used by public officials to evaluate projects is often done by the gambling industry itself." Accordingly, public policy and legal policy dictate that a state considering utilizing legalized gambling activities as economic development should rely primarily on nonindustry studies that are statewide or regional analyses and that have a strategic perspective. In this context, increased costs to the criminal justice system that are occasioned by increased legalized gambling activities must necessarily rely on the most authoritative and current reports available and extrapolate within a statewide or regional population base.

135

Such an analysis can frame the parameters for future debate and encourage more detailed studies. The present analysis focuses on only the potential for increased costs to a statewide criminal justice system as viewed in strategic policymaking. While other socio-economic cost-benefit issues should also be reviewed in state economic plans, these other issues are too broad for this analysis and are, therefore, not addressed. From the perspective of business activity, new businesses will tend not to locate or expand into those areas where crime is increasing at a rate greater than the national average. As a corollary, states with legalized gambling in general and locales with particular outlets for legalized gambling will be at high risk not only for failing to attract new businesses, but also for losing preexisting businesses. Preexisting businesses in areas where crime is increasing will be tempted to downsize, expand elsewhere, or even move entirely to another location. States and locales encouraging the gambling philosophy could easily have crime rates that increase exponentially above the national average. It is significant that strategic "business-oriented" reports have noted, for example, "the rate of increase in crime in Atlantic City [which] accelerated 150% (from a 5.4% to a 13.6% increase per year) after gambling was legalized" [according to the California Governor's Office of Planning and Research]. Given the nationwide preoccupation of states to legalize more and "harder" forms of gambling, it can be argued that those states without legalized gambling will be at a significant strategic business-economic advantage over those states that legalize gambling.

> *"States and locales encouraging the gambling philosophy could easily have crime rates that increase exponentially above the national average."*

In 1994, these socio-economic concerns were recognized and echoed by authoritative law enforcement officials; for example, Michigan Attorney General Frank Kelley has said:

> Many people try to argue that casinos bring positive results. They say that casinos mean more jobs—more money for the state—a different image. I would say to each of those statements that any positive impact would be so totally outweighed by the negatives that they should want no part of it.

Instinctively, at least some law enforcement officials appear to be concerned with the projected increases in costs to the criminal justice system, as well as the impacts on the preexisting social fabric that are occasioned by legalized gambling activities—particularly casinos. The analysis by Attorney General Kelley's staff and the conclusions are typical:

> According to [the] FBI figures, between 1977, when the first casino opened in Atlantic City, and 1986, just nine years later, the incidence of larceny per capita increased by four hundred and sixty-seven percent. Incidence of all crime combined increased by [one] hundred and thirty-eight percent—and this figure includes all categories of violent crime, including rape and robbery.

When Detroit was considering a vote on casino gambling back in 1988, I shared those statistics with a study commission and pointed out that a one hundred percent increase in crime in Detroit would paint a picture of absolute chaos that could barely be imagined. And, that *any money brought into the city would quickly be spent on an expanded law enforcement effort to control the crime.* (Emphasis added.)

As an expert with decades of experience, his conclusion was unequivocal: "I have been Michigan's Attorney General for more than thirty years, and there has never been an issue that has disturbed me any more than the proliferation of gambling in our state." From the business perspective, any issue that concerns a state's chief legal officer to such an extent should necessarily concern businesses and business executives.

## Delimitation of Costs

As in some other issue areas, it is sometimes difficult to calculate the increased "administrative costs" associated with legalized gambling activities. The data is preliminary in several regards, but some observations and conclusions can be made with regard to the administrative costs of monitoring and regulating casino gambling, states can profit by extrapolating from the costs experienced by similar gambling locales. In the absence of any comprehensive state plans relating to legalized gambling activities, state policymakers are basically relegated to utilizing this type of approach—particularly when short decision-making time frames are involved.

Given these constraints, it should be noted that the administrative costs of regulating just the "casino gambling" in Atlantic City, New Jersey, for example, are approximately $56 million to $59 million per year. These costs can be delimited m a variety of ways, e.g., as a function of "visits," or of local patrons vis-à-vis gambling tourists. From a state governmental perspective, however, these costs can be expressed as a function of the state budget. Since the 1991 fiscal year budget of New Jersey was $24.7 billion, the calculation is as follows: $56 million ÷ $24.7 billion = .23%. Of course, this number appears small, but it looms larger when it is combined with the projected socio-economic costs to New Jersey and then compared to the state revenues actually generated by legalized gambling activities.

> *"Any issue that concerns a state's chief legal officer ... should necessarily concern businesses."*

In a similar context, the Illinois State Police calculated that their law enforcement costs would increase by 50 percent, or $100 million per year, if a 1992 proposal for a $2-billion casino complex was approved for Chicago. Governor James Edgar estimated that this amount would just match the state's realistic share of the projected new tax revenues from the casinos; that is, $100 million. As a function of the state budget for fiscal year 1991, these increased state police costs would be: $100 million ÷ $25.1 billion = .398%. While the added tax revenues were also $100 million or .398 percent of the state budget, which appeared to be a breakeven proposition, there were other costs associated with legalized gambling activities that were not associated with traditional business activities. As calculated in a study sponsored by the proponents of the casino complex, the "regulatory" costs were calculated at $65 million per year and increased Chicago police and fire protection costs were $11.4 million per year.

> *"The Illinois State Police calculated that their law enforcement costs would increase by 50 percent, or $100 million per year."*

## Comparison with a New Orleans Casino

By comparison, the projected costs to the criminal justice system for a New Orleans casino, one-seventh to one-tenth the size of the proposed Chicago casinos, were $14 million per year, including increased police and corrections systems costs of $10.4 million, increased costs of $2.3 million for the district attorney's office, and increased costs to courts of $1.5 million. The obvious temptation to Illinois agencies was to multiply this $14 million per year by the greater size of the proposed Chicago casino complex (using the industry's own system of commonly utilized square-foot multipliers), which would yield increased costs to the Illinois criminal justice system of between $98 million and $140 million. However, in an attempt to minimize any problems of counting similar costs twice because of the different methodologies utilized in different studies and in different states, the higher costs that would tend to occur when trying to transpose the New Orleans casino estimates to the larger Chicago casino complex were not included in this analysis—although the latter two categories of increased costs to the district attorney's office and the courts probably would not involve any significant overlap with the Illinois figures. These costs ranged somewhere from a base of $3.8 million to an upper range of $26.6 million to $38 million (if the industry's square-foot multipliers were used). Therefore, projecting an additional $3.8 million in costs to the court system of Illinois was probably extremely conservative, but was not added to the basic calculations in the analysis that follows. Similarly, it was difficult to determine where to add Governor James Edgar's increases for the new prisons that would be required at a cost of $15 million per prison per year, and these costs were not included.

When the conservative Illinois costs are added together, the projected $500 million per year in estimated tax revenues to be paid by the proposed 1992 Chicago casino complex pale in significance. The relatively minor amounts paid in taxes become more apparent when it is recognized that the $500 million is really a "projection" that (1) does not materialize until the tenth year, and only at $371 million; (2) includes all taxes from "all" conceivable taxable sources; and (3) involves a dispersion (to a large degree) of taxes to the different local and state governments. Illinois Governor James Edgar believed that the state of Illinois could only expect realistically to receive $100 million in new tax revenues, which would not compensate for the increased state police costs of $100 million plus the increased regulatory costs of $65 million. Despite these constraints, the gambling proponents' own estimate of $500 million will be utilized in this example.

## A Billion-Dollar Problem

Even if it is assumed that the $500 million is the most accurate number, the $500 million shrinks to $323.6 million when deducting for the increased costs to the Illinois state police of $100 million per year plus the increased local police and fire protection costs of $11.4 million per year plus the increased regulatory costs of $65 million per year. However, the largest deduction to the projected tax revenues consists of the increased socio-economic costs due to the increased numbers of compulsive gamblers that the Chicago casino complex would generate. These costs are conservatively calculated at $3.7 billion [by the Better Government Association of Chicago].

> *"The [Chicago and Cook County population of] 5 million could be 'conservatively' multiplied by .0073, which equals 36,500 compulsive gamblers."*

Similar costs can be calculated by utilizing costs from socio-economic studies. Calculating the Chicago population and the surrounding Cook County population at 5.1 million, the population base would be approximately 5 million. Since "hard" casino gambling would be moving into an area that had only the state lottery plus horse racing and off-track betting, the 5 million could be "conservatively" multiplied by .0073, which equals 36,500 compulsive gamblers. This number of 36,500 compulsive gamblers multiplied by $52,000 per year yields an increased socio-economic cost of $1.9 billion.

Two additional subcategories of the socio-economic costs per year are "white-collar crime costs" of $4,123 per year and "intermediate incarceration costs" of $21,000 per year. Therefore, additional specific socio-economic costs related to compulsive gamblers interfacing with the criminal justice system would be:

Increased "White-Collar Crime Costs" = $4,123/yr. × 36,500 = $150 million

Increased "Intermediate Incarceration Costs" = $21,000/yr. × 36,500 = $766 million

Increased "Long-Term Incarceration Costs" = $2,400/yr. × 36,500 = $87.6 million

The total costs of these three categories would be approximately $1 billion. The long-term incarceration costs, specifically $87.6 million per year, are explained

139

in the following discussion.

According to the Compulsive Gambling Center, practically all compulsive gamblers commit crimes. General averages indicate that 75 percent of compulsive gamblers are not caught or the charges are not pressed. This latter instance is usually due to the fact that most compulsive gamblers commit their initial criminal activities against family members or close associates—for example, stealing money out of a family member's purse or wallet, or selling or pawning property belonging to family members.

## Incarceration Costs

The other 25 percent of compulsive gamblers usually find themselves in court and 60 percent of these, or 15 percent of the total number of compulsive gamblers, are convicted and must serve time in jail. The general long-term average cost of incarceration for a healthy compulsive gambler is $25,000 per year, and for an elderly individual, $50,000 per year. By comparison, the average Illinois cost of incarceration per prisoner was $16,000 per year. Taking the most conservative cost of incarceration, the costs of incarcerating compulsive gamblers per year before gambling is legalized in a state are:

.0077 × (state population) = number of compulsive gamblers before legalization

.0077 × (state population) × 15% × $16,000/year = cost of incarcerating compulsive gamblers per year before gambling is legalized

.015 × (state population) → .05 × (state population) = range of compulsive gamblers after gambling is legalized

.015 × (state population) × 15% × $16,000/year →

.05 × (state population) × 15% × $16,000/year = range of costs of incarcerating compulsive gamblers per year once gambling is legalized

As applied to the 1992 proposed Chicago casino complex, the calculations would consist of the previously calculated "increase" of 36,500 compulsive gamblers multiplied by the "long-term incarceration costs" of $2,400 per year, which equals "total long-term incarceration costs" of $87.6 million per year. To avoid confusion, it should be noted that the cost of $2,400 per year is expressed as a function of the total number of compulsive gamblers, whereas the cost of $16,000 per year is expressed as a function of only 15 percent of the total number of compulsive gamblers.

> *"The general long-term average cost of incarceration for a healthy compulsive gambler is $25,000 per year."*

The state of Illinois calculated that the actual tax revenues from the 1992 proposed Chicago casino complex would be $82.5 million in the first year of operation, while the lost tax revenues from other legalized gambling organizations in Illinois would be $100 million, for a net loss of $17.5 million. However, even if the larger projected tax revenues of the Chicago complex were presumed to be correct, the gravamen is that for theoretical tax revenues of $500 million (or more accurately, $257 million to $370 million), the following costs to the state of Illinois could be anticipated:

| | |
|---|---|
| Increased Ill. State Police Costs | $100 million |
| Increased Local Police and Fire Protection Costs | 11.4 million |
| Increased Regulatory Costs | 65 million |
| Increased White-Collar Crime Costs | 150 million |
| Increased Intermediate Incarceration Costs | 766 million |
| Increased Long-Term Incarceration Costs | 87.6 million |
| | $1.18 billion |

Of course, this $1.18 billion does not include the other socio-economic costs of $1.9 billion (which is quite conservative when compared with the reasonable $3.7 billion calculated by the Better Government Association).

## Solid Estimates

To be extremely conservative, the last category of long-term incarceration costs can range between $87.6 million and zero if it can be argued that somehow this category can be subsumed somewhat under intermediate incarceration costs. Similarly, the costs to the Illinois state police can range between $100 million and $42 million. Absent new data to the contrary, the other four categories seem to be fairly well established as solid estimates. Accordingly, the best estimates of increased costs to the criminal justice

*"The best estimates of increased costs to [Illinois's] criminal justice system ... appear to range between $1.03 billion and $1.18 billion."*

system with the introduction of legalized casino-style gambling in the major Illinois population base appear to range between $1.03 billion and $1.18 billion. It should be emphasized that these numbers were calculated by state agencies and academics in 1992—before significant or widespread riverboat gambling was in operation in Illinois, particularly in the Chicago area. Therefore, it can be argued that the influence of other legalized gambling activities on these calculations was minimal, and other states considering legalized gambling activities can extrapolate from these numbers and make some strategic calculations of increased costs to their criminal justice systems.

To express these costs to the Illinois criminal justice system (including regulatory costs) as a function of the entire population, the $1.03 billion to $1.18 billion can be divided by the taxpayer base that will have to support most of these costs; that is, the population of the state of Illinois of approximately 11 million. This type of per capita calculation is regularly utilized in the statistics promulgated by the U.S. Justice Department. Accordingly, the $1.03 billion to $1.18 billion divided by 11 million provides a range of $93 to $107 per person. These costs expressed as a function of each "new compulsive gambler" would be $28,200 to $32,300 per year. The other socio-economic costs of $1.9 billion per year would translate into $173 per Illinois resident or $52,000 per new compulsive gambler.

> *"Increased . . . gambling activities could precipitate fairly immediate increases to [Illinois's] criminal justice system of 40 to 50 percent."*

By comparison, the 1990 "preexisting costs" to the Illinois criminal justice system expressed as a cost per Illinois resident totaled $232.58 or specifically: (1) $125.08 police protection; (2) $26.44 courts; (3) $12.67 prosecution and legal services; (4) $3.34 public defense; (5) $63.72 corrections; and (6) $1.34 other justice activities. In summary, each Illinois resident must contribute $232.58 for preexisting costs to the criminal justice system. This amount should be compared with the $93 to $107 per person increases projected by studies as necessary to accommodate increased legalized gambling activities (e.g., via a large Chicago casino complex). Therefore, increased large-scale legalized gambling activities could precipitate fairly immediate increases to the state criminal justice system of 40 to 50 percent.

Similarly for other states, some important strategic approximations of increased costs to the criminal justice system can be calculated by multiplying these new "added" costs of $93 per person (the most conservative cost) times the population of the state. Obviously, these numbers need to be refined for different demographics, but they provide the starting point for the calculations. However, the number of new (or anticipated) compulsive gamblers can be calculated with some certainty, and therefore, the cost of $28,200 per year per new compulsive gambler provides a base point for costs to the criminal justice system (including regulatory costs).

## More Reliable Numbers

Of course, there is some error in these numbers, but as of 1992, these estimates appeared to be the best available. These numbers have much more "balanced" support from the academic authorities and from the field research than the numbers usually referenced by the legalized gambling interests.

It should be emphasized that as the Better Government Association of Chicago reported:

> We found that no one [that is, no expert] argues that casino gambling has positive societal effects, except for the purported secondary effects from the economic gains of more jobs and tax revenue. As a result, any debate over the societal effects of legalizing an additional form of gambling centers around the *extent* of the negative social impact.

This conclusion should be broader in its scope, because the negative societal impacts also affect business-economics, commerce, and legal and governmental policy. The costs that can be calculated fairly accurately—namely, the socio-economic costs, the criminal justice system costs, and the administrative costs to state governments—can be readily converted into economic costs affecting businesses and commerce in general. Accordingly, [what University of Illinois News Bureau editor Mark Reutter calls] "purported secondary effects from the economic gains of more jobs and tax revenue" are, in fact, overwhelmed by the socio-economic costs and are illusory benefits akin to "fool's gold."

# Local Gambling Operations May Collapse

by I. Nelson Rose

**About the author:** *I. Nelson Rose is a practicing attorney and professor at Whittier Law School in Los Angeles. He writes the nationally syndicated column "Gambling and the Law®."*

Gamblers like to make predictions. Of course, some predictions are easier to make than others. Predicting what will happen to legal gambling in the United States today is a relatively easy bet, because it has happened twice before.

Legal commercial gambling is one of the fastest growing industries in the United States and throughout the world. In part, this is because it is starting from a base of virtually zero, so the percentage increases year-to-year are spectacular. But in absolute dollars, the numbers are equally impressive.

According to industry publications every year Americans spend less than $8 billion at the nation's 25,000 movie theaters. This includes all ticket sales (less than $5 billion), plus popcorn, sodas and confectioneries. About the same amount, $7 billion to $8 billion, is spent on all forms of recorded music.

## Totaling Billions of Dollars

By comparison, in fiscal year 1992, the 36 operating state lotteries sold $24.36 billion in lottery tickets. Add in parimutuel betting on horses, dogs and jai-alai; total "action" in casinos and slot machines; wagers on sports; bets made in card rooms; and expenditures before prize payments in charity gaming and Indian bingo, and the total amount bet legally in the United States is estimated to be $330 billion.

Twice before, legal gambling has swept across America. The earliest settlements of America were funded, in part, by lotteries. Lotteries, both government approved and private, were not only allowed but actively encouraged during the colonial period. This era of widespread legal gambling ended with the spread of Jacksonian morality, aided by numerous well-publicized scandals. By 1862 Missouri and Kentucky were the only states that had not banned lotteries altogether.

Abridged from I. Nelson Rose, *Gambling and the Law®: Endless Fields of Dreams*, ©1995 by I. Nelson Rose. Gambling and the Law® is a registered trademark of I. Nelson Rose. Reprinted with permission.

The Civil War and the expansion of the western frontier brought about the Second Wave. The states of the old South needed a way to raise money to rebuild their devastated economies; they turned briefly to lotteries as a voluntary tax. However, the great Louisiana Lottery scandal of the 1890s led to the passage of strong federal anti-lottery laws (which are still on the books) and a complete prohibition of state lotteries, which lasted nearly 70 years.

> *"Lotteries, both government approved and private, were not only allowed but actively encouraged during the colonial period."*

Throughout the Wild West, gambling was ubiquitous. Sometimes, law enforcement ignored the casinos, because it was difficult to outlaw this typical frontier diversion. Frequently, gaming houses were explicitly made legal, so that governments could raise revenue through licensing and avoid the problem epitomized by Prohibition of having criminal statutes on the books that no one obeyed.

The rise of Victorian morality, accusations of cheating and the desire for respectability brought down the legal casinos in the West. At the same time, betting on horse races fell into disfavor and the tracks were closed. By 1910, the United States once again was virtually free of legalized gambling.

The Third Wave began with the Depression. Nevada relegalized casino gambling in 1931. Twenty-one states opened race tracks with parimutuel betting in the 1930s, with additional states allowing parimutuel betting in every decade since. The big boom began with the first legal state lottery opening in New Hampshire in 1964. By 1994, every state except Utah and Hawaii had some form of permitted commercial gambling; social gambling had been decriminalized everywhere in law or in practice; charity gambling was the rule, not the exception; and it became impossible to keep up with the various proposals for additional legalization being discussed in every state. All of this leads to the inevitable question: Why now?

## A Speculative Bubble

It is widely believed in the 1990s that anyone, including government, can get rich quick. All one needs to do to grab a piece of the action is to own, operate or tax some form of legal gambling. An endless flow of instant, unlimited wealth will follow. This delusion is a typical symptom of a classic speculative bubble.

Americans have an especially hard time understanding speculative bubbles, since we have little feel for history. When we think of historical eras characterized by wild speculation—such as the 1920s—we might imagine a toy balloon being overinflated: a market expanding unceasingly, until it explodes. The reality is more like watching a film of a roller coaster in reverse: a sustained runaway ride upward, with unexpected dips and bounces, followed by a relatively rapid descent to reality.

Even our view of crashes such as the [stock] market collapses in October 1929 and October 1987 reflect our hindsight view, compressing time and history into isolated great events, "Black Tuesdays." However, the recent collapse of the Japanese real estate and stock market bubbles, wiping out over $3 trillion in paper assets—63% of the value of the shares traded on the Tokyo Stock Exchange—took three years.

The craze to legalize gambling is not a stock market bubble. All bubbles grow out of unrealistic expectations, but pure market bubbles, like the one preceding the Great Crash of 1929, also need easy money for leveraged buying.

## Trading Frenzy

For connoisseurs of money mass manias, the current craze is more like the infamous South Sea Bubble than the equally infamous Dutch Tulipmania. In the 1720s, the government of England actively encouraged companies to exploit new opportunities created by the opening of the tropics, "the South Sea." By contrast, the Dutch craze for trading in tulip bulbs in the 1630s was purely a runaway market; government played no role. At the height of the speculative fever in England, one company was able to do very well selling stock "for an Undertaking which shall in due time be revealed," [according to John Kenneth Galbraith]. In the Dutch tulip markets, futures were created, aptly called "trading in the wind," [by Joseph Bulgatz]. Speculators paid enormous sums for contracts for

> *"It is widely believed in the 1990s that anyone, including government, can get rich quick."*

future delivery, hoping to sell them to a greater fool. While a small house in town cost about 300 guilders, a single tulip bulb sold for the outrageous price of 5,500 guilders. . . .

Unlike tulip bulbs, commodities or stock index futures, legal gambling can, in fact, generate revenue, but not on the scale imagined and not endlessly in the face of direct competition. As much as they might wish, not every town can become the next Las Vegas. There is a big difference between being the only legal casino on the East Coast and owning a riverboat in Iowa with $5 limits when there is a competing riverboat in Illinois with unlimited stakes a ten-minute drive away.

Why, in the 1990s, is there such a rush to legalize gambling? Speculative bubbles can be seen as a tiny bit of real value being blown all out of proportion. Gambling has boomed exactly because the law of supply and demand works.

## What Happens When Prohibition Is Repealed?

There is general agreement in the casino industry that North America can support a third major gambling center, between Nevada and Atlantic City. Unfortunately, many jurisdictions in the United States and Canada would like to believe they are going to be that center. There are people working in both countries to bring about more legal gambling in the belief that casinos will solve all of their locale's financial problems.

The reason for this grand self-delusion is relatively simple. We are coming out of a period of nearly complete prohibition. At the end of the Second Wave, legal casinos disappeared with the closing of the frontier. At the turn of the 20th century, the territories of New Mexico and Arizona were told by Congress to outlaw their gambling in order to be admitted as states. Even Nevada had outlawed all its casinos in 1909. Lotteries had already been eliminated by federal legislation, passed in response to the great Louisiana Lottery scandal of the 1890s.

By 1910, there were only three places one could bet legally in the United States: at racetracks in New York, Kentucky and Maryland. In that year New York outlawed racing. A few years later came Prohibition.

> *"As much as they might wish, not every town can become the next Las Vegas."*

(The era from 1900 to 1925 is a striking example of moral issues changing the law. Not only was virtually all gambling outlawed and prohibition of liquor enacted, but the first effective restrictions on illegal drugs and prostitution were imposed.)

Seventy years ago Americans could not bet or drink legally. In the 1990s, in states like Oregon, adults can bet on state-run Video Lottery Terminals [VLTs] (virtually indistinguishable from slot machines), purchase parlay cards from the state on National Football League games, and play the casino game of Keno through the State Lottery, in bars licensed by the state.

What happened?

Suppose prohibition of alcohol had just been repealed. The hypothetical owner of the first and only liquor store in a state would make a fantastic return on investment. But soon, if there were no government controls, there would be liquor stores throughout the state, as there are few barriers to entry. Excess profits would disappear; returns on investment would descend to normal levels.

## Government and Taxes

Government makes the situation worse. The fantasy that there is an endless supply of cash available, an infinitely elastic demand for gambling—this newly legalized vice—seems to hit politicians harder than entrepreneurs.

Sin taxes are always the easiest to raise. Casinos, like liquor stores and tobacco retailers, are easier targets than more politically acceptable businesses. Government's thinking is that people should not be gambling anyway and they will continue to make wagers, no matter how much the cost. So, even though half the gaming establishments in a jurisdiction might go bankrupt, the state continues to consider raising taxes on gaming.

Resorts International opened the first legal casino on the East Coast on May

26, 1978, spending $45.2 million to refurbish the old Chalfonte-Haddon hotel in Atlantic City. A first-year gross revenue of $224.6 million made it the most profitable casino in the world. The state of New Jersey, for merely allowing the casino to open, collected $18 million in taxes that first year. Indeed, in their first 15 years in operation, the casinos of Atlantic City, which never numbered more than 13, paid a total of $6 billion in local, state and federal taxes.

> *"The fantasy that there is an endless supply of cash available . . . seems to hit politicians harder than entrepreneurs."*

Twelve more casinos quickly followed. The Trump Taj Mahal, the thirteenth and last Atlantic City casino to open, cost over $1.1 billion. Its 120,000 square foot casino expanded the supply of casino floor space in the market by 18%. It had to win over $1 million per day on average just to break even. The Taj opened in April 1990; it declared bankruptcy in July 1991.

Although fiscal mismanagement, especially junk bond financing, played a role, inevitable competition and increased taxes dragged under half the new businesses. Thirteen casinos have opened in Atlantic City since 1978; 7 have been involved in formal bankruptcy proceedings: the Atlantis; Trump's Castle, Plaza and Taj Mahal; Bally's Park Place; Bally's Grand; and Resorts International, which filed twice in five years.

## The Growth of Casinos

The pace of change picked up in the early 1990s. Colorado opened limited stakes casinos in three small mountain towns in October 1991. By July 1992, the original 25 casinos had grown to 68. Taxes on casinos were raised, winter hit and within five months, by December 1992, over 21 casinos had closed their doors. Worse, taxes were raised on all real property, so many noncasino stores had been boarded up.

In January 1993, the small Mashantucket Pequot tribe, owners of the Foxwoods High Stakes Bingo & Casino in Connecticut that had opened in February 1992, began operating the only legal slot machines between Atlantic City and Canada. The initial 260 machines produced slightly over $2 million that first month. In July, the casino had 1,471 operating machines, earning $26.2 million for the month, for a daily average win of $575 per machine per day. That was twice as much as Atlantic City's daily average of $275 and four times the $140 per day won by $1 slot machines on the Las Vegas strip. By October the numbers had doubled again: the tribe now had 3,137 slot machines generating $1.625 million per day.

Political and economic pressure to break Foxwoods's monopoly in the northeast U.S. market made competition inevitable. In 1993, an Indian casino without slot machines was opened by the Oneida tribe in the middle of New York state; casino ships with slots started operating out of ports in Connecticut; an Indian tribe in Rhode Island won a court order allowing it to open a casino; and legislation for slot machines, Video Lottery Terminals, and more casinos on riverboats and on land were introduced in state legislatures in Massachusetts, Pennsylvania, Connecticut and every other jurisdiction north of Atlantic City.

## Other Boom Areas

The latest boom area with new casinos is Mississippi, both along the Mississippi River and the Gulf Coast. However, there is concern over what will happen to the gaming business in Biloxi/Gulfport when Louisiana and possibly Texas and Alabama open up casinos closer to the Gulf Coast's customers. Tunica, Mississippi—one of the poorest counties in this poorest state—also happens to be the closest county with riverboat casinos to the large Memphis market. How much business would survive if Tennessee legalizes casino gaming? The current return on capital investment is substantial enough that investors might not care too much about potential competitors in other jurisdictions opening five or more years in the future. However, there are serious concerns about other riverboats in Tunica saturating the regional demand for casino gaming.

The explosion of legal gambling has finally settled the question of whether availability creates demand. The traditional argument for legalizing gambling, or any vice, is that people are going to do it anyway, so it is better for the state to run it or regulate it than have the money go to organized crime.

> *"Thirteen casinos have opened in Atlantic City since 1978; 7 have been involved in formal bankruptcy proceedings."*

Of course, some people are going to gamble, even if the criminal penalties are enforced, which they are not. But people who live in cities with casinos nearby do gamble more than others. Take Minnesota, for example.

The first large, publicly released studies of casino customers found that the residents of Minneapolis–St. Paul became major consumers of legal casino gambling after casinos were opened nearby. Prior to 1990, when there were virtually no convenient casinos, the Twin Cities area was only the fourteenth largest feeder market in the country. By 1993, Minnesota had opened more legal, wide-open, full-scale casinos than Atlantic City, all on Indian land. That same year, Minneapolis–St. Paul had grown to be the fourth largest source of casino patrons. The number of casino gambling trips made by residents more than tripled in one year.

Some operators will always do well. Because people do not want casinos in their own backyards, quirks in the law will continue to give some operators virtual monopolies. But it is wrong to think of the boom in casino gambling as being limited to isolated mining towns and riverboats. The states themselves could conceivably become the largest operators of slot machines. . . .

The best and safest gambling operation is one designed for tourists, taking disposable income from nonresidents. Indian casinos are simply following Las Vegas's precedent. Ontario, Canada, is building its casinos on the U.S. border to capture American dollars.

This is not to say that local casinos cannot make money. They absolutely can, and can exist for years, so long as two vital points are understood:

1. Casinos, and this includes casino-style gambling like the state lotteries' Keno and VLTs, can hurt a small, but significant number of local citizens; and

2. A community with casinos cannot become another Las Vegas unless it is closer than its competition to a major population center.

Everywhere throughout history and throughout the world, where casinos have catered to local people, they have been outlawed in a few years. A casino acts like a black hole sucking money out of the local economy. No one cares if you suck money out of tourists, but large-scale casinos that do not bring in more new tourist dollars than they take away from local players and local businesses soon find themselves outlawed. There has been virtually no serious study on the topic, but it is highly likely there will be large increases in problem and underage gambling in communities with casino-style gaming, particularly if machines become omnipresent.

The other fear is federal intervention. So far, the federal government has left control of gambling to the states unless it had to become involved, [such as] with interstate horse racing and Indians, or there was a fear of organized crime. A large, nasty scandal in an almost wide-open state like Louisiana could bring federal oversight into every gambling operation, even casinos in Nevada.

## The Future

America's waves of legal gambling seem to last about 70 years—about as long as a human lifetime. This is probably not a coincidence, since we do not have memories of what life was like before we were born. Human beings have the remarkable ability to transmit information through the written word, even after we are gone. But we cannot as easily convey emotions linked to events and institutions of other times. What did it feel like to live during George Washington's time, when, it is said, it was easier to buy a lottery ticket than it is today?

*"There is concern over what will happen . . . when Louisiana and possibly Texas and Alabama open up casinos."*

What will the world look like in ten years? It is possible that every major population center of the United States and Canada, including Alaska and Hawaii, may soon have a casino-style resort within a two-hour drive. More casinos will create more customers, but at some point, perhaps relatively soon, the operators simply will be fighting for the same market.

The market for slot machines outside casinos might even be greater, because slots have been the major source of growth in U.S. casinos since the 1970s.

And then there is Las Vegas. While Atlantic City sees its market being eaten away by the opening of closer casinos of convenience, Las Vegas is reinventing itself. By the turn of the century it will be one of the world's leading family-oriented destination resorts, comparable to Orlando.

> *"The states themselves could conceivably become the largest operators of slot machines."*

Las Vegas has reached a critical mass of major attractions, a must-see unnatural wonder of the world. The buildings themselves have become the lures: the Excalibur, built as a castle; the Luxor as a pyramid; the Mirage, with its fiery volcano and white tigers; Treasure Island, a block-long set for staged pirate ship battles; and the MGM, a billion-dollar center of adult amusements. Las Vegas has changed from a gambling town to one of the very few manmade artifacts worth a trip across a continent: the Eiffel Tower and Taj Mahal rolled into one. But, while Las Vegas is becoming an artificial Grand Canyon, Atlantic City is a slum by the sea with casinos. Atlantic City is stuck in the casino business; Las Vegas understands it is in the entertainment business.

Without a major change of attitude on the part of the casino operators and regulators, Atlantic City may suffer the same fate as the nation's railroads. A hundred years ago, the railroad industry was confronted with the invention of the internal combustion engine. The train operators' universal response was to say they were in the railroad business, not the transportation business. And so they remained, until they all went bankrupt.

## Best Opportunities

The best business to be in over the next few years is *not* to be an operator, unless a company has a particular niche or a protected market close to a major population center. Rather, the best opportunities are for suppliers to the gaming retailers.

The companies that flourished during the California Gold Rush were rarely the miners; rather, they supplied food, clothing (Levi Strauss) and banking and shipping services (Wells Fargo). Of course, it is not wise to be the Pony Express when the telegraph and railroad come in; a company that makes rub-off lottery tickets also has to be able to make video gaming devices.

When will proliferation of legal gaming come to an end? We are still years away from the crackdown phase. The few scattered movements to limit the spread of gambling have so far been virtually universally unsuccessful. A few pauses in the runaway growth of gaming have occurred, such as in Iowa, but these were more the result of regional competition than from public pressure.

Even the collapse of large operators will not signal an end to proliferation. As many as half the racetracks in this country are about to go out of business, yet no one is talking about the end of gambling because of the tracks' demise.

We will know the end is near when we reach the silly phase, where any company can go public merely by saying it is going into the casino business. Scandals involving sports figures or public officials will begin to have an impact. Major candidates will run on platforms of putting an end to legal gambling.

State lotteries at first might retrench, by limiting their Keno and Video Lottery Terminals to age-restricted locations. The enactment in 1919 of the Eighteenth Amendment—Prohibition—shows that even the largest commercial ventures can be outlawed, if they offend public morals enough. But some state lotteries might suffer an even more inglorious end: they might just be ignored.

In two or three decades, most of the casino experiments on riverboats and in mountain towns may suffer the fate of all failed experiments, defeated by better-located, large, land-based competitors.

But the collapse of commercial gaming is years away. Today the smart bet is on the side of more legal gambling. Investment money will keep pouring in, giving the craze the feel of inevitable, continuing growth. For money managers, who must show greater growth of their funds than their competitors, it is as dangerous to be out of the growth stages of a national bubble as it is to be in when the bubble finally bursts. But the money will continue to pour in long after the market is saturated.

For the amazing thing about speculative bubbles is that you can tell people that they are building on a foundation of soapy water and they simply will not believe it.

# Riverboat Gambling Does Not Help Local Economies

**by Oliver Starr Jr.**

*About the author: Oliver Starr Jr., a former editorial page editor for the defunct* St. Louis Globe-Democrat *daily newspaper, is a freelance writer in Webster Groves, Missouri.*

Riverboat casinos are giant money-sucking machines. A $30 million riverboat casino operated by Harrah's can suck in $200,000 a day from bettors, assuming a typical daily loss of $50 per customer. This kind of high-stakes betting used to be called gambling. But liberals have come up with a new name—"gaming." It was formerly recognized as a vice. But it is now classed as "recreation" and "entertainment."

The difference is that state and local governments have taken over the gambling rackets, now known as the "gaming industry." The St. Louis Port Authority estimates that the new "gaming industry" on its riverfront when fully operational with four casinos will bring in "revenues" of $240 million a year and provide the city with $33 million in new tax dollars.

## The Gambling Fantasy

The truth is that state and local governments are hooked on the myth that they can gamble their way to prosperity—a notion every bit as ludicrous as Washington's belief that it can tax-and-spend the nation to boom times. Riverboat casinos are the ultimate expression of the fantasy—expressed in state-paid TV ads—that the way to become a millionaire is not through hard work and saving but to bet the grocery money against the long odds of lotteries and casinos.

Armed with these odds, gambling pros on the riverboats reel in chumps by the thousands and systematically strip them of their cash before dumping them ashore. It all takes place in an atmosphere of great fun and frivolity while local and state governments cheer them on in anticipation of sharing the loot. The people who own and run these boats are essentially fast-buck artists who jump in quick when there is a new gambling—excuse me, gaming—opportunity and

Oliver Starr Jr., "Riverboat Casinos . . .," in the Cultural Revolutions section of *Chronicles: A Magazine of American Culture*, vol. 18, no. 5 (May 1994), pp. 7-8. Reprinted with permission.

jump out fast when their "business" slows down. Witness how three of the five riverboat casinos in Iowa hoisted anchor after only two years when juicier "markets" opened up in other states.

The riverboat gambling law passed by the Missouri Legislature and approved by Governor Mel Carnahan calls for a $50,000 licensing fee (to keep the mom-and-pop casino operators out) and provides for the state to collect 20 percent of the "adjusted gross income" of these boats. But it is a safe bet that the social costs of teaching so many citizens to become habitual gamblers will largely nullify the gains that Governor Carnahan and the Democratic majority in the state legislature are gambling on. In virtually every case, increased gambling is accompanied by higher welfare costs, much greater costs for treating compulsive gamblers, and increased crime.

## The Craze Will Fade

There are three primary reasons the riverboat casino craze will likely end with a whimper. First, fierce competition is emerging as paddleboat owners from every state with a major waterway scramble to join the riverboat "gold rush." Illinois has already launched eight riverboat casinos, Missouri is scrambling to put a raft of new riverboats in the water, and Indiana has approved twelve more. The *President-Casino Mississippi*, which opened in Biloxi in August 1992, has already seen its competition increase from zero to at least six riverboats in the area. High-stakes land-based casino operators also have big plans for launching riverboat operations. As this frenzy heats up, winnings are bound to fall and many of these "dreamboats" will sink in a river of red ink.

Second, the flood of new gambling money being anticipated is not going to arrive. A study by the St. Louis Port Authority found that 5.7 million of the 7.2 million gamblers expected to patronize the new floating gambling joints will be from the St. Louis area. "This means that 80 percent of the money spent on gambling here would have otherwise been spent on other forms of entertainment—or remained in accounts in St. Louis banks," the *St. Louis Business Journal* reported. After the initial wave of "gulls" and compulsive gamblers has been fleeced, the public enthusiasm for this organized robbery almost certainly will wane. The supply of pigeons is not infinite.

Third, the Democrats who have ruled the Missouri Legislature for decades, along with tax king Mel Carnahan, will probably be thrown out by Missourians when they grow tired of the high taxes, rabid promo-

*"Gambling pros on the riverboats reel in chumps by the thousands and systematically strip them of their cash."*

tion of gambling, and new $300 million school tax law that makes puppets of local school districts.

St. Louisans would do well to consider the experience of Alton, Illinois, as told recently by John J. Dunphy, owner of a bookstore in that city. Dunphy reports that the arrival of the original *Alton Belle* casino at this city in 1991 brought more than $3 million in proceeds to the city government but that the effect on Alton business has been negligible. Dunphy says he has yet to have a blackjack player fresh off the *Belle* dash into his bookshop to purchase the works of Henrik Ibsen or Albert Camus. And even the local bars failed to get new business from *Belle* patrons. Other retailers have confirmed that those who come to try their luck on the *Alton Belle* just gamble and go home.

## Las Vegas East?

St. Louisans should ask themselves if they really want wall-to-wall riverboat casinos on their riverfront. That is what they are liable to get if the city fills four available berths with floating casinos. That noted philanthropist Donald Trump has indicated an interest in establishing a *world-class* casino in St. Louis and has said that he might toss in a convention center/hotel to sweeten the deal. But should St. Louisans aspire to see their city turn into Las Vegas East? They should also ponder the prospect of having their city government influenced by multimillionaire casino-boat owners. Pittsburgh mogul John Connelly, chairman and chief executive of President Riverboat Casinos, Inc., is sitting on a $390 million pile of stock in that company. As I was writing this, he was also about to become nearly $80 million richer by issuing two million shares of stock in his company (which will reduce his share to 32.4 percent) in anticipation of opening the *Admiral* casino on the St. Louis riverfront.

> *"Claiming these money-grabbing water palaces will produce jobs and prosperity is a stunt worthy of [circusman] P.T. Barnum."*

Connelly's influence in St. Louis is already attested to by the fact that for $20,580 a year his companies control six premium lease slots on the St. Louis riverfront, including three that could be used for gambling boats. The six include the permanently moored Robert E. Lee restaurant, the *Becky Thatcher*, *Huck Finn*, and *Tom Sawyer* cruise ships, and, in between these, the *Admiral* and vacant *President* and *Belle of St. Louis*, as well as an office barge. Connelly was also able to wangle state legislative approval, via Representative Jet Banks (D-St. Louis), to have his *Admiral* casino remain permanently moored on the St. Louis riverfront while other riverboat casinos have to cruise the Mississippi.

Iowa's riverboat gambling director, Chuck Patton, admits that casinos have brought an increase in crime to his state. When high-rollers turn the St. Louis riverfront into a gambling mecca, more police will be needed on the riverfront. But where will the city get the added police when it is already far short of the number of officers needed to fight St. Louis's escalating crime?

In 1994, the Missouri Supreme Court ruled that the statute authorizing riverboat casinos in the state was unconstitutional because it excluded certain types of gambling. Missouri's legislature hence authorized a statewide vote for a constitutional amendment [that passed] approving riverboat casinos.

Missourians should remember that government is supposed to protect the interests of citizens and that encouraging Missourians to try their luck against the long odds of riverboat games—at an average loss of $50 per customer—is a disservice to the people the government is sworn to protect. Claiming these money-grabbing water palaces will produce jobs and prosperity is a stunt worthy of [circusman] P.T. Barnum.

# Casinos Are a Burden on Local Governments

by Jeffry L. Bloomberg

**About the author:** *Jeffry L. Bloomberg is the state attorney for Lawrence County, South Dakota.*

[Editor's note: The following viewpoint is Bloomberg's testimony delivered to the U.S. House of Representatives Committee on Small Business during a hearing on the impact of casino gambling proliferation in September 1994.]

Since 1982 I have been a prosecutor, first as a deputy State's Attorney, and since 1986 as the elected State's Attorney of Lawrence County, a county of 21,000 in the Black Hills of western South Dakota.

Until November 1988, I had no background or interest in the issues related to casino gambling. However, in that year the citizens of South Dakota passed a constitutional amendment that allowed so called "limited" casino gambling in Deadwood, a town of 1,800 people and the county seat of Lawrence County. Perhaps because Deadwood was the first place outside Atlantic City and Nevada to legalize casino gambling, my office has been contacted by dozens of journalists, government officials, and private citizens seeking information on the effects of casino gambling on a small community.

Since that time, as I have traveled to various states that have been considering casino gambling, [I have seen that] the promoters of gambling have uniformly made the same pitch: "economic development, new jobs, and lower taxes." While these goals appear lofty, I believe it is imperative that government leaders and citizens scrutinize these claims very closely before opening the Pandora's Box of gambling, because, as we have learned in Deadwood, once gambling is legalized it is virtually an irrevocable decision.

## Dramatic Changes

No one predicted the dramatic changes that took place in Deadwood once gambling actually commenced on November 1, 1989. Within two or three

Jeffry L. Bloomberg, testimony before the U.S. House of Representatives Committee on Small Business's hearing "The National Impact of Casino Gambling Proliferation," September 21, 1994.

months, a main street that was typical of any small town was converted to a four-block strip of small casinos, now totaling eighty-two separately licensed gaming halls. Gone were the clothing, shoe, hardware, and grocery stores, as well as three separate car dealerships; they were all converted to gambling establishments. Many of the necessities of life such as clothing are no longer available within Deadwood, and customers of the town's only remaining grocery store walk a gauntlet of slot-machines as they exit with their purchases.

Real estate values sky-rocketed. Commercial properties that before gambling were valued at $150,000 sold for $500,000 one day and more than $1,000,000 the next. Of course this windfall was relished by the former property owners, but it did nothing for the auto mechanics, store clerks or other employees who were suddenly without jobs. They were faced with the decision of either moving away or finding new jobs in the gaming industry.

The town's economy, which was previously based on gold mining, timber, and family-oriented tourism, quickly became dominated by the gambling industry. According to one study, approximately 1,500 gaming as well as nearly 600 spin-off jobs were created by the legalization of gambling. Because of the geographic location of Deadwood within a mountain canyon, very little room exists for housing expansion; thus, most of the new employees live in surrounding communities and commute as much as fifty miles to get to their jobs.

This overnight transformation created enormous problems for the infrastructure of Deadwood and its city government. Parking, streets, water and sewer lines all proved to be inadequate. The city was faced with a dilemma. The needs were immediate, but cash flow from gaming taxes would not be sufficient for years.

Thus, the city council decided to sell bonds pledging revenues from predicted gaming and sales taxes to finance the improvements. The result was a municipal building boom which has updated the city's infrastructure, but which has financially tied the city's economic viability to gambling. If the citizens of Deadwood wanted to get rid of gambling today, they could not without total bankruptcy.

For the most part, the jobs that were created earn minimum wage or slightly better and are without benefits. Many are seasonal, and the employees face layoffs after Labor Day when the summer season has ended. Even many of the "licensed" support workers, such as blackjack dealers, pit bosses and other gaming personnel, depend on tips to make a living.

> *"If the citizens of Deadwood wanted to get rid of gambling today, they could not without total bankruptcy."*

The economic effect for the gaming entrepreneurs has also been a mixed bag. While only a handful of casinos have closed in the years since the birth of Deadwood's gaming industry, today they claim that over half of their businesses are operating at a loss. On the other hand, other gaming operations, those which combine ownership of multiple casinos in particular, appear to be making handsome profits.

## Taxes Increase, Not Decrease

As for the claim that gambling brings tax relief, this simply has not proven true. In fact, real property taxes for both residential and commercial properties have risen each and every year since gambling was legalized. This has occurred for several reasons.

First, because of the dramatic increase in property values, the assessments for virtually all property also increased whether they are gaming, non-gaming, commercial, residential, or agricultural in nature. Secondly, while gaming has generated nearly $6,000,000 annually in gaming taxes to the city and county, those amounts have been eaten up by increased administrative, law enforcement, and infrastructure costs. The city of Deadwood went from a pregambling 1988 budget of $1,430,919 to a 1994 budget of $9,113,796. As an example, the police force of five officers more than doubled to eleven full-time officers.

In my office we have also seen our caseload more than double. This increase in criminal caseload is attributable to two areas. First, the largest increase is attributable to the simple fact that there are more people working in and visiting Deadwood than before gambling. While it is true that any increase in visitors will statistically result in higher crime rates than before, I believe that the type of visitors we are attracting results in numbers higher than in a more family-oriented tourist community. Compare crime rates in Atlantic City versus Orlando, Florida, for a demonstration of this principle on a larger scale.

*"We have seen individuals who, prior to their exposure to gambling, had no criminal history. . . . Many of them had good jobs."*

But even if you attribute the bulk of the increase in crime to simply more people, a second category of increase is due to the nature of gambling itself. It is this group that I find particularly disturbing, for we have seen individuals who, prior to their exposure to gambling, had no criminal history. They were not junkies or alcoholics; many of them had good jobs; they became hooked on slot machines, and after losing all their assets and running all credit resources to their maximums, began committing some type of crime to support their addiction.

In general these crimes are theft, embezzlement, bad checks, and other forms of larceny.

## Desperate Acts

Oftentimes the individuals in this category have stolen thousands of dollars and become desperate. I think of the pizza restaurant manager who had a spotless record and embezzled $45,000 from his employers. Or the gaming-business bookkeeper who, having run up thousands in debt, committed suicide. Or the technical sergeant in the United States Air Force who, prior to gaming, had an exemplary ten-year military career, who became hooked on slot machines and eventually murdered a casino operator in a desperate attempt to retrieve $400 in bad checks he had written to the casino. [He] is now serving a life sentence without parole at the potential cost of over a million dollars to South Dakota tax-

> *"Probably most disturbing has been the growing dependence of local and state government on gambling dollars."*

payers, not to mention the loss of training dollars invested by the federal government, or most tragically the loss of human life.

Our office has also seen an increase in the number of child abuse and neglect cases as a result of gambling. These run the spectrum—from the children left in their cars all night while their parents gamble, to the children left at home alone while their single mothers work the casino late shift, to the household without utilities or groceries because one or both parents have blown their paycheck gambling.

Interestingly, we have not seen an increase in DUI [driving under the influence] cases and there has been no evidence of prostitution. In addition, I believe because of the extensive background investigations and regulation conducted by the South Dakota Commission on Gambling, there is no evidence of any involvement by organized crime. This fact might also be attributed to the low, five-dollar-bet limits authorized in South Dakota, which helps to minimize any efforts to launder illegal funds.

As to the claim that gambling promotes economic development, that was certainly true for Deadwood at the outset, but as competition from tribal casinos and other states has escalated, the growth in Deadwood gambling has stalled. It has been estimated that by the year 2000 everyone within the continental United States will be within a four-hour drive of casino gambling. When that saturation level has been reached, who then will want to fly or drive to Deadwood, or Elgin, Illinois, or Biloxi, Mississippi, simply to pull a slot-machine lever that they can just as easily pull in their hometown or state? Then gambling will survive almost entirely off of the local economy. One can only speculate as to what other businesses will suffer as a result. This principle has already been visible in Deadwood and the surrounding area where a number of non-gaming restaurants have closed due to their inability to compete with gaming-subsidized restaurants.

## Governments Depend on Gambling

Probably most disturbing has been the growing dependence of local and state government on gambling dollars. Because government officials have been unwilling to make the politically difficult decision either to raise taxes or cut services, they have turned to gambling as a supposedly "painless" revenue source.

The gaming industry in South Dakota, armed with large amounts of cash, has gone from being non-existent to being one of the most powerful lobbying forces in our state capital. Virtually every decision at city hall is made based on what is best for the gaming industry. Government is hooked on the money generated by gambling, and, I believe, in the long term the ramifications of this governmental addiction will be just as dire [for government] as for the individual who becomes addicted to gambling.

Does legalization of gambling bring about short-term benefits? The answer, at least for Deadwood, has been "yes," but it remains to be seen whether, in the long term the benefits will outweigh the negatives. Any community considering legalization should take that step only after careful consideration of both sides of this issue.

Chapter 4

# Does Indian Gaming
# Help Native Americans?

# Indian Gaming: An Overview

**by Ruth Denny**

**About the author:** *Ruth Denny is a freelance writer and contributor to* Utne Reader *magazine.*

The largest gambling center between Nevada and Atlantic City is, surprisingly, Minnesota, with fourteen casinos that together generated an estimated $900 million in 1991. The owners of these thriving gaming operations are the state's eleven sovereign Native American nations. Four casinos are operated on Dakota land in southern Minnesota, the other ten on Ojibwe land in the north.

As David Segal explains in the *Washington Monthly*, the Seminole tribe in Florida pioneered big-stakes reservation gambling by testing the limits of tribal sovereignty in 1979. "The Miami Seminoles defied a state law prohibiting bingo prizes of more than $100 and began offering $10,000 jackpots," he writes. The state sued, but in 1982 a federal appeals court ruled that since the Seminoles were a sovereign nation, state civil regulations did not apply to them. Tribes took note, and within five years 113 Indian bingo operations around the country were grossing $225 million annually.

## The Legal Go-Ahead

"Legal challenges from states abounded," Segal adds, "but in 1987 the Supreme Court decided that Indians could operate any form of gambling already permitted by the state—and could do so with their own regulations. In the fourteen states that allowed groups to run highly restricted 'Las Vegas nights' for charity, the door was opened for Indians to start up full-blown casinos."

In 1988 Congress passed the Indian Gaming Regulatory Act (IGRA) and after much debate about Indian rights and states' rights established an Indian Gaming Commission. The act's ostensible goal was to push tribal economic development and strengthen tribal government by promoting gambling—while at the same time protecting Native people from organized crime, which was sure to take an interest in the casino boom. But many Indian leaders felt that the act ac-

163

tually weakened their sovereign status—tribal governments normally deal directly with Washington—by allowing for more regulation by individual states and the Bureau of Indian Affairs. And Segal thinks that "the commission will probably remain ineffective. For one thing, it is woefully underfunded."

What the IGRA does procedurally is divide gambling into classes and then give a state the option to negotiate with the tribes as to whether specific classes of games will be allowed within its borders.

> *"The Indian gambling industry looks like a sure bet for economic growth."*

As Cynthia Montana writes in the Minneapolis-based Native American newspaper the *Circle*, "In places like California, Washington, [and] Wisconsin . . . where efforts to limit Indian gaming exist, the state can simply refuse to negotiate compacts. The tribe might sue a state for refusing to negotiate. So far, however, the Eleventh Amendment to the U.S. Constitution [which prohibits people of one state from suing another state in federal court] has successfully stopped tribes from winning."

## The Stakes and Costs

The stakes are high, because the Indian gambling industry looks like a sure bet for economic growth. In Minnesota, it is well on its way to becoming one of the state's largest employers, having created well over 10,000 jobs. And members of some Indian nations receive hefty checks as a share of the casinos' profitability.

Yet there are hidden, or not-so-hidden, social costs, and tribal people are paying them. Many of the problems that Native people had while living in poverty on reservations and in urban areas persist, and in some cases these problems—suicide, high dropout rates, alcohol and drug abuse, and tribal government corruption—have escalated along with the profits.

According to Montana, chemical dependency counselors on Minnesota's White Earth and Red Lake reservations say they are seeing many recovering alcoholics becoming addicted to gambling. In *Colors*, a Minneapolis journal for writers of color, Lee Ann Tallbear writes:

> New stories each week find their way into Indian conversations. Crazy decisions made by people with a lot of money. Payments made to people long accustomed to very little and in search of immediate satisfaction. Stories begin to surface about severe abuses. Crack. Cocaine. The effects—especially among the younger members of the community—of having no financial need or incentive to work. Where do we go from here?

Native people living off-reservation in urban areas, however, do not receive any direct benefits from the casinos other than employment opportunities. And even those opportunities have limits. Seventy-two percent of casino jobs in Minnesota are, in fact, held by non-Natives.

Each Native community deals with its casino profits differently. Three of the Dakota communities in southern Minnesota give out monthly payments—which vary from $2,000 to $4,000 per month depending on profits—to each enrolled member of the tribe. The seven northern Minnesota Ojibwe reservations have much bigger populations, but smaller operations because of their greater distance from the Twin Cities [Minneapolis and St. Paul], a major market for the casinos. Their profits are invested in improving housing, health clinics, schools, and sewer systems, as well as social service programs on or near the reservations.

The *Washington Monthly* reports:

> The Oneidas from Wisconsin watched their unemployment rate fall from 40 percent in 1976 to 17 percent in 1991, thanks to their gaming facility. With proceeds from their bingo hall, they have built a $10.5 million hotel and convention center and an environmental testing lab that has won state and federal contracts. They've subsidized their own Head Start program and built their own K-8 grade school. A high school is now in the works.

Rick Hill, Oneida tribal chairman, stated in his welcoming speech to the Native American Journalists Association conference held in Green Bay, Wisconsin, in 1992: "We have been reduced to gaming, but I feel at this time it offers the only chance we have for economic self-sufficiency."

Yet despite the enthusiasm it inspires in some, Indian gambling may have a hidden political cost to go with the social strains it brings. As

*"Indian gambling may have a hidden political cost to go with the social strains it brings."*

Tallbear explains in her *Colors* article, "Reduced federal support for services such as health care is already a fact for reservations with large casino profits. Is gambling a chance to rebuild a nation, or a hidden excuse to abrogate treaties?"

# Casinos Help Native Americans Thrive

**by Steve Thompson**

**About the author:** *Steve Thompson is a Chippewa member of the White Earth Mississippi Band in northern Minnesota.*

Since the opening of the first tribal-owned gambling casino, to the now multi-billion-dollar-a-year industry, the future of the Native American people has been taking shape. Since the days of Sitting Bull, tribal leaders have said that the Indian Nation would rise again. Unfortunately, the views of some government officials haven't changed much. They believe the Native American people do not pose a threat as long as they continue to live quietly on the reservations.

Some may argue that statement. They may say that those days are long gone, so why bring up the past. Some will even go as far as to say that those views never existed. It is this writer's opinion that those views did exist and continue to exist today. In my opinion, the only thing that has changed is the strategy. What was once attempted with gunfire, is now being done through government regulations and interference. In fact, not only is the government trying to regulate tribal-owned businesses *off* tribal land, they are trying to regulate tribal-owned businesses located *on* tribal land.

For whatever reason, it was the U.S. Government who felt it necessary to draw the lines and confine the Native American people to the reservations. Why do they now find it necessary to cross these lines and interfere with tribal business? In my opinion, they may feel threatened by the financial independence being created by the tribal-owned businesses.

## In Stronger Positions

It has become apparent that the financial and political position of the Native American population has strengthened considerably in recent years. This has opened many doors for the Native American people. Never before has there been such an increase in the number of businesses owned by Native Americans. Nor has there been such an increase in the number of Native Americans seeking

Steve Thompson, "Commentary," *The Prison Mirror*, January 1, 1994. Reprinted with permission.

college degrees.

As they all continue to educate themselves, we can expect to see a large decline in the number of Native Americans receiving any form of public assistance. We can also expect to see a reduction in the alcoholism rate among Native Americans. Finally, we can expect to see increasing numbers of Native Americans in positions of power as tribal business expands into the corporate world.

> *"The truth is, in the near future, the casino industry will be only a small part of the Native American's power."*

I find these changes very encouraging. The fact that these changes are being brought about *by* Native American people *for* Native American people makes it even more encouraging. It's been a long battle, but we are beginning to see these people demand the respect that they rightfully deserve. Not only as a proud, united people, but as an influential political and financial power.

What I find discouraging in all of this is that the U.S. Government seems almost resentful that Native Americans can take care of their own. In my opinion, they do not like the fact that these people are beginning to reclaim their independence. It is also my opinion that they think that by regulating tribal businesses, they will still have the upper hand. I hope they realize that their actions have only made the Native American people stronger and more determined to fight.

## Paving the Way for Expansion

In the near future, we can expect to see the casino industry completely saturated. This will be due to the number of casinos being opened on tribal land across the country. I've heard some people say that if it weren't for the casino industry, the Indian people wouldn't have anything. The truth is, in the near future, the casino industry will be only a small part of the Native American's power.

The casino industry has played a major part in strengthening the financial position of Native Americans across the country. It will continue to pave the way for tribal business as it expands to other industries. Tribal leaders are already discussing plans for expansion into such areas as manufacturing, construction, property management, education, etc.

The Native American people are serious in their quest. Tribal operations are largely increasing educational spending. By educating the Native American people, they will ensure a future for themselves. They will be the ones to oversee tribal operations and continue the fight for sovereignty into generations to come. They will be able to live independently, without interference from the U.S. Government. The Native American people will no longer live quietly on the reservations.

# The Media Should Recognize the Benefits of Indian Gaming

by Rick Hill

**About the author:** *Rick Hill is chairman of the Oneida tribe in Wisconsin and chairman of the National Indian Gaming Association, a Washington, D.C., organization representing Indian nations across the United States.*

On Sept. 18, 1994, CBS TV's *60 Minutes* aired a segment about the Mashantucket Pequot Tribe entitled "Wampum Wonderland." The story centered on the tribe's highly successful gambling and resort complex near Ledyard, Conn., and began as follows:

> It's a story rich in irony. Rich because it involves lots of money; irony because it's about Native Americans finally turning the tables on the white man. . . . Seven years ago, the Supreme Court ruled that Indian tribes can run their own gambling businesses on tribal land. Today, 90 tribes run 94 casinos. And as sovereign Indian nations, the tribes are free of state regulators, free of taxes and free of the rules that reign in the big-time casinos in Las Vegas and Atlantic City.

This set the tone for the remainder of the piece—one which could easily skew public perception about Indian gaming. The National Indian Gaming Association (NIGA) heard from many of our constituents regarding the negative implications portrayed in this piece. The following letter was sent by NIGA, with input and current statistics provided by the Mashantucket Pequot Tribe, to convey the tribal perceptions of the piece and offer suggestions on how to realistically respond to a vital and necessary industry.

## NIGA's Letter to CBS

The National Indian Gaming Association represents 122 federally recognized Indian nations from across the country. On behalf of those nations we are writ-

Rick Hill, "NIGA Expresses Outrage over '60 Minutes' Segment on Indian Gaming," *Indian Gaming Magazine*, November 1994. Reprinted with permission.

ing to express our outrage with your piece entitled "Wampum Wonderland." As it was littered with inaccuracies, half truths and innuendo, we are shocked that you allowed it to be aired.

We call upon you to correct the misconceptions that you conveyed to the American public [in] quickly developing a segment that inaccurately depicts the Indian gaming industry. We are confident that our member nations would be pleased to assist you as you work to make things right.

Because your interviewer apparently knows nothing of federal Indian law, which provides the underpinnings for much of what he observed, his interview builds upon the rhetoric of Indian gaming detractors. And their rhetoric generally is found in racism, market share or both. His "when did you stop beating your wife" approach to questioning suggested that he knew what he wanted to convey before developing the piece. And, clearly, his biases showed.

Federally recognized Indian nations are legitimate governments whose long relationship with the United States is amply visible in jurisprudential and legislative arenas. Since the 1820s, Indian nations have been recognized by the federal government as "domestic dependent nations." The inherent rights of these nations as sovereigns is amply codified and is found not only in a vast body of law, but in numerous treaties and the Constitution of the United States itself. It is not, as you stated, a "quirk of law."

We do not recall *60 Minutes* doing programs on Indian governments when their unique status merited

> *"We do not recall* **60 Minutes** *doing programs on Indian governments when their unique status merited them poverty, ill health, desperation and annihilation."*

them poverty, ill health, desperation and annihilation. But with one program, focusing on the most unique and successful of all Indian gaming operations in the country, you convey that anyone can be an Indian, Indian gaming is founded on schemes, and tribes are so affluent that they have to find ways to spend their money.

Let us share what is real and factual! The Indian Gaming Regulatory Act of 1988 did NOT authorize Indian gaming, but rather limited the Indian nations' rights by requiring that they compact with the states. In choosing to air the comments of local people who oppose Foxwoods [casino], you even had erroneous allegations about environmental impact (by law, impact studies must be conducted before development).

## No Mention of the Positives

You neglected to mention the 27,000 jobs that are created both directly and indirectly by the construction and operation of the casino (9,300 casino, 900 tribal direct hires), the support of the state legislature, and virtually every other conceivable benefit beyond the income of the Pequots. (And, on that point, should these people be maligned for operating one of the most successful, legitimate, professionally operated and regulated casinos in the world?) The Pequots annually pay in excess of $120 million to the state and you have an issue over their not paying corporate tax?! This is higher than the Connecticut corporate tax structure would require. You also did not mention the $500 million in goods and services purchased from Connecticut and New England vendors.

*"You have diminished the legitimacy of an industry in the eyes of millions of people."*

Had you researched, you would know that with the dramatic downsizing of the local shipyards, the already depressed area would be in desperation were it not for the employment opportunities afforded by the tribe. Instead, you chose to have locals say they didn't know what the tribe was doing. The Ledyard town planner recently announced how the casino is creating "an upswing in the real estate in the area." A feeble attempt at balanced reporting would surely have resulted in local residents who would have spoken positively of the tribe and the community's economic boom.

Your interviewer even challenged the Pequots' right to determine their membership. If someone is 15/16 something other than a U.S. citizen, should we say that person cannot be an American? Governments determine their own criteria for citizenship, and Indian nations exercise those authorities. . . .

Maybe you should do a piece on the history of Indian education and boarding schools. The philosophy of Colonel Richard Henry Pratt guided American policy in that regard. His famous quote, "Kill the Indian, save the man," likely contributes to why the Pequots know little of their own history. An exposé on how America systematically kept Indian people from knowing their history, culture and traditions and punished them for using their language might help your interviewer understand about "cultural deprivation."

Cheap shots like "The Royal Family of Connecticut," innuendo about Malaysian investors, etc. again show either the ineptness or the lack of ethics of your interviewer. Twenty years ago only one retired person lived on the reservation. Might the absence of any employment opportunities have contributed? It was shared that there were foreign investors. Would it have been fair to share that the Pequots approached 500 equally legitimate potential domestic lending sources—and no one would work for them? New England banks NOW are standing in line for Pequot business.

## States and Gaming

A program segment on state gaming, since state governments enjoy 35 percent of the nation's gaming revenue, might make an interesting program. Like the governments of Indian nations, they too use gaming in their economic arsenals to meet the needs of their constituents. Perhaps your interviewer could ask why state governments don't pay corporate taxes or tax on state lotteries. He could accurately point to the Pequots and their thousands of employees who pay federal income tax and query if they do too.

Perhaps the final thought is that you have diminished the legitimacy of an industry in the eyes of millions of people. Proceeds from Indian gaming are building schools, sewer systems, providing health, education and social services. The funds are providing the first leverage capital for economic development in the history of the relationship of the Indian nations and the federal government. Your misunderstanding and misrepresentation foments division between Indian nations and their neighbors. You should be ashamed! The First American has already had a Century of Dishonor!

We look forward to learning of your decision regarding, at a minimum, a retraction of the erroneous points noted above and a public correcting of the inaccuracies. We are optimistic that you will truly make things right by showing the realities of other gaming tribes and the remarkable things that are happening for our elders, children and seven generations as a result of this resource.

# Critics of Indian Gaming Are Wrong

## by Jon Magnuson

**About the author:** *Jon Magnuson is a Lutheran campus pastor at the University of Washington in Seattle and cochair of the Church Council of Greater Seattle's Native American Task Force.*

The "ghost trail" weaves through 7,000 acres across one of Washington state's largest Indian reservations. My informant tells me it carries no visible markings. For outsiders the path remains a hidden part of that indigenous community's spiritual geography. I'm told that some Salish avoid crossing the trail casually. They regard it as one that their forest spirits travel. Only initiates into the *Seyouwin*, or winter dance society, continue to perceive the trail; those who practice the thousand-year-old secret rituals are pledged to protect and honor it.

I stand in a parking lot with a longtime employee of the tribe's Treaty Protection Task Force, who musingly points out that the ghost trail ends a few yards in back of me at the doorway to the tribal casino, which operates 24 hours a day. This is my second visit to the tribe's gaming enterprise. We casually wander over to the renovated warehouse that now houses bingo games, roulette wheels and blackjack tables. . . .

## About Winning and Money

It's busy this afternoon. As in big-time casinos, there are no windows, no clocks and no places to sit down apart from gaming and bingo tables. Employees are cordial, floors spotless. State regulations prohibit liquor from being served here, and although food is available, it's apparent that no one has come to linger, eat or socialize. The atmosphere reminds me of Las Vegas and Reno. There is a feeling of peculiar seriousness in such establishments, perhaps because the rules seem so straightforward. This is about winning. And money.

As is true on most Indian reservations, this casino is leased to a national gaming organization, with a contract stipulating that it turn over full operation to tribal leaders in three or four years. Meanwhile, plenty of sophisticated marketing techniques have been put into place. Not long ago this nondescript ware-house was an empty building on the edge of a bay next to a lonely ferry dock. What was once an abandoned storage area is now an expansive, neatly ordered parking lot filled bumper to bumper with cars and vans. Each day hundreds of bingo and blackjack fans enter what was once a sleepy tourist and fishing town, oblivious to ghost trails, Indian treaty rights, or the ancient masked dances that still go on near here on rainy winter nights. I get myself some coffee, and my friend intro-duces me to a young tribal woman dressed in medieval jester's garb, working as one of the hostesses. She is friendly, and mentions with pride that 60 percent of the employees are tribal members. She's a single mother with three children. The pay is good, she says. My colleague, one of the tribe's cultural specialists, points, smiling, to a black-jack table. He says the dealer, a man with long dark hair, is one of the leaders of the *Seyouwin.*

> *"Twenty states now have Indian gambling, ranging from bingo parlors to casinos as big and glamorous as those in Nevada."*

This small but obviously lucrative casino is only one example of the sudden growth of legalized gambling on Indian reservations. It is also a sign of the sweeping shift in public morality that is under way in virtually every municipal-ity, Indian and non-Indian, across the country. Gambling has become an accept-able form of mass-market entertainment. In 1992 Americans spent more on le-gal games of chance than on films, books, amusement attractions and recorded music combined. That same year Americans spent three times as much money at Indian gambling casinos as on movie tickets. According to Wall Street fore-casts, spending on gambling will double within a decade. "If there weren't more demand than supply, we'd all be doing something else," says Bruce Turner, a casino analyst for Raymond, James, and Associates.

Twenty states now have Indian gambling, ranging from bingo parlors to casi-nos as big and glamorous as those in Nevada. Fifty-eight tribes are currently in-volved in gaming ventures. The Foxwoods casino in Connecticut is the single largest contributor to that state's tax coffers; it alone provided the state with $113 million in 1994. Minnesota, with its Native American gambling halls, cur-rently has more casinos than Atlantic City. Eager to jump aboard the economic boom, a promoter in northwest New Jersey has offered to donate land to the Delaware Indians if a few members of that tribe will come back from Okla-homa to sponsor a casino. . . .

## Mystic Lake

Driving south from Minneapolis, we take Highway 42 west off Interstate I-35. My companion, a former church worker for Indian ministry in northern California, says, "You gotta see this." He's right. Mystic Lake is Minnesota's most spectacular new gaming facility. Owned by the Shakaopee Mdewakanton Dakota tribe, Mystic Lake is a $15 million gaming entertainment center, the largest gambling casino between Las Vegas and Atlantic City. Crowning the facility is a tepee formed by searchlights extending hundreds of feet into the sky. The 135,000-square-foot casino boasts more than 75 blackjack tables and 1,000 video slot machines. One of its promotion brochures proclaims, "The excitement of Vegas . . . Without the desert." The Twin Cities' *Southwest Metro Entertainment Guide* reads, "If it's big money you're looking for, Mystic Lake Bingo offers games with mega jackpots. Megabingo starts at $500,000 and grows each night until someone cashes in." This is the pinnacle of Indian bingo, a dazzling feast of lights and sound where a new car is given away every night, where the food and beverage service is elegant and sophisticated, and where free shuttles from Minneapolis and St. Paul hotels arrive around the clock.

Walking through the doors, I'm taken aback by the glitter and noise of hundreds of slot machines and video games. The structure's circular design, our host says, symbolizes "the great circle of life, the four seasons, and the three cycles of life. Within the concentric circles of the main casino, all seven tribes of the Sioux nation are represented." I wander into the 1,100-seat Bingo Palace located at the west end of the structure and pause, disoriented by the mixture of spiritual and cultural images that frame this setting. A clergy friend from northern Minnesota had told me that the radio advertisements for Mystic Lake use a drum and the voice of an "authentic" shaman to lure customers to its gaming tables. Mysticism of a kind abounds here, but I'm not sure it is exactly what [Sioux holy man] Black Elk had in mind.

> *"On one level, the Native American boom in commercial gaming looks like a sure bet."*

On one level, the Native American boom in commercial gaming looks like a sure bet. In Minnesota, gambling is well on its way to becoming one of the state's largest employers, having created over 10,000 jobs. Members of some Indian nations receive checks as a share of casino profits. Three Dakota communities in southern Minnesota give out payments that vary from $2,000 to $4,000 per month, depending on profits, to each enrolled member of the tribe. The figures are staggering. After a lengthy legal struggle to regain the tribe's original 2,000-acre reservation, the Pequot nation finally got a financial guarantee from the Bureau of Indian Affairs and a loan from the Arab-American Bank in New York. Its casino opened in 1992 and was expected in 1994 to earn over $500 million for tribal members. The tribe has had to open a genealogy office to judge the claims of long-lost relatives to membership in the group, which is now up to 256 members, all of whom are at least one-eighth Pequot by blood.

Some of the tribes, like the Oneidas of Wisconsin, have gained respect and admiration from both Indian and non-Indian groups as they collectively have made decisions about how to use their windfalls of revenue. Thanks to their gaming facility, the Oneidas' unemployment rate fell from 40 percent in 1976 to 17 percent in 1991. With proceeds from their bingo hall, they have built a $10.5 million hotel and convention center, as well as an environmental testing lab that has won state and federal contracts. They have also subsidized their own Head Start program and built an elementary school. Other tribal councils, like Washington State's Suquamish, are using proceeds to purchase back reservation lands that were long ago taken away by state and federal policies. An attractive, state-of-the-art pamphlet for Mystic Lake concludes with some direct advocacy: "Tribal governments realize that casino gaming is not an end in itself. It is a means to achieve what no other federal economic development program has been able to in more than 200 years—the return of self-respect and economic self-sufficiency to Indian people."

## Criticism of Indian Gaming

The varied responses to Indian gaming emerging from Christian churches warrant special attention. As a non-Indian and a member of the clergy, I believe these responses reflect important deeper issues about ethics, spirituality and the complex face of racism and cultural identity. An immediate and common response was related to me in the form of a question by a denominational executive not long ago. "What are we going to do about Indian gambling?" he asked. In light of his strong, sensitive record of supporting treaty rights for Northwest tribes, he was finding himself in a moral quandary. He was pondering the dilemma of how the Christian community could affirm the proliferation of what has long been considered a vice by most Protestants. To best answer this question it is important to acknowledge that the issue poses several ethical and moral dilemmas. The first, and perhaps the most elemental, is the right of Native peoples to decide their own destinies, a right protected by treaty provisions. Only in states that already allow gambling are commercial Indian games of chance legal.

In the larger social context, it is unsettling that there has been so little opposition by church leaders to the proliferation of state lotteries. The exploitation of low-wage workers and the abdication of any corporate public commitment to building a solid, equitable tax system is dismally evident to economists, whatever their political loyalties. It might be good to clean one's own house before suggesting that Native Americans should clean theirs. For historical reasons, America's 200 Indian reservations face overwhelming internal and external conflicts in developing strategies for survival. As Rick Hill, Oneida tribal chairman, stated in his welcoming speech to the Native American Journalists Association in 1992, "We have been reduced to gaming, but I feel at this time it offers the only chance we have

> *"It might be good to clean one's own house before suggesting that Native Americans should clean theirs."*

for economic self-sufficiency."

Some perceive the results of Indian gaming as a humorous kind of revenge. Thomas Donlan, writing for the financial weekly *Barron's*, reminds us that one of the fundamental principles of economics is that a fool and his money are soon parted. What can be said in favor of a gambling casino, he says, is that it concentrates fools, money and those who would part the two, thus contributing to economic efficiency through moral decay. Donlan enjoys the irony. The people who were "de-

> *"The defense of aboriginal rights in courts has been won over and over again in the last half of the 20th century."*

feated by imported alcohol and disease," then corrupted by paternalistic management, he writes, "now find themselves, through a legal loophole, able to erect institutions to corrupt their oppressors."

## Native Cultures

A second popular response to the rise of gaming in Indian country is often moral indignation and masked anger. This is voiced quietly by many political liberals and whispered privately by progressive church leaders. Such an emotional response is probably rooted in what anthropologists call "nostalgic imperialism," an unconscious sentimentalizing and romanticizing of that which a dominant culture has destroyed. It is a fascination with indigenous people and culture, *exclusively* from an historical and artistic point of view. Such an "emblematic" relationship with Native cultures, anthropologists suggest, is a form of racism that many of us, including many Native Americans, share. In other words, others in the culture can gamble, but not the "noble American Indian."

While creative, powerful traditional values are still embodied in the remnants of Native spiritual religions and customs, it is important to remember there is no more "pure," unblemished spiritual teaching in indigenous cultures than there is in the varieties of Christian expression. The question "How could Indians be involved in commercialized gambling?" betrays our own longings for an innocent culture in touch with the best of earth and heaven. A good corrective might be to recognize that among Native Americans there is no consensus on the commercial gaming boom. The Mohawks of New York State have broken out in armed conflict over casino operations. The struggle to protect big-time tribal operations from organized crime continues. Traditionalists around the country grapple with tribal governments over the direction in which their communities are moving.

## Special Privileges

A third response to the increase in commercial Indian gaming is the plea by some for an "even playing field." The accusation that Native Americans have been given special privileges reflects a superficial reading of American history, as well as an ignorance of treaty rights and the historical relationship of tribes to the U.S. government. One of the more entertaining legal struggles against the explosion of Indian gaming has been waged by Donald Trump, seeking better odds for his own gambling ventures. Trump has sued the federal government for supposedly giving tribes regulatory breaks. His testimony before the federal courts was embarrassing and amusing to many Native American journalists, as he showed little if any understanding of the peculiar but critical history of the tribes' right of sovereignty, which has been affirmed since the earliest days of the Constitution. The defense of aboriginal rights in courts has been won over and over again in the last half of the 20th century. That legacy will undoubtedly remain part of our country's ongoing jurisprudence.

I'm on my way to British Columbia for a two-day stay at a Benedictine monastery. I turn on my car radio and hear an advertisement for the Lummi Indian casino 50 miles to the west. Switching stations, I find a public radio broadcast of a speech in Vancouver by a recent recipient of the Visiting Scholar Award sponsored by Simon Fraser University's Institute for the Humanities. The announcer introduces the speaker as Ovide Mercredi, grand chief of Canada's 600,000 aboriginal people. Although schooled as an attorney, his thoughts are expressed in typical Native style, in a personal, informal and somewhat circuitous way. Mercredi's closing remarks are about the future of his people, the recovery by his children and grandchildren of their culture, traditions and religion. "We're growing stronger," he says. "When we reclaim what once was ours, you will see us differently. We will win it back, buy it back, the land that was taken from us. You will hear our voices. Our Indian culture is renewing itself. In the years ahead," he concludes almost matter-of-factly, "you're not going to like us very much."

# Indian Casino Gambling Should Be Discouraged

**by William Safire**

**About the author:** *William Safire is a nationally syndicated columnist for the* New York Times.

The Washington Redskins are winning; "Native Americans" are losing.

While the politically correct fret that the word "redskins" may be taken as an ethnic slur, they ignore a far more serious assault on the character and traditions of our aboriginal Americans.

With the cooperation of greedy tribal leaders and their fast-buck white lawyers, tribes from the Chippewa in Wisconsin to the Barona in California are being victimized and corrupted by promoters of organized gambling.

## How the Boom Started

It began in seeming innocence in the early 1980s with bingo games on the reservations. Then half the states in the United States, under the delusion that good ends could be achieved by bad means, legalized gambling. (It's called "gaming" or "off-track betting" or "casino promotion of tourism"; never use a dirty word like "gambling.")

Because Indian reservations retain a form of sovereignty that limits control by state governments, shrewd gambling operators saw a way to get around local restrictions and steal a march on the local casinos. The Supreme Court held in 1987 that states that permitted gambling could not deny its triumphs, glories and spoils to Indian reservations.

That opened the floodgates to those who wanted to exploit the special status of Indians. Today, gambling dens fronted by Indians are a billion-dollar-a-year business and mushrooming; tribal lands are illuminated by neon; tribes reaching out for more suckers are litigating with state officials about whether one-armed bandits are illegal slot machines or merely "technological aids" to bingo players.

The corruption of the original American ethnic group is taking place under the cover of a public relations campaign to show how gambling is good for impoverished Indians. Profits go to the tribes, goes the story, which then build schools and hospitals and lift the unemployed families off welfare.

Baloney; malarkey; oompah. The few facilities gambling built are Potemkin villages [impressive facades concealing undesirable truths]. Casino gambling will help the average Indian as much as the New York State Lottery has provided great new facilities for the average schoolchild. The great benefit of gambling profits to the public has always been a sham; it has

> *"Big-time gambling is an organized vice deserving of no government promotion or identification with a single ethnic group."*

proved itself to be the most regressive and shameful tax on any state's books. New Jersey and Nevada, those paragons of state virtue, have led the way.

## Number of Indian Gaming Facilities

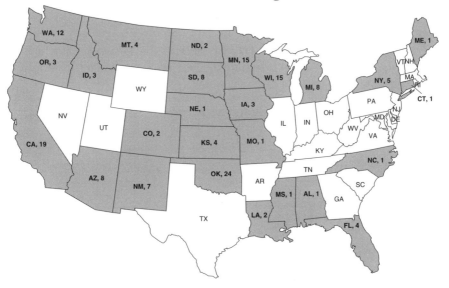

Source: *Indian Gaming* magazine, January 1995.

[For a long time], investigative media shied away from this national scandal. Many have been intimidated by immediate charges of racism by Indian "leaders" who benefit most from the deals like those being set up across the country by Grand Casinos Inc., a company whose over-the-counter stock is being promoted by non-Indians.

What a perversion of affirmative action; is this the proper answer to the massacre of innocent Indians at Wounded Knee?

In fact, the corruption of gambling is ripping many tribes apart. The Mohawk fighting along the U.S.-Canadian border in 1991 was based largely on control of gambling money. The introduction of slot machines all but insures further mob penetration and moral degradation.

Big-time gambling is an organized vice deserving of no government promotion or identification with a single ethnic group. All lotteries are con games, manipulating our something-for-nothing lust. (I throw away any junk mail with a picture of Ed McMahon on it.)

Is there no tribal leader courageous enough to come forward to tell Indian children they come from the stock of Sitting Bull and Crazy Horse and that their role models need not be George Raft and Meyer Lansky?

## Stop Promoting Gambling

Are there no genuine friends of a poverty-stricken group willing to put aside tut-tutting about misperceived slurs long enough to call attention to the real cultural and moral crisis facing the Indian nations today?

We cannot deny Indians their right to compete with states in attracting suckers of all races. The answer is to get both state governments and Indian tribes out of the gambling business. Public promotion of betting is wrong; it corrupts people and politicians; it should never be the goal of public policy.

If we fail to stop the casinoization of the reservations, we will surely change the name of the football team to honor the next generation of aboriginal Americans. We'll call them the Washington Croupiers.

# Indian Gaming Has Harmed Many Tribes

## by David Segal

**About the author:** *David Segal is an assistant editor for the* Washington Post *daily newspaper.*

Plastic garbage bags stand in as roofs; faucets along a dirt road serve as showers. A 12-year-old might call this a scout camp, but the Kickapoo tribe of Eagle Bend, Texas, calls it a nation—and it's clearly a nation in trouble. A quarter of the population is unemployed, more than half is illiterate, and much to the embarrassment of tribal leaders, the signal crop in the community vegetable garden is marijuana.

By the looks of it, the Kickapoo reservation needs several basic things, including electricity, plumbing, and a school. But it *wants* only one thing: bingo, and step on it. "We're desperate for the money," says Julio Frausto, a tribal leader. And the Kickapoos are not the only ones. Since Congress passed the 1988 Indian Gaming Act, which guaranteed tribes the right to run gambling enterprises on their reservations, more than a hundred tribes from North Dakota to Florida have gotten into the act, eager to translate blackjack and bingo into better education and opportunity.

### Enter Wayne Newton

But while the Kickapoo look to Las Vegas for inspiration, they might be wiser to the first glance a few hundred miles north, to Miami, Oklahoma.

When the leaders of the Seneca-Cayugas there hired Wayne Newton Enterprises to run their high-stakes bingo parlor in October 1990, they thought their troubles were behind them. The parlor had been shut down for several months after the tribe terminated its contract with a British management company that failed to turn a profit after running the hall for a year. But now they had a real Las Vegas concern working for them, and Wayne himself—half American Indian—came to the grand opening to give away the evening's big prizes. Sure, the tribe was asked to throw in $224,000 to help restart the operation—over and above the $300,000 it had already spent to build the hall—but Wayne was going to ante up $125,000, he was sending his best people, and anyway, business during November was good. No worries.

By December, worries. On most nights the huge hall, with its mirrored ceilings and pastel interior, was packed with 1,400 players. But profits were

> *"Tribes with gaming operations have been beset by difficulties ranging from graft to fratricide."*

nowhere to be found. Neither, for that matter, was Wayne's $125,000. In December 1991, Newton Enterprises' own ledger sheets reported a gross of $12.5 million for the year, improbably offset by enough expenses to leave a debt of $360,000,

which the company asked the tribe to cover. For the whole year the Seneca-Cayugas received $13,000—barely a seventh of the salary of Newton Enterprises' on-site manager. The final outrage came in December, when two jackpot winners were unable to get their checks cashed at the bank. The tribe retaliated by surrounding the bingo hall with pick-up trucks while Newton's security forces barricaded themselves inside. After a tense five-day standoff, a federal judge ruled that the hall was to be returned to the tribe. The question of who would pay the hall's debt is now headed for arbitration.

## From Graft to Fratricide

Although tribes have always kept criminal and financial data to themselves, and while the government seems equally disinclined to discuss the subject of troubles in Indian gaming, there's a growing body of evidence that what happened to the Senecas is not unusual. Since high-stakes, Indian-owned bingo parlors made their first appearance in the late seventies, tribes with gaming operations have been beset by difficulties ranging from graft to fratricide. What Congress envisioned as a fast track out of poverty and unemployment for American Indians has evolved into a billion-dollar-a-year industry that has added precious little to social services on reservations throughout the country.

"If we get the money from bingo, we're going to set up a vocational training program," says Kickapoo administrator Frausto. "Even if the kids don't go to college, they'll have a trade." Perhaps. But they may also get more than they bargained for. In one extreme instance, the Mohawks of upstate New York split into pro- and anti-gambling factions and commenced a brief civil war because profits from their seven on-reservation halls were going exclusively to hall owners and their non-Indian management team. Two tribe members were left dead.

While it's easy—and partially correct—to blame American Indians for the unfolding gambling fiasco, the real culprit may be bureaucrats in Washington, D.C. After all, Indian gaming is an experiment that might convince even [conservative economist] Milton Friedman that government regulation is in order:

inexperienced, financially desperate Indians entering a slick and crime-infested business. But the Indians don't want help, and the commission the government created to regulate Indian gambling, the National Indian Gaming Commission (NIGC), is equally disinclined to provide it, preaching laissez-faire as tribe after tribe gets taken. The shame is that a few tribal success stories suggest that, if properly run and carefully regulated, Indian gambling can pay off as promised—in housing and modern plumbing, scholarships and jobs. Instead, as the Kickapoos break in the tables without expertise or government assistance, the deck has quietly been stacked against them.

To anyone familiar with the effects gambling has had on other communities that have legalized it, the Indians' venture into gaming may sound less like a shortcut to prosperity than a quick way to finish off tribal life once and for all. Wherever it's been tried, gambling has been accompanied by a dramatic increase in violent and property crimes, alcoholism, and drug abuse. Yet there is surprisingly little breast-beating on the reservations about how gambling could destroy what is left of Indian culture. (Could names like "Stands With 17" be far behind?) One reason is that Indians are a little more modern than we think. Another is that, after a decade of penetrating budget cuts, they have few other options.

## Government and the Reservations

Indian gaming took hold in the eighties, as most everything else on the reservation was withering away. While funds for education decreased only slightly in the Reagan-Bush era, other aid programs plunged. In 1980, the National Health Service Corps sent 155 physicians to reservations; a decade later it was sending 7. Housing and Urban Development, which had authorized 6,000 new units of Indian housing during Jimmy Carter's last year as president, was building only 1,500 new units by 1988. The Economic Development Administration, which had funded bricks-and-mortar projects, was slashed to near extinction, while the Community Services Administration, which granted money for development projects, was wiped out altogether.

"The Reagan cuts devastated tribes," says Frank Ducheneaux, who served as counsel on Indian Affairs for the House Committee on Interior and Insular Affairs during this period. "Since most have high rates of unemployment and poverty and rely heavily on the government for social services, Indians had to find alternative sources of funding." And as the need for alternative funding became evident, the legal grounds for gaming were being won.

*"The shame is that a few tribal success stories suggest that, if properly run and carefully regulated, Indian gambling can pay off as promised."*

The first test came in Florida back in 1979, after the Miami Seminoles defied a state law prohibiting bingo prizes of more than $100 and began offering

$10,000 jackpots in a 1,200-seat hall. The state sued, but in 1982 a federal appeals court ruled that since the Seminoles were a sovereign nation, state civil regulations did not apply to them. Tribes nationwide took note, and within five years, 113 bingo operations around the country were grossing $225 million annually. Legal challenges from states abounded, but in 1987 the Supreme Court decided that Indians could operate any form of gambling already permitted by the state—and could do so with their own regulations. In the 14 states that allowed groups to run highly restricted "Las Vegas nights" for charity, the door was opened for Indians to start up full-blown casinos.

> *"Indians are especially vulnerable to mafia infiltration because few banks make loans to tribes."*

A year later, Congress bestowed its approval with the Indian Gaming Act, which advocated gambling as "a means of promoting tribal economic development, self-sufficiency, and strong tribal governments." Yet Congress wasn't altogether sanguine about gaming—nor should it have been, considering the then-vivid example of Atlantic City, where the felony crime rate skyrocketed in the first few years of legalized gambling. (Las Vegas was steadier, ranking either first, second, third, or fourth in per capita felonies in the country's metropolitan areas between 1960 and 1984.) Nevertheless, Congress agreed that the Indians had both the legal right to establish gaming parlors and little prospect of raising badly needed money from other sources. So to shield Indians "from organized crime and other corrupting influences" and ensure that "the Indian tribe is the primary beneficiary of the gaming operation," it devised a complicated system of regulation. Yet [up to 1992], no government or private agency had examined the successes or failures of Indian gaming—Congress didn't apparently have much of a plan for overseeing how its well-intentioned rules would work. According to the FBI, troubles began almost as soon as the gaming did—and those troubles have included organized crime.

## Grift Horses

When Stewart Siegel, a dealer and manager at casinos from Las Vegas to the Caribbean, was hired to run the Barona reservation's bingo hall in San Diego, California, he brought a pro's touch to the reservation's games: Grand prizes like cars and $60,000 in cash were regularly won by planted shills, who then gave the money back to Siegel. After pleading guilty in 1986 to four counts of grand theft, including bilking the tribe of $600,000 a year, he joined the witness protection program and started talking. Testifying before the Senate Select Committee on Indian Affairs with a hood over his head, he claimed that he knew of at least 12 halls that were controlled by the Cosa Nostra [an alleged mafia organization] but guessed that nearly half of all Indian casinos were tainted by it, either directly through management and investors or indirectly through suppliers.

The allegation is hardly far-fetched, given the economics of starting up a gaming hall. Indians are especially vulnerable to mafia infiltration because few banks make loans to tribes; their land, which is sovereign, cannot be foreclosed. So when tribes look elsewhere for start-up money, well- and not-so-well-concealed mafiosi are often their most willing backers. According to the FBI, the trendsetting Seminoles unwittingly hired the mob when they opened their hall in 1979. (The FBI routed them out.) Two years later, the Cabazons, a tiny tribe in Riverside County, California, retained Rocco Zangari, a member of a Southern California organized crime family, to run their card room. When tribal vice-chairman Alvin Alvarez accused the management of skimming profits, he was forced out of office. Months later, he and two other critics were found shot to death. The case has yet to be solved.

## Management Companies

Disorganized crime may be just as threatening. Under the most common contracts that tribes negotiate with management companies, the Indians are promised 60 percent of "profits after expenses," a clause that often means the tribe gets nothing. Examples of management companies cooking the books are legion. On the Mohawk reservation where the intratribal gambling war broke out, non-Indian investor Emmet Munley was found by his Indian business partner to have deducted $186,000 in traveling expenses and $120,000 in accounting fees. At the Seneca-Cayuga hall, Wayne Newton Enterprises was clearing $20,000 to $30,000 a month, according to Don Deal, who used to work for the company and saw the accounting sheets, while the tribe earned next to nothing. The Winnebagos of Wisconsin got a Halloween party and a back-taxes bill from the IRS for $800,000 but have yet to get any profits from their management company, the Genna Corporation.

Even worse, gambling has cut off the little federal support the Winnebagos had before gaming, says tribal chairwoman Jo Ann Jones. Allegations that the Genna Corporation has bought off half of the Winnebagos' tribal council in lieu of sharing the profits have so riven the tribe that [as of March 1992] members have been unable to meet and approve applications for government programs. Since June 1, 1990, all their federal grants for housing, education, and other social services have ceased.

> *"Gambling . . . constantly tempts those involved with large sums of immediately available cash and easily fudged ledgers."*

So are the Genna Corporation and those other management companies corrupt? No one—neither the tribes nor the government—has taken the trouble to find out. While in Nevada and New Jersey the mere scent of ill repute will get one barred from even the lower echelons of casino management, aspiring Indian casino managers are currently disqualified only if the FBI—which runs finger-print checks on request—discovers a felony conviction. The NIGC is supposed to be doing more sophisticated background checks, sniffing out the mafia and making sure tribes are getting a fair count from their management companies. But the commission is clearly not doing enough homework. Wayne Newton Enterprises' only other experience in Indian gaming, with the Santa Ynez of California, ended in bankruptcy. Emmet Munley was unable to get a gambling license through the Nevada Gaming Control Board on two occasions because he associated "with persons of questionable and unsavory character." (The NIGC's colleague, the Bureau of Indian Affairs [BIA], which must approve any contract between a management company and a tribe, has also been less than vigilant in sifting out undesirables. Indeed, it was a BIA agent, Thomas Burden, who originally recommended Emmet Munley when the Mohawks were searching for investors.)

> *"Gambling is no panacea for deep social ills that could be billions of dollars and decades away from a cure."*

What has the NIGC been doing since it was written into existence in 1988? Mostly finding office space; it wasn't until February 1991 that it settled on permanent quarters, and even then it needed an additional eight months to publish its first set of regulations. . . .

## Slow Motion

Slow motion is a standard feature of federal bureaucracies, but the commission has also been hindered by the combined resistance of Indian leaders—many of whom see the commission as patronizing and unnecessary—and the states, which have their own interest in making sure the halls are functioning responsibly. Adjudicating between two sovereign entities makes painstaking debate on the commission's every move inevitable. A set of revised regulations on what types of electronic machines will be allowed in bingo halls was heatedly debated for months in hearings in five cities across the country.

Even after it publishes all its regulations, the commission will probably remain ineffective. For one, it is woefully underfunded. The New Jersey Casino Control Commission employs over 400 people and spends $23 million per year to keep an eye on Atlantic City's 12 casinos. The Indian Gaming Commission spends $3 million per year to oversee more than 150 halls. And what the NIGC lacks in financial way, it won't be making up with regulatory will. [Former commissioner] Tony Hope presided over a relatively hands-off commission. "There will be no micromanagement from D.C.," he insisted.

The style is the legacy of a Republican policy, initiated by Richard Nixon in 1970 and expanded upon by Ronald Reagan and George Bush, to encourage Indian self-determination by allowing tribes to make their own decisions wherever possible. When James Watt headed the Department of the Interior, he in-

structed BIA to review contracts between Indians and bingo hall managers only
when tribes requested it, even though long-standing law requires that all such
contracts get BIA approval. The NIGC has taken a similarly minimalist approach in its role as watchdog.

That the growth of Indian gaming coincides with this new governmental dis-
interest is a historical accident and not a very fortunate one. Washington's liber-
tarian impulses may arguably be long overdue in other realms of Indian life, but
they are misplaced in gambling, an industry that constantly tempts those involved with large sums of immediately available cash and easily fudged
ledgers. What is true for the owners and managers of casinos in Atlantic City
and Las Vegas is true for the Indians: Without strong, vigilant, and impartial
oversight, they are easy marks for the mob and all types of hustlers. . . .

## Regulation Roulette

Because many Indians currently rely on far-flung, low-paying migrant work
to survive, the promise of jobs is often a major incentive to tribes considering
gaming. But these Vegas-scale operations will not ease unemployment. They
need to be located near or within easy access of major population centers; most
reservations, however, are in the hinterlands.

> *"Government now has an obligation to tribes to make sure that gaming is run legally."*

The jobs issue is even more important than it first appears because it is
most often those halls and casinos
employing and involving tribe members that succeed. While the Winnebagos went broke and the Mo-
hawks turned to gunplay in squabbles over outside control, several tribes have
been quietly fulfilling the gaming act's promise of more jobs and social services
by operating their own shops.

Before the Mille Lacs Chippewas of Minnesota opened their Grand Casino in
April 1990, 60 percent of their families lived below the poverty line; 45 percent
were unemployed. By December, only a handful lived in poverty, virtually none
were unemployed (most had gotten jobs in the casino), and the tribe had become the county's biggest employer. A modern sewer system, school improvements, and a health clinic are on the way.

The Oneidas [in Wisconsin] watched their unemployment rate fall from 40
percent in 1976 to 17 percent in 1991, thanks to their gaming facility—which is
run with no outside management help. "I can't imagine why so many tribes are
willing to give away 40 percent," says Bobby Webster, part of the tribal management team. With proceeds from their bingo hall, they have built a $10.5 mil-
lion hotel and convention center and an environmental testing lab that has won
state and federal contracts. They've subsidized their own Head Start program
and built their own K-8 grade school. A high school is now in the works. While
most reservations have been losing members, the Oneidas have seen their num-

bers swell by a third in the past 15 years.

Still, even when it works this well, gambling is no panacea for deep social ills that could be billions of dollars and decades away from a cure. Even among the Oneidas unemployment is still high, and drug and alcohol problems persist. But if a few tribes can make a little progress through gaming, perhaps more can. And in the absence of other sources of funding, it means a few more Indian kids educated and employed and fewer houses with trashbag roofs.

## Government's Obligation

Yet in their current hands-off mode, the NIGC and the legislators who created it are repeating the mistakes of previous would-be benefactors who threw plots of land, and then money, at tribes. By their passivity, they're effectively ensuring that good programs are flukes, not formulas—and that beggared but eager tribes like Eagle Bend's Kickapoos will be playing against the odds.

Keeping decent information about what works and what doesn't, and then providing technical assistance for start-ups, should be the minimal role of the slumbering NIGC. But it's not enough. While some Indians might paint any oversight effort as an infringement on their rights of sovereignty, this is the wrong moment for the government to be daunted by that charge. After a green light from the federal courts, program-slashing by successive administrations, and a reluctant thumbs-up from Congress, the government now has an obligation to tribes to make sure that gaming is run legally and in the interests of the people it was intended to help—in short, that gambling is the "means of promoting tribal economic development, self-sufficiency, and strong tribal governments" Congress declared it would be in the eighties. The last thing the Kickapoos need, after all, is another broken promise.

# Indian Gaming Is Problematic

## by Robert Allen Warrior

**About the author:** *Robert Allen Warrior, a Native American, is a former con-tributing editor for* Christianity and Crisis *magazine.*

American Indian political theorists have often pointed to the municipality of Monaco as an example of what they mean when they say that small Native American groups can be politically viable. The comparison is becoming more and more apt as national Indian leadership embraces casino gambling as the panacea for tribal economic woes.

With the opening of an Indian casino in Connecticut, national attention has come to an ongoing debate about the desirability of high-stakes gaming as a means of economic development. Without doubt, bingo and gambling can bring millions of dollars into a native community, but many people inside and outside Indian country worry that corruption, organized crime, and social deterioration follow these enterprises like a shadow.

### The Pequots

The Mashantucket Pequots opened their Foxwoods High Stakes Bingo and Casino on February 15, 1992. Employing 2,300 people, Foxwoods offers roulette, craps, blackjack, and poker. Waitresses wear buckskin minidresses slashed to the hip. A sales display of Indian pottery is set up just past the cash machines at the entrance. People in Connecticut, much less the rest of the world, did not even know these Pequots were still around, until the casino opened.

The Mashantucket are taking advantage of the 1988 Federal Indian Gaming Regulatory Act. Congress wrote the act to embody a decade of U.S. Supreme Court decisions recognizing the rights of Indian groups to engage in whatever forms of gaming are allowed in the states they are in. Even if states allow only one-night Las Vegas nights or church bingo, Natives can do those things year round. Further, the money from gaming is tax-free.

Robert Allen Warrior, "Indian Country Crap-Shoot," *Christianity and Crisis*, May 11, 1992. Reprinted with permission.

189

On the heels of Foxwoods' opening, ABC and NBC both featured reports on Indian gaming and the *New York Times* followed events at Mashantucket closely. The general tone of much of the reporting has been: Sounds good, but what about corruption and organized crime?

## A Choice of Champions

*Times* columnist William Safire was the most concerned. In a January 1992 column he asserted that gambling surely will be the "demon rum" of the 1990s for American Indians and wondered when responsible and moral Native American leaders would stand up against this scourge. It's always fun when some national pundit goes on a brief vision quest into Indian issues and emerges with such a sure sense of knowing what's happening in Indian country. In response, syndicated Lakota columnist Tim Giago called Safire a "pompous, aristocratic ignoramus," and added, "if he had written the same malarkey about African-Americans, he would have been tarred and feathered as he left his office."

Importantly, Giago's paper, the *Lakota Times*, had been carrying the banner of Indian gaming for months. "Indian gaming: It's legal, it's desirable and it's here to stay" was the headline of an article in November 1991 in a special tabloid insert devoted to Native gambling enterprises. Chock full of ads from Indian casinos and bingo parlors around the country, the insert assures and reassures readers that blackjack and keno are the economic panacea Indian communities have been waiting for.

Following the insert, [three subsequent] issues of the *Lakota Times* featured multiple front-page stories on gaming and most other issues have at least one. On February 12, 1992, six articles, two op-ed pieces, and two letters about gaming appeared in the first section of the paper. In all of these articles and various op-ed pieces, the paper accuses critics of Indian gaming of being paternalists who don't think Indians can do anything for themselves.

Giago's advice for Safire and others who believe that Indian gaming is organized-crime infested is: "Go to a casino owned and operated by an Indian tribe. If you find one Mafia connection at any one of them, I will personally buy you a big, Cuban cigar." This is certainly a proper reaction to Safire and others who take upon themselves the burden of helping all of us poor, ignorant, susceptible Indians, but Giago's all-but-uncritical championing of Indian gaming leaves much to be desired. While he may be right in saying that gaming has been "more good

> *"Questions remain about Indian gaming that . . . conservative native leaders do not want to ask."*

than bad" for Indian communities, questions remain about Indian gaming that Giago and other conservative native leaders do not want to ask.

For instance, Giago would have gone bankrupt giving out cigars had Safire and others gone to upstate New York and Quebec to visit Akwesasne [a Mohawk reservation in New York and Canada] a few years ago when gambling and smuggling started a civil war among Mohawks there. According to several published reports (and even more off-the-record comments), gambling operations there were indeed linked to organized crime. But perhaps more importantly, Akwesasne illustrates a fundamental problem of gaming: the continued presence of irresponsible, unaccountable tribal governments in many Indian communities. The fact is, most councils undertake these gaming operations with precious little input from local people. Without a government vehicle through which local community concerns can be heard and standards created, the probability of abuse and corruption is extremely high. Among the Mohawks, for instance, the U.S. government–created tribal council supported gambling while the followers of the traditional longhouse staunchly opposed it.

> *"Our national leadership seems to prefer gambling away the future of their communities in a blind crap-shoot."*

Bingo and gambling are most successful in areas that can draw large non-Indian clienteles. In more isolated areas, the vast majority of money comes from Indian families and does little to invigorate devastated economies, not to mention the reservation social problems gambling can aggravate.

At the same time, strong, responsible leadership can turn gaming into a highly positive venture. The Osage bingo in Pawhuska, Oklahoma, does brisk business among Indians and non-Indians alike and helps fund important local projects. The main point here is that gaming is a mixed bag and will continue to be for a long time.

## The White Man's Cut

One thoughtful letter to the editor that recognizes how complex the situation is did manage to find its way into the *Lakota Times*. In that letter, Wallace Wells of the Crow Creek Sioux Tribe in South Dakota predicts that all of these gambling enterprises will be for naught once state governments get tired of seeing millions of dollars going into reservation economies without getting a cut for themselves. Eventually, Wells argues, states will legalize gambling. Won't this lead, he asks, to "some more empty buildings because people with money will rather go to a town than to a reservation" to gamble? Wells points also to increased criminal activity and the eventual oversaturation of gaming facilities as reasons for Indians to be more reflective before embracing gambling.

These concerns are important; the *Lakota Times* and others messianically championing gaming would do well to take them to heart. Unfortunately but not surprisingly, our national leadership seems to prefer gambling away the future of their communities in a blind crap-shoot.

# Organized Crime May Infiltrate Indian Casinos

## by James Popkin

**About the author:** *James Popkin is a senior editor for the weekly magazine* U.S. News & World Report.

Seated in the largest Senate hearing room in 1989 with a hood over his head to protect his identity, the witness identified only as "Marty" had some confessions to make. Not only had he helped the mob set up and run a high-stakes bingo hall on an Indian reservation, he testified, but he had padded expenses and robbed the tribe of over $600,000 a year.

But even Marty's sensational tales of filling bingo halls with helium and awarding $60,000 cars to paid shills paled in comparison to his next news flash. Marty told members of the Senate Select Committee on Indian Affairs that 12 other Indian bingo halls also were controlled by the mob. "Organized crime is destroying the Indian reservation," he said in a slow, mechanical baritone, his voice deliberately altered through the use of a special machine.

### Serious Doubts Raised

Years later, the leaders of the Indian gambling industry are still smarting. Marty's apocalyptic visions of Mafia domination have been proven wrong, they argue, adding that Indian-owned casinos and bingo halls are more heavily regulated than the glitz palaces in Atlantic City and Las Vegas. But while it's true that the industry has grown much more sophisticated and has weeded out the most venal operators, many questionable characters remain. From dozens of interviews with federal, state and local law-enforcement officials and from documents obtained through the Freedom of Information Act, *U.S. News & World Report* has learned of a number of cases that raise serious doubts about the integrity and inviolability of Indian casinos.

Devastated by unemployment, substandard housing and schools and crippling alcoholism, many Indians have come to see gambling as "the new buffalo"— the first true economic opportunity in two centuries. But buffalo never paid dividends like a one-armed bandit. In Connecticut, the sprawling Foxwoods Casino owned by the Mashantucket Pequots could conceivably gross $1 billion [per] year and net half that amount. On the Shakopee Mdewakanton Dakota reservation near Minneapolis, the Mystic Lake casino takes in so much cash that tribal members sometimes receive dividend checks for up to $20,000 a person per month, one official with the Bureau of Indian Affairs says. And in July 1993 near Syracuse, N.Y., the Oneida Indians opened the $10 million Turning Stone Casino, expecting to rake in well over $100 million a year.

Now that 73 tribes in 19 states offer or will soon offer full-scale casino gambling, the big boys have taken notice. Atlantic City casino owner Donald Trump sued the U.S. government for allegedly giving an unfair advantage to tribes setting up casinos. And he's out to prove the fledgling industry is corrupt. "A lot of the reservations are being, at least to a certain extent, run by organized crime," says Trump. "There's no protection. It's become a joke."

## Mob Infiltration

Mobsters did, in fact, prey upon Indian gambling during the 1980s. Besides Marty, whose real name was Stewart Siegel and who managed a California bingo hall for the Barona Indians before he died of cancer, Indian gambling's cast of characters was like something out of an Edward G. Robinson movie. In 1993, for example, reputed Chicago mob boss John "No Nose" DiFronzo and his gambling expert, Donald "The Wizard of Odds" Angelini, were convicted of conspiracy and fraud in a failed attempt to take over gambling operations at the Rincon Reservation near San Diego in the late '80s. The Chicagoans had hoped to skim profits and launder mob money, FBI wiretaps show. In 1980, California's Cabazon Indian tribe hired as their poker-room manager one Rocco Zangari, identified as a mobster in Senate testimony. He was subsequently fired. Later, after tribal Vice Chairman Alfred Alvarez complained to local newspapers about poker-room skimming, Alvarez and two others were shot dead; the case has never been solved.

"There's probably been a learning curve, and people have been burned," says Rick Hill of the National Indian Gaming Association. But Las Vegas was an open town for mobsters in the 1930s, he adds, policed only by a sheriff. "You always have to look at things from a historical perspective."

*"Mobsters did, in fact, prey upon Indian gambling during the 1980s."*

Trump's hyperbole notwithstanding, the vast majority of the 175 total Indian casinos and bingo halls are honest and clean. Many employ Las Vegas or Atlantic City pros and have vigilant in-house security teams. Several management companies are publicly traded and have passed overlapping layers of government scrutiny. The FBI does not see a "coordinated, concerted effort" by organized-crime families to raid the Indian gambling industry, says Jim Moody, chief of the FBI's organized-crime section. There are no "publicly known" cases of current mob infiltration.

But the threat remains. The bureau had six ongoing investigations as of August 1993. . . . And when asked which crime families are interested in Indian gambling, Moody replied: "I don't know any that aren't."

## The Pittsburgh Road Paver

The FBI is investigating a Pennsylvania asphalt-company owner who manages a major casino in Minnesota and is expanding into tribal gambling in California, Oklahoma and Ontario, Canada, *U.S. News* has learned. Angelo Medure, 64, president of Gaming World International, has no criminal record and has passed the background checks required to manage the Shooting Star Casino in Mahnomen, Minnesota, owned by the White Earth Band of Chippewa. No charges have been filed against him. But the FBI became suspicious when it learned Medure leases a New Castle, Pennsylvania, warehouse to a pasta firm that was run in the 1980s by reputed mobsters.

The Pennsylvania Crime Commission says that Henry "Zebo" Zottola, 57, was president of Rocca's Italian Foods and that Louis Raucci Sr., 63, was an investor and employee. Zottola helps collect payments for the Michael Genovese crime family from local loan sharks, bookies and drug dealers, the commission says. Raucci was convicted in 1990 on racketeering, narcotics and tax violations and is serving a 27-year jail sentence.

> *"There are no 'publicly known' cases of current mob infiltration. But the threat remains."*

In an interview, Medure initially denied knowing Raucci or Zottola. Later, he said he had met Zottola at the pasta plant several times but claims he was unaware of Zottola's background. Confidential telephone records obtained by *U.S. News* confirm their relationship. A 24-page summary of calls made in 1986 from Zottola's Pittsburgh home reveals that Zottola called Medure's house and his trailer home in New Castle 6 times on March 21, 1986. On May 9, Zottola called Medure's condominium in Pompano Beach, Florida, and Medure's construction company. Medure says he has no organized-crime links and claims Zottola simply called to discuss warehouse remodeling plans.

Zottola acknowledged in August 1993 that he called Medure repeatedly in 1986 to discuss the warehouse. He admits being friends with men who the crime commission says are Pittsburgh mobsters but claims he has no link to the Mafia and is just an honest carpet salesman.

Although Zottola never admitted it to local FBI agents when they questioned him in May 1993 about Medure, the calls did not stop in 1986. Zottola called Medure in 1992 to discuss selling him video-poker machines to be used at the Minnesota casino. Medure confirmed the call but says he told Zottola he was not interested. "[Medure] told me that anything he put on that reservation had to be approved by the state of Minnesota. And I just forgot about it after that," Zottola adds.

The White Earth tribe has had some curious business dealings in the past. In 1987, before Medure became involved, Carmen Ricci sold 30 video-poker machines to the tribe. New Jersey officials describe Ricci as an associate of the Nicodemo Scarfo crime family. "At that time they were legitimate businessmen," tribal Chairman Darrell "Chip" Wadena says.

> *"The White Earth tribe has had some curious business dealings in the past."*

Medure profits handsomely from his casino deal. His firm gets 35 percent of casino profits—at least $3 million a year. Chairman Wadena fought to increase Medure's take by 5 percent, at his own tribe's expense, but a federal mediator refused. Medure had plans in 1993 to manage casinos for the Hopland Band of Pomo Indians and the Cloverdale Pomo Indians in Northern California, and the Ratportage First Nation near Kenora in Ontario. His firm also planned to manage a bingo hall for the Seneca-Cayuga tribe in Miami, Oklahoma.

## The Strip-Bar Owner

Restaurant owner Robert Sabes was well known in Minneapolis as a millionaire businessman. So locals were hardly surprised when he created a successful casino management firm called Gaming Corp. of America. But troubles began in 1993 when Mississippi gaming regulators learned that Sabes owned a topless bar in Minneapolis where the entertainment was managed by Michael Peter, a flashy South Florida millionaire with a nationwide chain of strip-tease bars called Solid Gold. Peter was indicted in 1991 on extortion and kidnapping charges, and the case [was sent to] state court. Federal agents seized thousands of Peter's documents at about the same time, citing concern over possible organized-crime ties. No federal charges have been filed.

Sabes denies any mob links and says he had "an arm's length" relationship with Peter. But the embarrassment and the licensing delays to come persuaded Sabes to sell his Gaming Corp. stock in April 1993 and leave the publicly traded firm. Although one tribe quickly cut all ties to the restaurateur, others continue to seek his business. In July 1993, Sabes won preliminary approval from Arizona's Yavapai-Apaches to manage their proposed casino north of Phoenix.

Evidence of a more troubling relationship may jeopardize those plans, too. In testimony to the Wisconsin Winnebago gaming commission released in August 1993, Sabes admits also doing business with James Williams, a partner in Peter's strip-bar empire and once a major bingo hall operator for Indian tribes and charities from California to Florida. Williams was convicted in 1987 of failing to pay taxes on some $300,000 he earned from bingo halls. Florida police records call him a "close associate" of Anthony Accetturo's, whom the FBI has identified as a capo, or boss, of the Thomas Luchese crime family of New York. Williams, who did not return phone calls, admits in the police files only to meeting Accetturo three times in the 1970s.

In an interview, Sabes admitted that he signed papers with Williams as early as Nov. 9, 1988. That was just four months before Williams was locked up, prison officials say. But he says he did not learn of Williams's conviction or alleged Mafia ties until 1990.

## The Bingo Paper Supplier

When Florida's Miccosukee Indians opened a 2,000-seat bingo hall west of Miami in 1991, they hired Tamiami Partners to run it. Two years later the tribe kicked the firm out, alleging mob ties. Tamiami partner Cye Mandel denies the charges and has sued the tribe for cutting him out of the venture, which in 1992 grossed $35 million. One thing is sure: Tamiami did sign a contract with a bingo paper supplier authorities have linked to the mob.

After a bidding process, Tamiami began buying supplies from Frank Nannicola of Warren, Ohio. Nannicola is the son-in-law of Charles Imburgia, who, according to the Pennsylvania Crime Commission, is a member of the Genovese crime family in Pittsburgh. A 1992 crime commission report claims certain bingo operations in the Youngstown, Ohio, area "are obligated to purchase bingo supplies from Nannicola."

Nannicola says his firm sells supplies in 25 states and got the Tamiami contract because of superior service and price. He denies that his father-in-law or his business has mob ties: "The Pennsylvania Crime Commission should get some new employees and some new information."

Despite the allegations, the National Indian Gaming Commission has never done a background check on Nannicola Wholesale or Tamiami Partners. One reason: Although Congress created the commission in 1988 to regulate Indian gaming, its rules didn't take effect until February 1993. The commission has a massive backlog of old and new management contracts to review.

Just such snags prompted members of Congress to meet in 1993 to discuss tightening Indian gambling laws and a new Senate bill. National Indian Gaming Association Chairman

*"The commission has a massive backlog of old and new management contracts to review."*

Rick Hill says the tribes want the cleanest industry possible. But they also want to ensure that a few questionable characters do not bring ruin to an industry that employs thousands and has helped tribes build much-needed schools, hospitals and homes. "It's a bread-and-butter issue," Hill says. "We need Indian gaming to survive."

# Bibliography

## Books

| Vicki Abt, James F. Smith, and Eugene Martin Christiansen | *The Business of Risk: Commercial Gambling in Mainstream America.* Lawrence: University Press of Kansas, 1985. |
| --- | --- |
| John C. Burnham | *Bad Habits: Drinking, Smoking, Taking Drugs, Gambling, Sexual Misbehavior, and Swearing in American History.* New York: New York University Press, 1993. |
| Charles T. Clotfelter and Philip J. Cook | *Selling Hope: State Lotteries in America.* Cambridge: Harvard University Press, 1989. |
| Committee on the Judiciary, Subcommittee on Patents, Copyrights, and Trademarks | *Prohibiting State-Sanctioned Sports Gambling.* Washington: U.S. Government Printing Office, 1992. |
| J. Dombrink and William N. Thompson | *The Last Resort: Success and Failure in Campaigns for Casinos.* Reno: University of Nevada Press, 1990. |
| Educational Research Service | *State-Run Lotteries: Their Effects on School Funding.* Arlington, VA: Educational Research Service, 1993. |
| Ken Estes | *Deadly Odds: The Compulsion to Gamble.* Newport, RI: Edgehill, 1990. |
| Governor's Office of Planning and Research | *California and Nevada: Subsidy, Monopoly, and Competitive Effects of Legalized Gambling.* Sacramento, CA: Governor's Office, 1992. |
| Rick Hornung | *One Nation Under the Gun: Inside the Mohawk Civil War.* New York: Pantheon, 1992. |
| Illinois Fiscal & Economic Commission | *Wagering in Illinois: A Report on the Economic Impact of Existing and Proposed Forms of Gambling.* Springfield: Illinois Fiscal and Economic Commission, 1992. |
| Eric H. Monkkonen, ed. | *Prostitution, Drugs, Gambling, and Organized Crime.* New York: K.G. Saur, 1992. |
| National Indian Gaming Association | *Speaking the Truth About Indian Gaming.* Washington: National Indian Gaming Association, 1993. |
| Mark Siegel, Alison Landes, and Carol Foster | *Gambling: Crime or Recreation?* Rev. ed. Wylie, TX: Information Plus, 1992. |

# Bibliography

| William N. Thompson | *Legalized Gambling: A Reference Handbook.* Santa Barbara, CA: ABC-CLIO, 1994. |
| Michael B. Walker | *The Psychology of Gambling.* Tarrytown, NY: Pergamon Press, 1992. |
| Lynn S. Wallisch | *1992 Texas Survey of Adolescent Gambling Behavior.* Austin: Texas Commission on Alcohol and Drug Abuse, 1993. |
| Craig A. Zendzian | *Who Pays? Casino Gambling, Hidden Interests, and Organized Crime.* New York: Harrow and Heston, 1993. |

## Periodicals

| Jerry Adler | "Just Say Yes, Hit Me Again," *Newsweek*, June 21, 1993. |
| Scott Armstrong | "California Prospects TV Betting," *The Christian Science Monitor*, April 26, 1993. Available from 1 Norway St., Boston, MA 02115. |
| Gary S. Becker | "Gambling's Advocates Are Right—but for the Wrong Reasons," *Business Week*, September 6, 1993. |
| Sheila B. Blume | "Compulsive Gambling: Addiction Without Drugs," *The Harvard Mental Health Letter*, February 1992. Available from PO Box 420448, Palm Coast, FL 32142-0448. |
| Pierre Briançon | "Betting with the Indians," *World Press Review*, December 1993. |
| George Brushaber | "You Bet, We Lose," *Christianity Today*, February 7, 1994. |
| Francis X. Clines | "Gambling, Pariah No More, Is Booming Across America," *The New York Times*, December 5, 1993. |
| *The Economist* | "Fifty Ways to Lose Your Wallet," March 26, 1994. |
| Earl W. Foell | "For Bettor, For Worse," *World Monitor*, March 1993. |
| *Glamour* | "Should States Profit from Legalized Gambling?" May 1994. |
| Paul Glastris | "Beware of Greeks Bearing Chips," *U.S. News & World Report*, July 24, 1994. |
| Hardy Green | "Give Lands Back to the Indians? You Bet," *Business Week*, August 1, 1994. |
| Pam Greenberg | "Most States Hold Off on Legalized Video Gambling Decisions," *The Fiscal Letter*, July/August 1993. Available from 1050 17th St., Suite 2100, Denver, CO 80265. |
| Ronald Grover | "Will Too Many Players Spoil the Game?" *Business Week*, October 18, 1993. |
| Gayle Hanson | "Gambling: Playing Their Ace to Get Out of the Hole," *Insight on the News*, June 21, 1993. Available from 3600 New York Ave. NE, Washington, DC 20002. |
| David Holmstrom | "Gambling Ventures Reverse Poverty of Only Some Indians," *The Christian Science Monitor*, July 8, 1994. |
| Michelle Ingrassia | "Betting: When It Becomes a Problem," *Newsweek*, June 14, 1993. |

# Gambling

Jenny Labalme — "The Great Riverboat Gamble," *Southern Exposure*, Summer 1994.

Bill Lueders — "Buffaloed: Casino Cowboys Take Indians for a Ride," *The Progressive*, August 1994.

Richard MacPhie — "Gambling on Casino Jobs," *Colors*, September 1994.

Edward J. McCaffery — "Why People Play Lotteries and Why It Matters," *Wisconsin Law Review*, 1994.

Richard A. McGowan — "Lotteries and Sin Taxes: Painless Revenue or Painful Mirage?" *America*, April 30, 1994.

Barry Meier — "Casinos Putting Tribes at Odds," *The New York Times*, January 13, 1994.

Peter Passell — "Foxwoods, a Casino Success Story," *The New York Times*, August 8, 1994.

Gary Putka — "New England States Step Up Wagering on New Casinos," *The Wall Street Journal*, September 2, 1994.

Betsy Reed — "America's New Addiction," *Dollars and Sense*, July/August 1994.

William C. Rhoden — "High Stakes; Low Sense of Values," *The New York Times*, July 21, 1993.

I. Nelson Rose — "The Future of Indian Gaming," *Journal of Gambling Studies*, Winter 1992. Available from 72 Fifth Ave., New York, NY 10011.

Lydia Saad — "Gambling Attitudes: Americans Frown on Sports Betting," *The Gallup Poll Monthly*, December 1992.

Ivan Solotaroff — "The Book on Gambling," *Esquire*, September 1994.

*USA Today* — "Controlling Addiction to Gambling," April 1994.

*U.S. News & World Report* — Special section on casino gambling, March 14, 1994.

George Vecsey — "Gambling on Athletes Is Not Allowed Here," *The New York Times*, July 19, 1992.

Jennifer Vogel — "A Lotto Bunk," *Utne Reader*, November/December 1993.

Rick Wartzman and Pauline Yoshihashi — "Gambling Industry Says Tax Means Snake Eyes, but from Washington It Looks Like a Natural," *The Wall Street Journal*, March 31, 1994.

Steve Wiegand — "The Canvas Casino: California, Indian Tribes Battle Over Gambling," *California Journal*, August 1993. Available from 1714 Capitol Ave., Sacramento, CA 95814.

John D. Wolf — "Confronting Casinos," *The Christian Century*, August/September 1993.

Justin Zimmerman and Danielle Starkey — "Will Gambling Save the County Fair? Another Endangered Species Threatened by Budget Cuts," *California Journal*, July 1993.

# Organizations to Contact

The editors have compiled the following list of organizations concerned with the issues debated in this book. The descriptions are derived from materials provided by the organizations. All have publications or information available for interested readers. The list was compiled on the date of publication of the present volume; names, addresses, and phone numbers may change. Be aware that many organizations take several weeks or longer to respond to inquiries, so allow as much time as possible.

**BMT Communications**
7 Penn Plaza
New York, NY 10001-3900
(212) 594-4120

BMT Communications is a marketing and retailing magazine publisher. Its periodicals include *International Gaming and Wagering Business*, a monthly magazine that covers the gambling industry and frequently editorializes on gambling issues.

**California Council on Alcohol Problems (CCAP)**
803 Vallejo Way
Sacramento, CA 95818
(916) 441-1844

The council is composed of members of various religious denominations who are concerned with the harms of gambling. It believes that gambling is socially disruptive, politically corrupt, and morally dangerous. Its publications include fact sheets, pamphlets, and the quarterly newsletter *Capitol Re-Cap*.

**Canadian Foundation on Compulsive Gambling (CFCG)**
505 Consumers Rd., Suite 605
Willowdale, Ontario, Canada M2J 4V8
(416) 499-9800
fax: (519) 255-9888

An organization of business and health professionals and others, CFCG provides executive summaries of surveys of Ontario residents' attitudes and behavior regarding gambling. It publishes pamphlets on compulsive gambling and teen gambling and has produced a high school curriculum and educational video about problem gambling.

**Coalition for Gambling Reform**
121 Lowry Lane
Wilmore, KY 40390-1218

The coalition publicizes the social and economic costs of gambling, including the threat casinos pose to communities. It publishes the monthly newsletter *Gambling Economics*.

**Gamblers Anonymous (GA)**
PO Box 17173
Los Angeles, CA 90017
(213) 386-8789
fax: (213) 386-0030

GA is an organization of compulsive gamblers who seek to stop gambling and to help other compulsive gamblers do the same. It publishes pamphlets on compulsive gambling, a list of local Gamblers Anonymous meetings, and the monthly *Lifelines Bulletin*.

**General Board of Church and Society**
100 Maryland Ave. NE
Washington, DC 20002
(202) 488-5600 / (800) 967-0880

This department of the United Methodist Church believes that "gambling is a menace to society; deadly to the best interests of moral, social, economic, and spiritual life; and destructive of good government." It urges Christians and others to abstain from gambling and opposes state promotion and legalization of gambling. The board provides an anti-gambling information packet that includes position papers, pamphlets, and article reprints.

**Institute for the Study of Gambling and Commercial Gaming**
College of Business Administration
University of Nevada
Reno, NV 89557
(702) 784-1110

The institute offers courses and degrees in management and other areas of gambling. It holds national and international conferences on gambling and publishes proceedings from them. The institute produces quarterly reports on current issues and trends in legalized gambling and copublishes, with the National Council on Problem Gambling, the quarterly *Journal of Gambling Studies*.

**Michigan Interfaith Council on Alcohol Problems (MICAP)**
PO Box 10212
Lansing, MI 48901-0212
(517) 484-0016

MICAP is an organization of religious leaders and others who seek to address the problems of alcoholism. It publishes the biweekly newsletter *MICAP Recap*, which often includes editorials and other information about the negative effects of legalized gambling and opposition to casino gambling in the greater Detroit area.

**National Congress of American Indians (NCAI)**
900 Pennsylvania Ave. SE
Washington, DC 20003
(202) 546-9404

NCAI is an organization of tribes representing six hundred thousand Indians that seeks to protect, conserve, and develop Indian natural and human resources. It believes that gaming is a right of Native American tribes and an aspect of tribal sovereignty. It also believes that the 1988 Indian Gaming Regulatory Act (IGRA) was a concession to the federal government and states and that further concessions are unwarranted. NCAI publishes a quarterly newsletter, the *Sentinel*.

### National Council on Problem Gambling
John Jay College of Criminal Justice
445 W. 59th St.
New York, NY 10019
(212) 765-3833 / (800) 522-4700

The council includes health, education, and law professionals, recovering gamblers, and others concerned with compulsive gambling. It conducts seminars and training programs on the identification and treatment of compulsive gambling behavior. The council publishes books, brochures, videos, the quarterly *Journal of Gambling Studies*, which explores the psychological behavior of controlled and pathological gamblers, and the quarterly *National Council on Problem Gambling Newsletter*.

### National Governors' Association (NGA)
444 N. Capitol St.
Washington, DC 20001-1572
(202) 624-5300

NGA is an association of governors of the United States and its territories. It serves as a body through which governors influence the development and implementation of national policy. NGA is concerned with the states' roles in federal gambling legislation and has published several *Backgrounder* papers on legalized gambling.

### National Indian Gaming Association (NIGA)
904 Pennsylvania Ave. SE
Washington, DC 20003
(202) 546-7711
fax: (202) 546-1755

NIGA is an organization of Indian tribes that operate bingo games or gambling casinos. It works for the successful operation of Indian casinos as well as effective tribal, state, and federal regulation. NIGA publishes the quarterly newsletter *Moccasin Telegraph*.

### Public Gaming Research Institute (PGRI)
15825 Shady Grove Rd., Suite 130
Rockville, MD 20850
(301) 330-7600
fax: (301) 330-7608

PGRI studies various issues concerning the gambling industry, including legislation and marketing. It publishes the monthly magazines *Indian Gaming* and *Public Gaming International*, the latter devoted entirely to North American and international lotteries.

# Index